EVEREST

IT'S NOT ABOUT THE SUMMIT

Twenty years of preparation, two years of devastation
on the world's highest mountain

Ellis J Stewart

Published in 2016

Copyright © Ellis J Stewart.

An Everest Dream Book

Edited by Pinnacle Editorial
{P}
www.alexroddie.com/pinnacle-editorial

A CIP catalogue record for this title is available from the
British Library.

This book is dedicated to everyone who has ever embraced the Everest Dream, and to all those dreamers who sadly died on the mountain in 2014 and 2015 including Pasang Temba, Kumar and Tenzing

&

to my beautiful children, Aaron, Lara and Isla. Aaron you can read it now, Lara and Isla you will have to wait.

Everest – It's Not About The Summit

Contents

FOREWORD BY BRIAN BLESSED

"This book is a celebration. It is a tale of extraordinary courage and sustained, tenacious endeavour. Books about intrepid adventurers and explorers always fire my imagination and leave me begging for more. Such people are our dreams made flesh and blood. Ellis fits the bill perfectly; he is the personification of the spirit of adventure. Many factors of awe-inspiring magnitude face those who seek adventure among the highest peaks: climbing difficulties, avalanches, vertical scale, climatic conditions and frightful altitude problems. Ellis with supreme courage coped with fatigue, cold, insomnia, diminished appetite, avalanches and earthquakes. This man is truly a staggering individual. His achievement is a clarion call to all who wish to fulfil their dreams. I salute him."

Brian Blessed OBE

PROLOGUE

The time was rapidly approaching 4.00am. I knew this because for the past hour or so I had been fixated on the game 'Doodle Jump' on my iPhone.

Sleep had once again evaded me. To calm my nerves a little, I decided to accept that insomnia was perfectly commonplace at altitude. I focused on moving this four-legged digital creature up a never-ending series of platforms without falling. Bloody frustrating it was. I knew that 4.30am would soon come around and put me out of my misery – in more ways than one.

I had arrived at Everest Base Camp over a week earlier and spent the last seven days settling in. Slowly, I began adjusting my body to the extreme high altitude and the frigid night-time temperatures. A few days earlier I had climbed three quarters of the way up the Khumbu Icefall and then back down to Base Camp. Now my team and I were about to climb all the way through the Icefall to Camp One, where we would stay a night before pushing further up the mountain. Apart from the nerves, I felt confident and prepared to take the next step in my relentless pursuit to stand on the highest point in the world.

A year ago almost to the day, on my first attempt to climb Everest, sixteen Nepali Sherpa mountain workers, ferrying loads up the route in preparation for that season's climbing, had been tragically killed.

On that occasion, my team members and I were only a few hours away from reaching the mountain. An ice serac the size of a small mansion had calved away from a hanging glacier on the mountain's western shoulder, triggering a deadly avalanche that crashed down into the Icefall. The Sherpas didn't stand a chance. From hearing the crack as the ice released, they would only have had seconds to react. Nearly all directly in the fall line were instantly killed or seriously injured.

For a year at least, this tragedy was the darkest and most catastrophic day in the mountain's history. It became the single largest loss of Nepali workers on the mountain since the 1922 British attempt in Tibet, when seven porters died after a group-induced avalanche.

On a cold and misty Saturday morning in April 2015, it was my team's turn to enter the Icefall once more. We were to assemble in our dining tent that morning ready for a 5.30am start. Stepping out into the freezing early morning air, I noticed a trail of head-torch beams snaking its way up through the ice. These guys, whoever they were, had clearly been up several hours before our team – some were even nearing the top of the Icefall. I gave the whole absorbing scene a few more seconds of my time and then hurried over to the mess tent, where hot milky tea, two boiled eggs and porridge awaited.

After final kit checks and pats on the back, we were on our way. Shortly after 6.00am my crampons' front points bit into the solid blue ice of a small serac at the entrance to the ice.

As dangerous as the Icefall can be, its sheer striking beauty is undeniable. Towering walls of snow and ice surrounded me in every direction.

That morning, after starting out with the four team members plus our guide Tim, we quickly spread out over a considerable distance along the route. The thick mist that had hung around all morning was now beginning to close in. I found it increasingly difficult to make out the terrain ahead.

I began to experience an overwhelming feeling of tiredness. It was only my second day on Everest, and already I felt out on a limb and completely spent. Other than the altitude, I had no obvious answer. I had trained incredibly hard before both of my attempts on the mountain, so I found it difficult to believe this had anything to do with fitness.

Several times that morning I thought about turning back and retreating to Base Camp where I could rest, regroup and figure out what the hell was causing this extreme lethargy. High on Everest was not a place to suddenly find out that my body couldn't cope with the demands of extreme-altitude climbing.

As soon as these thoughts of retreat crossed my mind, I brushed them aside. I continued with my slow plod, which I was banking on to get me to the top.

Several hours into the climb and still the debilitating exhaustion wouldn't leave me. Yet with each step up, I was one step closer to the top of the Icefall and eventually Camp One, where I could rest.

Only Alex, the youngest member of our team, remained with me. The team members were no longer visible to each other as the weather continued to close in. By mid-morning we could no longer see more than a few metres in front of us. I was very conscious that we had, by now, slipped to the very back of the team.

Our guide Tim came through on the radio to check on our whereabouts, as he had done several times that morning. He informed us that we were doing well, to just keep going and he would wait for us higher up. I sensed that things were not going so well. Yet I was still in the game, still moving up, slowly but ever so surely.

After another half an hour, we met up with Tim. The final ladders of the Icefall just happened to be the steepest and most exposed of the entire route. These ladders, lashed end to end up a sheer wall of ice some 50ft high, were the final barricades before the end of the technical climbing. After that the gradient eased all the way into Camp One, still some twenty minutes away.

I reached the top of the final ladder and, in worsening conditions, took off my pack to retrieve my water bottle. For the first time that morning since leaving Base Camp, I finally allowed myself to relax and rest a little, feeling that Camp One was surely close by.

And then it happened… I began to hear cracks in the ice all around me. The stable ground we had been inching slowly up was now moving with Tim and me on top of it. Alex must have been 50m further on, but he may as well have been on the moon – I couldn't see anything or anybody.

Once again, Everest had come alive. Only this time I was in the firing line. That same firing line that last year had claimed sixteen lives. Fearing I was about to be added to the mountain's roll call of people in the wrong place at the wrong time, I closed my eyes and waited for my demise. The mountain gods were clearly angry. In their wake was about to be left a trail of tragedy, heartache and shattered dreams.

The Khumbu Icefall

PART ONE: AN EVEREST DREAM

The secret to getting ahead is getting started – Mark Twain

You are about to read my story about how I attempted to climb Mount Everest, the highest mountain in the world. They say that every story must have a beginning, middle and an end, but this story will be slightly different – it will have a beginning, middle and a tragedy, followed by another middle and one further huge cataclysmic tragedy.

As an introduction to who I am, I want to share a description from a speakers' website I am registered on. It says this:

Ellis is not a professional mountaineer who routinely visits the Himalayas to climb. When he left for Everest he was a pretty unlikely fellow from a non-traditional climbing background who just simply harboured a big dream to reach the roof of our planet. Little did he realise what would happen in the attempts at achieving this goal.

As you will learn, a lot of my life and my ambition to climb Everest happened by chance. Opportunities presented themselves or I created them from nothing. Either way I grabbed every opportunity with eager hands.

In life I believe that we are our own worst adversaries. It is far easier to convince ourselves that we can't do something than it is to convince ourselves that we can. This is why most people's dreams remain just that. However, if you can tell yourself that something is right for you and that you can do it, then why can't you? You don't need anyone else telling you that you can't.

Growing up, I had always fancied myself as a climber or explorer, so I took the steps needed to enable the realisation of a dream. I believed climbing the highest mountain in the world was an achievable goal.

These first steps to the mountain began in my youth in the streets and alleyways of a town in Northern England, where the seeds of my dream were firmly planted. Allow me to take you there.

My early years were interspersed with attempts to collect as many scars on my body as I possibly could. By the time I was five years old I had done a grand job of this. My *pièce de résistance* is an eight-inch scar consisting of thirty stitches, shaped rather like the Nike sportswear logo, which runs down the front of my right thigh. This is from an unfortunate fight I had with a misplaced Luke Skywalker figure on the living room floor, resulting in a Superman-style flight through a glass door. Needless to say I lost. As a result the fact that I have a scar on my body that normally accompanies the slogan 'Just do it' says a lot about the person I have become.

My mam insists to this day that I deliberately tried to injure myself for all the attention and treats I would receive when I finally returned home from my hospital visits. My Star Wars figure collection grew handsomely after each accident. I considered that maybe a broken limb or two might actually get me a Millennium Falcon spaceship if I was lucky.

As I matured from a toddler to a small boy, this quest to injure myself showed no signs of slowing. Further trips to the hospital would become all too regular. From scalding the palm of my hand on a plugged-in iron – which required an extensive skin graft and a two-week stay in hospital – to deciding to use my body to stop a car, by running ahead of the lollipop lady on a pedestrian crossing, nothing, it seemed, was out of reach for this wannabe stunt kid.

Growing up in Hartlepool, a small seaport town in the north-east of England, didn't offer many opportunities to become acquainted with mountains or the outdoors in general. That would come much later.

To me, playing outside in the street offered infinitely more opportunities for exploration and adventure than being stuck inside. I was always the last kid in at night, and even when I was called home, I was very reluctant. By being outside, I was getting a lot of natural exercise and this meant I soon slimmed down and became a normal healthy child, albeit a highly accident-prone one.

I never knew my real father, on account of my mam divorcing him when I was three years old. He had a drink problem which sadly would get the better of him at the time. My mam did what all good parents should do in a similar situation – to put me first, which she did, so we left.

We moved in with my nana whilst my mam began rebuilding our new lives. I have good memories of those few years living in my nana's big old house, and it was during these few years of my childhood that I had my first experience of climbing.

As the crow flies, my infant school was just around the block from nana's house, but on the ground it wasn't so easy. Mam had to walk me all the way to the top of a road and then down another to get there.

From the bedroom window I spotted a shortcut. Using a few well-placed bricks and a metal hook, I was able to scale the wall and leap down into the neighbour's garden on the other side, where school was a mere hop, skip and a jump away.

This garden-creeping was my first real taste of adventure. I was never caught, although I did come very close on one occasion. The owner of the garden I had been illegally crossing each day had been waiting for me at school home time. He tried to grab me from behind a rose bush. He was too slow though and I easily escaped his clutches.

Scampering through his garden became a challenge and I would get quicker each time. I perfected my evasion techniques too. I could hear "You little bugger!" or "I'll get you next time!" over my shoulder as I scaled the wall back to the safety of my nana's old house.

When I was around eleven years old I went on a school residential trip to a local outdoor activity camp in Carlton in the North Yorkshire Moors. I had plenty of experience of time away from home, thanks to my lengthy hospital stays. After our first day and night away, some of my classmates had already become homesick, yet I just took it all in my stride. In fact, I felt completely at ease. This school camp was my first full experience of the outdoors and I took to it like the proverbial duck to water.

At 7.00am each morning after breakfast we were issued with leather walking boots that were two sizes too big, a luminous orange cagoule and a blue daysack for our packed lunches. We would then head off out for the day's activity. On the last of these activity days, we were taken for a walk to the top of a local hill, which I had often seen from the car window when passing through this part of North Yorkshire. Near to the villages of Newton-under-Roseberry and Great Ayton, Roseberry Topping dominates the skyline overlooking nearby industrial Teesside. This distinctive cone-shaped peak was the hill we were dragged up that day. I have ascended it over a thousand times since. It was my first 'mountain', which would set me on my journey to Everest.

Looking back, I now know it isn't a mountain at all – nowhere near. Yet it had a profound effect on my childhood and certainly felt like a mountain to me back then.

Ascending Roseberry Topping as a child unlocked a whole new world of discovery for me. I had my eyes opened to the fact that there was more to being outdoors than front streets, back alleys and neighbours' gardens.

There was a whole world of adventure out there waiting to be discovered, and I was eager to do the discovering.

Ellis at Carlton Camp

When I was thirteen I joined a local Royal Marine cadet unit in Hartlepool. My three years as a cadet were an enjoyable period of my youth and no doubt helped to cement discipline and a sense of pride. I am sure this was one of the character building blocks that made me the ambitious go-getter I became.

I soon immersed myself in the sporting opportunities that being in the cadets offered.

As well as being in the football team, I also joined the cadet rowing team and took part in competitions around the country, racing other crews from across the UK. It reached a point where I began to enjoy the rowing events more than I did playing football, and I became a lot fitter for it.

My schoolwork began to suffer because all I could think about was the cadets. I now had a career goal in mind. When I left school I was going to sign up for the Royal Marines.

Very soon, I was to experience the first major setback in my young life so far.

Persistent ear infections plagued my early teens. After one of many surgical interventions during this time, an Ear, Nose and Throat (ENT) consultant dropped a bombshell. Scarring caused by the operations and infections had damaged the hearing in my right ear, to the point where I had lost three quarters of my normal hearing capacity.

Losing the hearing was bad enough but this was nothing compared to how I felt when I realised this was the end of my military aspirations. The recruiting officers for the Royal Marines wouldn't even look at me, let alone medically examine me, if they knew I had significant hearing loss. I couldn't understand why this had happened. Overnight my whole world collapsed and everything was taken away from me.

This cruel blow came at a time in my life when everything seemed to be working out. When I turned sixteen I had become a sergeant in the cadets, something that I was justifiably proud of. Even the Royal Marine officers who conducted the cadet sergeant's exam said I would make an excellent marine.

I began a course in Leisure Management at the local college and stayed in the cadets for one more year, praying for a miracle cure for my partial deafness. When I realised no cure would arrive I knew it was time to leave. For the first time in my life I had hit the bottom, and I had to learn to climb and claw my way back to the top – something I would learn to do over and over again throughout the next fifteen years.

As a seventeen-year-old college student with no means to support myself, I needed to do something. That something soon came knocking. Due to a chance encounter whilst helping a much older friend with a mobile disco, I was offered an implausible opportunity that, once again, would change the course of my life for the next several years. Needless to say, I grabbed it.

I was standing on my own one evening behind a DJ booth at a birthday party when someone approached me. He introduced himself as the manager of a wine bar in the town centre. He went on to say that he was looking for a new DJ for a weeknight slot, and would I be interested in applying? My friend, the DJ whose equipment I had been temporarily looking after, was at the bar.

I don't know what possessed me, but I didn't reveal that I wasn't the real DJ. I cued up and began to play *In the Navy* by the Village People, a camp classic from the 80s.

All the while the real DJ was chatting up the barmaid, oblivious to the opportunity that I was about to steal away. But it was too late – I had already agreed to go down to the bar for a try-out. The only slight drawback was that I had to bring my own records to play, which he assumed I owned as *'young man, there's no need to feel down, I said young man'* blasted out of the speakers.

A day later I solved this problem by borrowing £50 from my mam and buying the entire UK top ten on 7" vinyl record from the local music shop.

As the big night came around, I was beginning to regret my indiscretion at not owning up and admitting that I wasn't a real DJ. It was too late, though – cometh the hour, cometh the man. I loaded my recently purchased records into my bag, which included amongst others: *Bring Your Daughter to the Slaughter* by Iron Maiden, Cher's *Shoop Shoop* song, *The One and Only* by Chesney Hawkes and *Do the Bartman* by Bart Simpson. As eclectic a mix of music as you will ever find.

What followed was in my eyes a disastrous evening as I wondered what the hell I was doing. I felt completely out of my comfort zone.

What the bar manager hadn't informed me was that Thursday night was also karaoke night. This meant that, in between songs, I also had to get to grips with the machine that played the karaoke songs and pass the microphone to random strangers, who then proceeded to sing wildly out of tune.

The Tom Cruise film *Top Gun* was only five years old at the time, and still hugely popular. That night, I had to listen to three different renditions of *You've lost That Loving Feeling* by The Righteous Brothers and the same number of women screaming and cackling their way through Berlin's *Take My Breath Away*.

By the end of my hour, I had lost the will to live. I buried my head in my hands, sure that I was about to be shown the back door for what must have been the worst DJ performance the bar had ever seen.

The bar manager came up to me and shook my hand. "Unbelievably good. In fact, it was brilliant – when can you start?"

"Really!" I replied, completely gobsmacked.

Apparently, it wasn't so much my skills on the turntables that had impressed – he was quick to point out that they hadn't. It was more my patter on the microphone that won him (and the entire bar) over. I had the bar in uproar with my choice of songs and my mickey-taking tactics on each person that came up to sing.

The bar manager thought I had brought a collection of comedy songs to play that night. I didn't have the guts to tell him that my choice of music was deadly serious. Still, the manager and the entire bar thought it was side-splittingly funny. I went home £75 richer and with a new regular Thursday night slot as an in-house DJ.

I do not recall the exact date in question when my life changed forever, but I do remember the evening as if it were only yesterday. That evening threw me head first into a journey that would leave its mark in so many unimaginable ways.

I attended a talk in the local town hall, which I had seen advertised as '*Rock and Ice – an evening with Doug Scott*'. I was, at the time, vaguely aware that Doug Scott had climbed Mount Everest and it was this that attracted me to the talk.

Ever since I had climbed Roseberry Topping over ten years before, I had taken an interest any time I saw the word 'Everest' or 'mountaineer' published in a newspaper or book. I knew Everest was the highest mountain in the world and I also knew where it was, vaguely. Somewhere near a place called Kathmandu, or as I thought 'Katmandoo'.

Without realising it, I had been taking more than a passing interest in the mountain, yet I had never met anyone in real life who had actually been there. I quickly bought a ticket.

As I would later learn that evening, Scott and another mountaineer called Dougal Haston became the first British subjects to stand on top of the mountain in 1975. Haston sadly died in a skiing accident two years later, but Scott was still very much alive and I hung on his every word that night in the Hartlepool town hall.

Ironically, he barely mentioned Everest in his talk. It was an illustrated lecture about his harrowing ordeal descending The Ogre in Pakistan in 1977, two years after his Everest heroics. Scott broke both of his legs above the ankles on the descent.

As one of the old school of hard-lined British alpinists, Doug Scott had served his time on some of the most dangerous and downright ridiculously difficult mountain faces on the planet. I was seriously in awe of the man.

I wasn't sure when, or even how, but from that moment I knew that I wanted to experience mountaineering myself. Clearly, I didn't want to replicate Scott's descent of The Ogre, but a spark ignited within me that night.

With Everest I suddenly had a new interest and a mountain I wanted to know everything about. Climbing it seemed like one hell of a challenge, akin perhaps to walking on the moon or reaching one of the poles. The challenge of Everest, and the opportunity it offered for achievement and pushing my boundaries, had me under its spell almost the minute I left the town hall.

Although at first I didn't appreciate just how pivotal this evening would become, Everest had just walked up to me and smacked me square on the chin. From that moment on my life would never be the same again.

Eyes now open to the adventure possibilities that mountains offered, I began to take steps towards a deeper understanding of what drove men and women to climb them.

To help me answer that question, I began reading stories of historical expeditions. I picked up on a quote George Mallory had written during his attempts on the north side of Everest in the twenties.

People ask me, 'What is the use of climbing Mount Everest?' and my answer must at once be, 'It is of no use. There is not the slightest prospect of any gain whatsoever. Oh, we may learn a little about the behaviour of the human body at high altitudes, and possibly medical men may turn our observation to some account for the purposes of aviation. But otherwise nothing will come of it. We shall not bring back a single bit of gold or silver, not a gem, nor any coal or iron... If you cannot understand that there is something in man which responds to the challenge of this mountain and goes out to meet it, that the struggle is the struggle of life itself upward and forever upward, then you won't see why we go. What we get from this adventure is just sheer joy. And joy is, after all, the end of life. We do not live to eat and make money. We eat and make money to be able to live. That is what life means and what life is for.

It became apparent to me that Mallory had got it spot on. Climbing Everest wouldn't serve any useful purpose, other than satisfying my own needs and desires. But be that as it may, over the next several years I became intoxicated with the mountain and its deep history.

Starting the physical process of achieving my Everest dream was still a few years away, but I continued my education by reading more and more and as often as I could.

From the outset it became obvious that people die on Everest, and often. It was hard to dismiss fatalities on the mountain as minor occurrences.

This assumption was compounded further after reading Chris Bonington's book *Everest The Hard Way*. This book documented an expedition to the mountain in 1975, which was a huge success, albeit tainted by tragedy.

Doug Scott completely omitted the experiences of his Everest climb from his talk that evening. So it was left to Bonington's book to fill in the blanks for me.

It was late in the day when Doug Scott and Dougal Haston reached the summit of Everest on the 24th of September 1975, which meant they had to endure an emergency bivouac on the mountain's south summit, the highest ever attempted. Both men survived the night and were able to drop down to Advanced Base Camp the following day. Pete Boardman and Pertemba, the expedition sirdar, followed this initial success two days later with further summits. In fact, the expedition would have been a glorious success if it weren't for the fact that one of the team members, Mick Burke, went missing shortly after it was assumed he reached the summit. His body was never found.

It is fair to say that reading about all the fatalities and terrible accidents on Everest sent a shudder down my spine but not enough to stop my curiosity. I began a love affair with the mountain and began to think about what it would be like to climb it. Yet I did not have the first clue how I could do that. Everest for now would have to wait.

One evening I was looking through the local newspaper when a job advert caught my eye. The headline *'Outdoor Pursuits Enthusiasts Required'* jumped out from the pages. The local council was looking to recruit several individuals for training to become instructors in various outdoor pursuits.

Once qualified, you would be expected to work with disaffected and disadvantaged school-age children.

'You will be required to participate in governing body certification schemes in canoeing, camp-craft and rock climbing', the advert went on to add. 'Rock climbing!' Those two words stood out more than the other activities mentioned and the grey matter began to kick into action. I had never rock climbed before, but I had seen climbers on the crags and buttresses of North Yorkshire, and it fascinated and intrigued me at the same time.

It was time to polish up the résumé and apply to become a trainee rock-climbing instructor. Sure it was a multi-disciplined role, but all I saw was the word 'climbing'.

I duly applied and waxed lyrical about my outdoor credentials, which amounted to nothing at that moment in time. However, don't forget this was the guy who had landed himself a job as a DJ with no experience at all. I was sure I could pull off the same trick again. On the application I was pretty keen to stress how much knowledge I had about mountains and, in particular, Everest. One question asked what my biggest achievement was to date. 'Climbing Everest, at some point over the next few years', was my rather brazen answer.

I admitted that I had never climbed before – well, not with a rope and harness and all the usual paraphernalia that you use to climb up rocks. I was not so sure they would be impressed with the trees and garden walls I'd climbed in my youth but I mentioned it anyway.

The recruitment officer responsible for selecting the candidates for the instructor roles was clearly impressed with my answers, garden wall and all, as I was interviewed and chosen for one of the positions. "Everest you say? We shall see!"

It was through this outdoor instructor position that I began my transition into a climber. Although the days out on rivers in open canoes and kayaks were exhilarating, it was climbing on the crags of the Wainstones – a rocky outcrop in the Cleveland hills – that really excited.

Ironic as it is now looking back, it became pretty obvious from the outset that I was never going to be the most gifted rock climber to grace Yorkshire's rock faces. I was a tad awkward and clumsy and my technique was awful. "What technique?" Simon the instructor would say. But what I lacked in ability I more than made up for with sheer determination and passion. No matter what route we tackled, I would always reach the top. My style of climbing may not have been graceful, but it worked for me and I enjoyed every minute of my apprenticeship on the rock.

After familiarising myself with the lore and practice of rock climbing, my attention began to wander towards the mountains. Although scaling gritstone outcrops was at once gripping and terrifying, a chance weekend's navigation exercise in the fells of the Lake District had come along, as part of a training programme to receive a Basic Hill Walking Leader's certificate.

I had enjoyed hill walking intermittently on and off over the past several years and I felt at ease sloshing up and down fells in all kinds of weather. This was England after all, where it rains more often than not. After walking the fells on the navigation course, I found myself returning at each and every opportunity I could. I quickly began to realise that I preferred a day spent scrambling and hiking my way to the top of a hill rather than edging up slowly attached to a rope.

I had now participated in, and learned the basics of, rock climbing, scrambling and navigating around the British hills and I treasured ever minute of it. However I didn't last long in the role and I left shortly after a year. Being a DJ and an outdoor instructor was taking its toll on me. The DJ job paid a lot more money than supervising kids in canoes, so it was an easy choice to make.

In the mid-eighties something monumental happened in the world of mountaineering that would ultimately pave the way for people like me to one day go to Everest.

Throughout the sixties, seventies, and most of the eighties, Everest had been a mountain reserved for the elite – a preserve for those who had earned the opportunity to step foot on its hallowed faces. You needed to be at the top of your game to have a crack at the peak, and this was apparent in the nationally selected cream-of-the-crop climbers who were to be found on the mountain's slopes during these decades.

However, a colossal tilt in the make up of attempts on Everest occurred on the 30th of April 1985. An American businessman by the name of Dick Bass reached the summit, completing a quest to become the first person to climb the highest mountain on each continent. Becoming an accomplished mountaineer in the process, Bass had no idea that his achievement would help to seed an industry that has grown ever since: the quest for the Seven Summits. It took the businessman from Oklahoma four attempts to scale Everest but eventually he did, ably guided by the fellow American mountaineer and filmmaker David Breashears.

Upon guiding Bass to the summit, Breashears had unwittingly created a whole new way to climb the mountain. If you had the necessary finances, three months spare and the desire to climb the highest mountain in the world, then Everest was open for business.

It didn't take long for people with these three qualities to cotton on to that fact. Within a decade, Everest went from the sphere of elite mountaineers to a mantelpiece photograph for people from all walks of life. The dawn of commercial mountaineering had begun.

PART TWO: THERE BE DRAGONS

Listen to the mustn'ts, child. Listen to the don'ts. Listen to the shouldn'ts,
the impossible, the won'ts. Listen to the never haves, then listen close to
me... Anything can happen, child. Anything can be. – Shell Silverstein

In 1995 I briefly dated a girl called Nicola, whose parents lived in a small town called Seascale in Cumbria. With its proximity to the Lakeland fells, and in particular the highest mountain in England, Scafell Pike, I loved spending weekends at her parents' house.

One summer's evening I left Hartlepool to visit Nicola. In my possession I had a four-pint milk carton full of water and three chocolate bars. Over thirteen hours later, I arrived in Seascale completely dehydrated and exhausted and close to collapse. A friend had lent me his expensive Marin mountain bike while he was working away in the Royal Marines and said I could use it.

Cycling over a hundred miles across the country was probably not what he had in mind. A year earlier, the official coast-to-coast (C2C) cycle route had opened. The night I left my house on my friend's bike, I attempted a sea-to-sea bike ride of my own. Instead of following the official route, I planned on just tearing across the main A-roads and motorways. I reckoned this would knock hours off the under-24-hour time.

I set off in good spirits, confident in my fitness and route-finding ability. The first thirty-odd miles went by in a breeze. I felt full of zip as I wheeled the last mile or so into Barnard Castle in County Durham. I found a bench and enjoyed the first of my chocolate and took a large gulp of water to refuel the system.

The route for the next fifty-five miles into Keswick, in the heart of the Lake District, presented no major route-finding difficulty. I cycled along the A66, a major road that bisected northern England, connecting Cumbria in the west with Durham in the east. This was as foolhardy as it sounds. Most sections of the road are single-lane carriageways. Trucks and lorries would hurtle past at sixty miles an hour, literally only inches away from hitting my shoulder and, at best, knocking me off the bike or, at worst, decapitating me. Regular toots from lorry drivers' horns let me know what they thought of my foolishness.

Luckily, it was late at night and the traffic had eased off. I carried on cycling and, slowly but surely, I edged closer to Keswick. To add insult to injury, it began to rain and I was soaked to the skin.

A bit further along the road, I came to a set of unmanned roadworks that had a few flashing orange traffic-management lamps. I didn't think they would miss one, so I secured it around my seat post with a bungee cord that was conveniently wrapped around the bike's frame. At last, any vehicles coming up from behind could now see me.

It began to get light as I cycled past fields and farmhouses along country lanes with sheep dogs barking. I ran out of water at Keswick and, with no shops open, I couldn't replenish my supplies. I was becoming really dehydrated and my energy levels were dropping fast.

After being dive-bombed by one or two bats – one of which caught me in the face and felt like a knife slash – and crashing off the bike when I took a corner too fast, I could take no more. If I didn't get water and fast, I was done for. I would be found dead in a ditch at the side of the road in a few hours' time, with strange scratch marks on my cheek, a traffic lamp around my saddle, an empty milk carton and a deluxe AA travel map of Great Britain. It would be the strangest mystery the police, in this part of rural Cumbria, would have to solve for years.

And then, as if by divine intervention, a light came on in a house up the lane. A chap wearing Sellafield-branded overalls was on his way to the start of his daily shift at the power station. I figured that, if I made up some story about doing a charity bike ride from Hartlepool Power Station on the north-east coast to Sellafield on the north-west coast, it would be more believable than just admitting that I was some imbecile who decided to ride a bike across the A66 to see his girlfriend.

To his credit, he not only allowed me – a perfect stranger – into his house at five in the morning and gave me water, but he also made me a bacon sandwich and offered to drive me the rest of the way down to Seascale. The best of humanity was alive and well that morning, and I found it in a little cottage just outside Ennerdale Bridge.

Feeling refreshed and energised, I cycled the rest of the way down into Seascale, revelling in the fact that I had just cycled the entire width of Northern England on a whim.

I surprised Nicola and her family at 6.30am when I knocked on the door. "Hi, have you missed me?" I said, as a bleary-eyed Nicola opened the front door. I must have looked exactly like I had just ridden 140 miles on my bike across the country.

"What the hell are you doing here?" came the response. Not quite the reaction I had in mind.

The overriding lesson I took from this mini adventure was that I had taken myself out of my comfort zone. I had attempted something which, although reckless and foolhardy, could be completed with nothing more than mind over matter, three mars bars, four pints of water and a bacon sandwich.

Coco Chanel, the famous French fashion designer, once said, "You live but once, you might as well be amusing." Amen to that.

Later that same year, I became a British Champion in the sport of Dragon Boat Racing. The Hartlepool Powermen Dragon Boat Racing Team powered home in first place in the 500m grand final of the National Championships. I had joined the team a few years earlier after first experiencing the sport as a cadet, but I didn't become a 'first choice paddler' for two years. During that time, I would religiously turn up for every training session and attend every race. I was so enthralled with the sport that, for a while, it threatened to eclipse my love of mountains.

As well as racing in Dragon Boats I was cementing my love for mountains at every opportunity I could.

The first time I walked to the top of Scafell Pike was in the winter of 1995. Nicola's family invited me to spend the Christmas period with them, and I didn't need asking twice.

I secretly had one eye on the distant fells, which you could clearly see from her parents' house, glistening away under fresh snowfall in the winter sun. The back garden offered spectacular views of the entire Scafell range. But when you stood out the front, the views couldn't have been any more different, as you peered towards the reactors of Sellafield nuclear fuel reprocessing plant.

A few days after Christmas, Nicola and her family arranged a day of shopping. I figured this would be a perfect day to walk to the top of Scafell Pike, which had looked tantalisingly close all week.

With no offer of a lift, I knew that I was going to have to walk the twelve miles just to get to the bottom of the mountain. I woke early, sorted my pack with food and provisions for the day and was off out the door before anyone else had stirred. If you are going to climb the highest mountain in the world then starting with the highest mountain in England is a good start.

I covered the walk to the mountain in three hours and arrived at the campsite at the head of the valley shortly after 9am. I then spent a glorious day in the fells, reaching the top of the pike after four and a half hours. I was unfamiliar with this part of the Lakes, but had a map and compass – which luckily I knew how to use thanks to the outdoor courses I had attended.

Blue skies and crisp, clear air stayed with me all day. The crunch of the new snow underneath my feet was intoxicating. I revelled in one of the best days I had ever spent in the British mountains. In all the times I have been back to Scafell Pike since, I have never experienced better conditions or clearer views than I did that first day over twenty years ago.

Not content with just reaching the top of Scafell Pike, I continued and topped out on Great End, Great Gable and Kirk Fell before descending back down to the inn on the valley floor. I was smitten. I had completed a horseshoe of fells, and it struck ten o'clock at night when I dragged my weary body to the bar in the Wasdale Head Inn.

Situated at the head of a remote and unspoilt valley, the inn styled itself as the birthplace of British mountaineering. A quick glance at the walls, adorned with pictures of a bygone era of climbing, meant it was hard to dispute. Samuel Taylor Coleridge, the English poet and philosopher, descended a rock climb on Scafell in 1802, the peak adjacent to the one I had just that day ascended. This was a good eighty years before the Golden Age of early British climbing.

The inn was a mecca for the climber and mountaineer and, as I sat warming myself round the fire that night with a pint in hand, a deep feeling of contentment and belonging swept over me. I felt like I had truly arrived and discovered my life's passion.

The inn was full that night, but after I explained that I had a twelve-mile walk back to Seascale and had no tent, the landlord agreed to let me sleep in the bar for free. I helped him tidy up the bar and clean the tables to show my appreciation. I kept the fire going long after the last guest had retired upstairs, and I blissfully fell asleep to the sound of crackling wood in the fire and snow gently falling outside.

My girlfriend's father arrived to pick me up the following morning, as my feet were blistered from the previous day's efforts. As I packed my bag to go, I noticed a small church at the head of the valley, which I had completely failed to see the day before. The Church of St Olaf is one of England's smallest churches and it was easy to see why.

I went across to take a closer look. The church had a long association with climbers and, as I studied the south-facing window, I noticed an etching of Napes Needle on Great Gable, a famous rock climb of the area. The etching was accompanied with the following quote:

I will lift up mine eyes unto the hills, from whence cometh my strength.

After jotting it down on a scrap of paper I hurriedly put it away inside my pocket. On the 25th of April 2015, I carried that scrap of paper and the words upon it inside my pack.

I concluded my relationship with Nicola not long after that weekend when she realised I was more into the location of her parents' house than her.

I continued as a member of the Dragon Boat team for several more months and enjoyed every moment in the team. Competing far and wide from Canada to Europe I clocked up some amazing life memories. There were also some not so good, such as the time I almost died of hypothermia when the boat capsized in Derwent Water in the Lake District, resulting in a day in Keswick Hospital. Maybe I will save that for another book.

Dragon Boat Racing increased my sense of teamwork and discipline. I left the team after four glorious years, with a new sense of pride and achievement.

A good friend of mine believes that we should spend our lives collecting memories, rather than material assets and possessions. I am inclined to agree, and I was about to put that belief to the test over and over again during the next twenty years.

Once again my journey to Everest was about to take a different course. It would ultimately prove to be a tumultuous period of my life, with many twists and turns, and much sorrow along the way. This path would however eventually lead me to the foot of Everest for the first time. In doing so, the mountain went from being the out-of-reach dream of a disillusioned chancer to a life's mission I was determined to achieve.

During one of the final Dragon Boat events I raced in, I met a girl called Vikki from a rival team. She came from Milton Keynes in Buckinghamshire.

A few months later I packed up all my belongings, quit my DJ job and left home to be with her. For the first few months our relationship developed nicely and everything was bliss. I just needed to find a new focus in life, and a new way to earn money.

Entering a university course for three years did cross my mind, but it would have been a struggle to make ends meet. I was no spring chicken, and I did not see how university would help me go to Everest. For now, university would have to wait – but then so would Everest. Living in a new area of the country meant I needed money. I needed a new job.

One day, while looking through the classifieds of the local newspaper, I saw a job advertised for an outdoor shop not far from where I was living. The job requirements were listed as having experience in the outdoors, a passion for climbing or hill walking, and experience in retail sales. I had two of the three criteria and was confident I could land the position. I applied and was offered the job on the spot.

My starting salary was £7,750, which would rise to £9,250 after a year's employment. Although not great money in anyone's book (in fact, there were probably better-paid positions doing pretty much anything else, come to think of it), I cared not. I would be talking about, and selling, climbing equipment and clothing five days a week. This also allowed me to enthuse to customers and fellow staff members about how I was going to one day climb Everest. "You mark my words," I would often say. "Yes, Ellis, of course you will," was the usual dismissive response.

I quickly settled in to the daily working life in the aptly named Outdoor Shop in Stony Stratford, a small market town on the outskirts of Milton Keynes. Considering that the nearest mountains were 175 miles away in North Wales, the shop stocked a vast array of highly technical outdoor kit. Clientele mostly consisted of climbers, mountaineers, walkers, and people off to backpack around the world.

The owners of the shop were a couple of chaps called John and Phil. Phil appeared to be the financial guru behind the business, and was responsible for the accounts and books, whereas John was the hands-on shop-floor guy, responsible for buying in all the shop's stock. He also happened to be an Alpine mountaineer who, along with his wife, was on a quest to climb every mountain in the Alps over 4,000m – a feat he was well on the way towards achieving by the time I started at the shop.

John would fly off to the mountains most weekends and come back having scaled a few more peaks. In his early forties, he was a strong, skilled and confident mountaineer.

Sadly I never saw eye to eye with John. I respected him because he practised what he preached, but that is where our relationship ended. However, if a customer came into the shop with a question about climbing in the Alps, or a query about a piece of technical kit beyond my level of comprehension, he was the first person I would seek out.

I think a large part of the problem with John was that he never respected me back. The shop mainly employed young climbers, and some of them were very vocal. At every opportunity they were keen to talk about their weekends spent climbing E1 rock routes in the Llanberis slate quarries in Wales. I was more silent and reserved, and I don't think it did me any favours.

I was good at my job; in fact I was very good. A girl walked in one Thursday evening with her parents. She was off on a expedition to Borneo and wanted a good pair of walking boots and a waterproof jacket. Several large carrier bags of kit later, and £2,000 lighter, they left the shop.

When I look back at my time in the shop now, I think I kept quiet because I didn't have as much to brag about. My weekends and free time were not spent climbing or hill walking as much as I would have liked.

I had a new girlfriend who wanted to spend time with me. Although we met in a Dragon Boat, she didn't share my same love of mountains and the outdoors. Therefore, weekends were spent doing 'couple things' together, like walking along canals and going out for meals. When it came to selling in the shop, this dented my confidence. If a customer approached me, wanting to know which crampon was best for a forthcoming climbing trip to France, or asking if I could assist with a choice of climbing rope, I would go and find one of the guys and ask them to help out.

One part of the shop that I loved was the book department. On quiet days, I would spend many an hour here. The stories of climbing and mountaineering really caught my imagination. Employees were allowed to buy books at trade price, which meant my mountaineering and Everest collection grew larger on a monthly basis.

I began collecting old Everest books as a hobby after a friend of Vikki's, whose parents ran a pet shop up the road, found a box of old books in the attic. One of the books was about Everest.

I knew immediately that it must be worth something. It was an immaculate first-edition copy of *Everest: The Unfinished Adventure* by Hugh Ruttledge, about one of the failed British attempts on the north side of the mountain in 1936.

I read the book in its entirety, and then had it priced. I was astounded to hear that it was worth upwards of £250. Not bad, considering it was destined for a charity shop. I still have the book to this day.

On one particularly quiet day, even by the Outdoor Shop's standards, I clocked a new book for sale on the shelf. It had just been put out that day. The image on the front cover drew me to it. I recognised it immediately as the South-East Ridge of Everest. A climbing rope was being whipped out over the edge of the ridge, clearly by strong winds. I picked up the book and read the subheading: *A personal account of the Everest Disaster*. The book was *Into Thin Air*.

I recalled hearing something on the news about a storm on Everest the previous year and that climbers had been killed, but until *Into Thin Air* came out, I wasn't familiar with all the details of what had happened high on the mountain. The book would change all that. Within a year of its release, it had become a huge success and would end up topping *The New York Times* non-fiction bestseller list, and would also be honoured as Book of the Year by *Time* magazine.

The book details an attempt to climb the mountain in the spring of 1996 by American writer and mountaineer John Krakauer.

Originally Krakauer was only meant to go to Base Camp and write a report on the commercialisation of the mountain for *Outside* magazine. However, he saw an opportunity to realise a childhood dream and asked his editor if it would be possible to climb the mountain instead. The editor agreed and Krakauer signed on with the New Zealand guiding company Adventure Consultants – a name I would become very familiar with in a few years' time.

The book covers the events that took place on the mountain from the author's perspective. Eight climbers died, and several others became trapped on the mountain, when a freak storm blew in on the night of May 10th 1996. It became the deadliest season on the mountain until recent times, with the most recorded deaths in a single day.

The book was as controversial as it was gripping, and it became a genre-defining edition in the annals of mountaineering literature. For most people sitting at home on their comfy sofas with no intention of ever visiting Everest, it offered a glimpse into the world of high-altitude commercial mountaineering.

It is not my job to retell the events of that ill-fated year on the mountain. This is *my* Everest story to tell. That story has been well documented through further books, of which Anatoli Boukreev's *The Climb: Tragic Ambitions on Everest* is one of the best. There have been TV documentaries, media columns the world over, and now even a major Hollywood movie that replay events from that year on Everest.

I read the book intently over three days. Krakauer wrote so candidly about tragic events, but there was something else much more profound that screamed out from the pages of the book. After reading *Into Thin Air*, my dream to climb Everest became more real, almost visceral. I can't explain it, but I knew from that moment on that one day Everest would be a part of my life. Call it a sixth sense if you will, but one book had opened a portal to an enticing prospect.

Could someone from Hartlepool, who started out climbing garden walls, really climb Everest? After reading *Into Thin Air*, I began to believe in the possibility that I could. One way or the other I was determined to find out.

Whilst working in the Outdoor Shop, Vikki fell pregnant. Everything changed overnight. In a few short months I would become a young dad, at the tender age of just 24, and I needed to earn more money. Everest dropped down my list of priorities.

Working in the Outdoor Shop came with a reputation. It was renowned for being one of the finest independent shops in the UK. This meant I effectively had a free pass into my next job as assistant manager of a shop in the nearby town of Aylesbury. But first, I had to deal with a few more pressing matters.

In August 1997, my son Aaron was born. In naming Aaron, I had consulted an A-Z baby name book, and was prepared to spend some time scanning the options. But I needn't have worried. The first name I came to in the boy's section stuck. According to the book, the origin of Aaron was Hebrew and meant lofty, exalted and high mountain man. *That will do,* I thought; *Perfect!* Vikki agreed.

Thirteen months later, I married Vikki, the girl I had met Dragon Boat racing and since lived with for the past two years.

We went for a one-week honeymoon in Scotland, where I dragged my new bride to the top of Ben Nevis and went looking for the Loch Ness Monster. It is safe to assume it wasn't the most romantic of starts to a marriage. I wondered if Vikki realised what she was getting herself into.

I began working in Ramblers shortly after returning from Scotland. The customers in Ramblers were, as the name implies, predominantly walkers. Still, it was a quaint little shop and I enjoyed the daily gossip with the walking fraternity, as much as I did chatting with climbers.

The shop manager, a chap called Andy, was a local Scout leader. One day, he happened to mention an event that he thought would be right up my street.

Some young Brit had just reached the summit of Everest and was giving a talk about it in a week's time at a private school. The Scouts had organised the talk and I could attend if I so wished. He went on to add that it was by someone called Wolf something or other. "Yes I am interested in going," I said. "Mind you, I have never heard of any British climber called Wolf."

A week later, I listened to Bear Grylls give a pretty good account of his recent expedition to climb the mountain. At the time, long before he became the household name he is today, Grylls was just this posh kid thrust into the limelight as the youngest British person to successfully reach the top. He would go on to write a book about it, called *The Kid Who Climbed Everest*.

Bear's book did a good job of bringing the mountain down to a level that the armchair enthusiast could appreciate.

Becoming a father at a young age meant that certain sacrifices had to be made. As much as I longed for weekends roaming the hills and countryside, I had a young family to support. For a few years, my passion for the outdoors had been well and truly nullified.

Right now, climbing Everest – or any mountain for that matter – seemed as far away as ever.

There and then, I made a deal with myself that, before the turn of the century, I would somehow visit Everest. It was already the back end of 1998, so I knew I had to get my skates on.

In the summer of 1999, cracks in my marriage were beginning to show. We had been very young when we met, and we rushed head first into living together, having a baby and getting married before we really got to know one another. I was about to take a job requiring significant amounts of time away from the family, and this certainly didn't help.

A position had become available as a sales rep with the outdoor clothing brand Páramo. The job involved covering the whole of the UK. Derek, the current sales rep, would often visit the walking shop in Aylesbury – we were one of their biggest stockists in the south-east of England.

On one visit, he mentioned that he was moving up to become sales director, which meant they needed someone to step in to his shoes. I had only worked in outdoor retail for just over two years, but already I was feeling bored and needed more stimulation.

Being a rep would be a much bigger challenge. I would have incentive-driven targets to achieve and would get to be my own boss. I applied for the position and was invited to an interview. I travelled down to East Sussex and had to give a presentation to the entire company sales force on Páramo products. The situation got the better of me. Overcome by nerves, I gave a shocking presentation. At one stage I froze, having seemingly forgotten how to speak. I recovered, though, and was able to regain my train of thought and complete the presentation. It was a complete shambles.

On the train home, I was 100% convinced that my application wouldn't be taken any further. A few days later, a letter dropped onto the doormat. A 'Dear John' letter, I assumed, telling me thanks, but no thanks. However, they invited me back for a second interview; this time I could give a presentation on a topic of my choice. This was a second chance that I was not going to mess up. When the day came, I delivered a much more polished presentation on the history of climbing Everest. I travelled back home much more confident and happy with my performance.

The following morning, the sales director called to offer me the job. "Can I ask?" I said. "Why did I get a second interview when I did so badly with the first one?" His answer still stays with me to this day. "Because," he said, "You finished what you started." He went on to tell me that, had I not been able to recover when I froze, they would not have brought me back in. The fact that I was able to take a moment, and then finish the presentation, showed that I could handle a crisis.

I put the phone down, having learnt a very valuable lesson. Always finish what you set out to achieve. This became a philosophy I would now apply in my goal to reach Everest.

In my new career with Páramo, I was given a brand new car, a company laptop and a mobile phone. I had never owned a phone before, so this was completely new to me. I remember receiving my first ever text message. I had just started with the company and was attending a training course in a hotel, with another employee, when the phone beeped. 'Meet you in reception at seven o'clock for drinks', I read on the screen. *Wow, that's clever,* I remember thinking, *but it will never catch on.*

In my role as sales rep, I would be driving all across the UK, visiting retail shops to sell them Páramo clothing, as well as giving structured training sessions to shop staff. What appealed most was spending time in areas of the UK that would enable me to get outdoors. I worked out that, if I was very clever booking my appointments, I could spend most afternoons either hill walking or mountain biking. This job seemed too good to be true. In a few months' time, I would discover that it *was* too good to be true.

The year 2000 became the best year of my life, and the worst, both at the same time. I have poignant memories of the start of the new century. I would resign from my position with Páramo and go through an emotional break-up from my wife.

I ended up working ten-hour shifts in a warehouse and I came very close to having a complete breakdown. One thing and one thing only dragged me back from this precipice of despair: a lump of rock and ice 29,035 feet high, thousands of miles away in the Kingdom of Nepal.

The year started out badly enough when, on the stroke of midnight on New Year's Eve, I lifted Vikki up on the dance floor at a party. In doing so, I struck her head on a sparkly disco mirror ball. The ball dropped to the floor, smashing it into a thousand pieces. As omens go, this one was pretty bad. She wasn't best pleased.

Everyone probably has memories of where they were when 1999 rolled into 2000, and the start of the 21st century. I had visions of being somewhere exciting and memorable – Sydney Harbour perhaps, or maybe Times Square in New York. Instead, I was at a line-dancing party in a church hall in Hartlepool, with a load of rooting and a tooting cowboys and cowgirls. Not exactly what I had in mind.

Only a few months in to the sales rep position, and already I was feeling like I had made a mistake. If I thought that being an outdoor rep would bring me plenty of opportunities to be outdoors, I couldn't have been more wrong. In fact, it took me further away than ever.

Because I was on the road Monday to Friday, visiting retailers, I was keen to get back home at weekends. My plans to be out on the hill after my appointments were nothing short of fantasy. The cold harsh truth was that, when not at an appointment, I would be back in the car, off to another part of the country. Mountains were just a blur I saw out of the car window as I sped from place to place.

I became depressed again, sinking back to that low I had experienced all those years earlier when I couldn't join the Royal Marines. I became introverted and seriously down in the dumps.

It wasn't the company's fault. They had put their faith in my ability to do the job – a job that, on paper, I thought I would really enjoy and throw myself into. But I had to experience it before realising it wasn't for me. Eating in hotels and motorway service stations also meant that my waistline was starting to get bigger. I was not in a good place at all.

I recall the day I made up my mind to quit. I had put it off all day long, too nervous to inform the sales director of my decision. I was just four months in to the job, so I knew this was not going to go down well. Finally, just before the end of the day, I plucked up the courage to tell my boss that I was out.

He took it surprisingly well. I think the first word out of his mouth was "Fuck". But once he got that out of the way, he listened to my reasons. After agreeing that I shouldn't stay in a job I wasn't enjoying, he wished me well. We began arranging all the formalities of handing back the company car, laptop and phone.

I knew what I had done that day was pure madness. I didn't, as yet, have another job to go to. I hadn't even consulted Vikki. She was going to be furious. By quitting my position with Páramo, I had hammered the first nail in the coffin that was soon to become my doomed marriage.

For my own well-being and state of mind, I felt a lot better – liberated from the pressure of the sales job. It hadn't worked out and I had to accept that, although it was now a scar on my résumé, one that I would have to work hard to correct.

Sure enough, the news didn't go down well with Vikki.

"So what are you going to do now?" Vikki threw at me. "You need to work."

Of course, she was right. I knew that the situation I had put myself in wasn't perfect. I also had a two-and-a-half-year-old son to take into account. Dreams of climbing Everest weren't going to help me much in my present predicament.

I got wind of the fact that an indoor snow slope was due to finish construction in May, and inside there would be retail shops that needed staff and managers. I applied for a position as a floor manager with one of them. It was only February though, and May was a long time off for someone earning no money.

As luck would have it, Vikki's brother worked in a warehouse as a supervisor for a large engineering parts company. He told me that he could probably get me a job to tide me over.

I took the job and began working long shifts, walking up and down aisles and aisles of nuts and bolts and other parts. My job was to pick these parts and place them in a tray with an order sheet. Once I had picked that order, I would then place it on a conveyor belt, where it would go through to a packing department to be shipped out. I would then start all over again with another order. I was expected to pick up to fifty orders on a ten-hour shift, day in day out, with half an hour for lunch.

As jobs go it was right up there. I settled in to the tedium, just grateful that I was earning money. It was soul-destroying work and I switched off to the monotony of it all.

If things were bad with my working life, then my home life was becoming unbearable. Vikki and I were not getting on. Each day, when I returned home from walking the picking line, we would argue and fight. Vikki lost both of her parents to cancer when she was only sixteen and, consequently, was forced to grow up fast. She became a responsible adult long before a teenager should have to. Because of this, she needed a sense of normality and security in her life.

It began to dawn on her that I wasn't the person to provide this. Although we had married and had a child, she sensed that I wasn't ready to settle down into a nine-to-five career, a nice family home and a few holidays a year. We had made a terrible mistake and we both knew it.

Neither of us regretted having Aaron. We placed him at the centre of any decisions we were about to make. Luckily, he was very young, which offered him a level of protection. Not that I condone any marriage break-up, but I always think it is less damaging for younger and more naïve children.

I don't really remember the day that my marriage ended, but I do remember the words that Vikki said that day. "I am done. I want a divorce."

Could my life actually get any worse than it was right then? I was twenty-six years old, living in Milton Keynes, working a dead-end job and about to become a divorced dad to a two-year-old. At the time everything was as bleak as could be. I had experienced a fair degree of adversity in my quarter of a century on the planet so far, and this was another one of those times.

A wise man once said that, in times of adversity and change, we really discover who we are and what we are made of. I was about to find out.

Having ascertained that my marriage was definitely over, I began to plan for my immediate future – even though I did not have a clue what that future was. Vikki wanted me out of the home so she too could move on with her life. That was fine with me, as long as the transition wasn't disruptive to Aaron; the only problem was that I didn't know where I was going to go. I couldn't afford a place of my own on the meagre wage I got for being a human robot. May, and the snow slope shop job, was still a long way off. One morning, whilst I was riding to work on my bike, the answer came to me as if by divine intervention.

I was crossing a road when a truck appeared from out of nowhere. I had to slam my breaks on hard to avoid ploughing into the side of it. As I picked myself up from the floor, I was about to launch a torrent of abuse at the driver, when I noticed the sign on the side of the truck. There in letters three feet high was the word 'EVEREST', followed by the advertising strapline *'Fit the Best'*.

So, looking past the fact that I was almost wiped out by a double-glazing-window truck, what I saw was Everest – *Be the Best*. Right there and then, I knew what I was going to do.

I went to work that day and handed in my notice with immediate effect. Three days later, a plane screeched off the tarmac at Heathrow's Terminal 2 runway, heading for Kathmandu in Nepal. I sat sipping a coffee in seat E14, watching all my troubles drift away beneath me. As I flew across the rooftops and clouds of London to the start of my new life, I knew that my direction had once more changed course. This time I was heading straight for Everest.

PART THREE: THE ROAD TO EVEREST

The distance between your dreams and reality is called action

As seat-of-the-pants decisions go, this was the most spontaneous thing I had ever done. I had convinced myself that, to get over the break-up of my marriage, I would do the one thing I had promised myself before the end of the previous year: visit the mountain of my dreams.

However there was one slight drawback to my plan, as was often the case in my life. I was pretty broke when I quit the job with Vikki's brother. So how was I going to be able to afford a trekking holiday? I had recently withdrawn my last £1,000 life savings to see me through while I looked for somewhere new to live. This would have gone a long way towards paying a security bond and the first month's rent on a place, but once again I defied all logic and common sense by deciding to fly halfway across the world and live for the moment.

The moment I decided I was doing this, I booked my flights and bought a guidebook to trekking in Nepal. Everything became clear for the first time in years. I knew in my heart that I was doing the right thing; if I was ever going to climb Everest, then I had to *see* the mountain first.

The flights cost £550, which left me £450 for spending money. I skipped on the insurance to keep the cost down.

"Everest!" Mam said. "What? When? How?"

"Don't ask," I said. "Just trust me."

Mam was upset at the breakdown of my marriage, having experienced two divorces of her own. She was genuinely concerned for my welfare when I told her that I had booked a return flight to Nepal to trek to Everest.

"When are you leaving to do this?" she enquired.

"Actually tomorrow," I answered.

"WHAT!" she shouted back at me down the phone. "Have you lost your bloody mind?"

"Probably. But I'm going to Everest to get it back."

I had no intention of renting a grotty bedsit and staying in a thankless job just to scrape a living. What I wanted to do was *really* live.

I knew that Aaron was going to be OK with his mum, and besides, I was only talking about a four-week trip. It wasn't as if I was off to travel the world for a year. Still, my decision to go to Nepal didn't go down too well at all. I assured Vikki this was the best thing to happen, as it would give us both the breathing space we needed to get over the break-up.

"I can't believe you are actually going through with this!" Vikki threw at me on the eve of departure. "You know what you are doing is abandoning your son," she further added, heightening the guilt I already felt. I knew I had to do this, though. It was the path I desperately wanted to take – no, needed to take.

I said as much back to Vikki. "I don't expect you to understand why I am doing this, and I am not asking for your acceptance. But this is just something I must do," I added. I felt terrible, guilty, excited and anxious all at the same time.

As I boarded the coach to Heathrow, on my way to catch the flight, I was apprehensive, but content for the first time in a long time. The date was 5th April 2000.

Once in Nepal I had planned to walk the whole way to the mountain from the road's end at Jiri. This was for a few reasons. Firstly I wanted to soak up as much of the experience as I possibly could. Walking through the lower agricultural terraced lands of rural Nepal would allow me to immerse myself in the culture and customs of the country and its people. But secondly and more significantly it was a lot cheaper; I couldn't afford to buy a return air ticket to Lukla.

Walking from Jiri added ten additional days of trekking before I even reached Lukla, but the extra time would enable me to enjoy everything the longer trek would offer.

Touching down in Kathmandu the following evening was a huge culture shock. I had never visited somewhere with such a high level of poverty and deprivation. In Kathmandu, it confronts you head-on the second you leave the international airport building.

There was no shortage of locals jostling and pulling at me for attention. I settled on one, who offered me a free ride into town, if I was willing to book a night in the hotel that he was clearly earning commission from. I had no problems with that. He soon had my bags thrown into the back of an old car with the rear windscreen missing. The car – if you could call it that – had seen much better days.

As I hurtled towards Thamel (the tourist quarter of the city) through the back streets of Kathmandu, everywhere was eerily dark and quiet. Piles of rubbish were stacked high outside crumbling red-brick buildings. Candles cast a pathetic glow over doorways where dogs were fed scraps of leftover dinner, which were thrown out into the streets. A cow walked out into the road, forcing the driver to take evasive action.

Ancient ruins and religious artefacts jostled for space, crammed in next to trinket shops and very basic-looking hotels with names such as Hotel Manaslu, the Annapurna Guesthouse and the Everest Hotel. There was no doubting the mountains of the Himalayas were the real tourism pull in this part of the city.

I arrived at my destination in a ramshackle, almost dystopian part of the city. Checking in to the hotel I was informed there was a power outage. This explained why everywhere was cloaked in darkness.

These rolling blackouts, I would come to learn, were when power was intentionally shut down in parts of the city. Nepal's already delicate electricity supply had, at times, huge demands placed on it. To avoid a total shutdown, rolling blackouts were brought in by the electricity company to cope with the demand. It was a daily occurrence in Kathmandu. As I made my way to Thamel, parts of the city were experiencing one of these blackouts. There had also been a general strike that day, which had turned violent; as a result, a large number of Thamel's bars and restaurants remained closed. I decided I would spend my first full night in Kathmandu in the safety of my hotel room.

I knew I would have to be frugal with my spending but luckily Kathmandu was very cheap, as I discovered over the following few days before I began the trek. I was trekking to Base Camp quite literally, as the Lonely Planet guidebook stated, 'on a shoestring'.

To reach Jiri from Kathmandu involved a ten-to-twelve-hour bus journey from the bus station in the centre of the city. I can't say I was looking forward to this part of the journey, but still, I would get to rub shoulders with the locals and experience a completely different culture to any I had witnessed first hand before.

On my first full morning in the city I found a tour operator who could sell me a bus ticket and also one for my pack. I was advised to keep my pack with me at all times, and not put it up on the roof of the bus.

I booked my bus ride to Jiri at 5.30am the following morning. This meant I had the rest of the day to explore Kathmandu, which I was eager to see. My journey to Everest had well and truly began. I spent the rest of the day away with the fairies, grateful to finally be in Nepal.

In my short time in Kathmandu, at the beginning of the trek, I took in most of the major historical and religious sites. I found the whole place highly absorbing and spiritual. A steep long stairway brought me to the monkey temple, named because of the holy monkeys that lived on one of the temples on the site. This climb in the humid mid-day sun made for an early bout of exercise.

As a non-Hindu, the temple was out of bounds for me. However, there were lots of other religious and spiritual artefacts and shrines around. I did what all good tourists do, and that was to snap away with my camera. Back then, there were no such things as smartphones and digital cameras. I didn't know if the pictures I was taking were any good. I would just have to snap away and hope that some would turn out half-decent.

On the other side of the river I witnessed a Hindu cremation. I was respectful of the occasion and declined from taking any photos. The body was dipped into the river three times before the cremation began, then wrapped in a white sheet and a funeral pyre lit on top of it. On completion of the cremation, a member of the group swam in the river. Hindus believe that the river purifies people spiritually; all funeral mourners from a cremation are encouraged to dip in the river. I was fascinated with the whole spectacle.

I arrived at the bus station the following morning and was given two tickets – one for me, and one for my bag. I also left a bag of clothing, that I wouldn't need until I returned to Kathmandu, at the Marco Polo guesthouse. All I had with me was clothing and equipment that I would need for the trek. Even so, there was a fair bit of weight in my pack. I hauled it aboard what the driver assured me was a roadworthy vehicle.

Jiri, nestled at 1,935m above sea level, was a neat little settlement in a fertile valley. There were many lodges there, mainly used by the locals, as most people tended to miss this part of the trail out, opting instead to fly to Lukla. Before reaching Jiri, I had the long bus journey to complete before I could revel in my first full night on the trail, away from the hustle and bustle of Kathmandu.

Jiri was actually only 110km from Kathmandu, but due to the nature of the terrain and the roads, it was a slow methodical journey with constant stops to let people on and off. It was all uphill too as we huffed and puffed our way along single-track roads. We never seemed to be able to go for more than a kilometre or so without some interruption.

With the top speed of the bus a whopping 40mph, I settled in for a long day. Further along the road, we stopped to let an old lady get on with two ferret-like animals in a cage. I actually had no idea what they were. But for the next hour they made their presence known, screeching and chirping away loudly.

The bus was packed that morning and there wasn't a spare seat to be had. An older chap got on and I promptly offered up the seat my pack had been occupying. I made the driver pull over so I could stick my pack up on the roof with the rest of the luggage. "No, no," he said. "You have paid for seat." I told him that I didn't mind. I couldn't possibly have my pack on a seat whilst someone else, considerably older than me, stood up. I don't think he understood my objections though and just stared at me as if I were mad.

At the next stop, another older local boarded and I offered up my own seat this time. I reckoned that I was going to be on my feet for several hours a day from tomorrow anyway, so what difference did several hours today make? The driver looked back at me, perplexed. Clearly, chivalry wasn't practised in rural Nepal.

After a few more hours of steady climbing along the valley, we stopped in a more established town for an hour's lunch stop. I noticed that the bus was having a wheel changed. We had driven for at least an hour with the front tyre as flat as a pancake. I can't say I had noticed to be honest – the road was as bumpy and rough as hell anyway. We could have had four flat tyres and it wouldn't have made a jot of difference.

All the bus passengers headed across the road into what looked like a local Nepali diner. I followed them. It was lunchtime and I was hungry. A cheeseburger and fries would have gone down very well, but there was only one dish on offer. It was the local food of choice in this region of the world: dal bhat.

Each region of Nepal has its own take on the dish, but the main ingredients are always the same: rice, vegetables and lentils.

To someone like me, used to a rich western diet, it was incredibly bland. Still, not being one to insult or disappoint, I eagerly ordered a portion. I was given a plate overflowing with rice and vegetables on one half and a heavily laced garlic and lentil soup on the other.

I sat down at a long table with everyone else, but then realised I didn't have any cutlery. I made the universal sign, pretending to use a fork, to show the server what I needed. He showed me that I needed to use my hands to pick up the food.

I looked around to see how everyone else was doing this. You poured the garlic soup over the rice and veg and then brought it to your mouth to eat it. I proceeded to do likewise, but was instantly reprimanded for using the wrong hand. In Nepali cuisine, you use the right hand to eat. The left hand is for certain toilet purposes and should never touch food. I was told I was allowed to hold a cup with my left hand, but never food.

I ate every last scrap of the dal bhat, not wanting to offend. The server rewarded me with another full plate. *Oh no,* I thought. There was no way I could eat another serving. Still, not wanting to insult my host, I tried my best to eat the new helping. I washed the lot down with two Diet Pepsis.

Back on the bus, we continued on our way. Within fifteen minutes, I knew I was in trouble. I felt half a kilogram of rice and veg start to come back up. I motioned to the driver to pull over, and not a moment too soon as I heaved my lunch all over the side of the road. I glanced back at the bus and saw everyone laughing at me. What a pathetic introduction to Nepali food. I quickly began to feel better, but it had been a tad embarrassing.

A few passengers got off after one more stop, which gave me my seat back. As I sat watching rural Nepal go lazily by out of the window, I got my Sony Walkman out of my pocket and decided to listen to some music. Back in the year 2000, the iconic iPod still hadn't been invented. All of my music was on cassettes, which you listened to on a portable cassette player. For those of you reading this born after 1995, I am afraid you will have to ask your parents what these were.

The Walkman was the iPod of its time. Mine was a bright yellow sports model and stuck out like a sore thumb. I still cringe to this day when I look back at photos of my first visit to Nepal. All I see is that hideous Walkman attached to my belt.

I got chatting with the young local sat in front of me, who took a great interest in listening to my music. I was listening to The Corrs, the Irish sibling quartet, who were hugely popular at the time. I had the hots for Andrea Corr, the lead singer. I told my new friend that she was my girlfriend back home. This was met with much whooping and cheering.

I spent the last few hours into Jiri walking up and down the bus, allowing all the other passengers to take a turn listening to the music coming from this strange yellow brick. My friend followed behind, telling everyone the singer was my wife. *If only,* I thought! The ten or so hours went quickly and I have fond memories of my first introduction to Nepal outside of Kathmandu, apart from vomiting up my first dal bhat, of course.

As the bus came to a stop, I hauled my weary self up onto the roof to retrieve my pack. It was still there, as I was confident it would be. The second my feet hit the dirt, I was whisked away by a teahouse owner. He gave me a key for a room and wasted no time in having my pack taken inside. I was happy with this. I hadn't planned where I was going to stay from night to night anyway, so was grateful for a room to find me.

A couple from New Zealand shared that first night with me in the lodge. Ken and Kelly were trekking to Base Camp too. I got on well with them both instantly, and as this was the first day of the trek, there was a strong possibility that I would be seeing plenty more of them.

That first night in the lodge I felt more alive than I had been in years. I allowed my mind to wander to Everest. I imagined what it would be like, finally standing at the foot of the Icefall, looking directly into its jaws and seeing its icy teeth glisten.

I drifted off to sleep, listening to my new Irish wife's dulcet tones, covering a Fleetwood Mac classic: "Yeah, thunder only happens when it's raining, players only love you when they're playing. Yeah, women they will come and they will go, when the rain washes you clean you'll know, you'll know." *You've got a point there, my love,* I thought, as sleep overtook me.

From Jiri, I had planned a leisurely fourteen-day trek to Base Camp, following the main expedition route through the Khumbu Valley. This was the way the British team went in 1953 on their journey to the mountain. I felt honoured to be following in their footsteps. The surrounding fertile land was timeless. It probably didn't look any different than it had forty-seven years before when Edmund Hillary, John Hunt and company passed through.

That morning, I had peanut butter on toast and lemon tea for breakfast, before beginning my first day's trekking. I stopped for lunch at a *Shivalya*, a bustling little village with a handful of lodges.

After lunch I set off with Ken and Kelly, but was keen to get some air into my lungs and a sweat on, so I pushed ahead.

I chose a teahouse to stay for the evening in Deorali at an altitude of 2,705m. I ordered a dinner of fried potatoes and yak cheese and joined in a game of cards with some fellow trekkers, including an American couple, a chap from Canada and a girl from Sweden. I retired to my very basic and flimsy wooden-walled bedroom at 7.30pm and updated my journal – something that would become standard practice from that point on.

As the trek advanced, the daily pattern over the next few days emerged: arriving at a teahouse by mid to late afternoon, ordering an evening dinner, washing and changing into warm clothing, and then finding a seat in the large communal dining area that all teahouses and lodges had.

For the first few days of trekking, I found my own steady pace. I idly drifted each day away, lost in my thoughts as I listened to my Walkman, taking in the stunning scenery all around me. I had to pinch myself on more than once occasion to be sure I was actually there, trekking through the lower foothills of the Himalayas, on my way to Everest.

On the third day of the trek, I reached an attractive village called Junbesi that clung to the side of a hill. The lodge I chose was very clean, tidy and spacious. In the dorm that night, I got talking with a Canadian girl called Monica, who was part way through a round-the-world trip. We instantly got on and chatted away a good few hours, putting the world to rights.

The following morning dawned with clear blue skies. It was a great omen for what would become a hugely memorable day for me – the day I would finally see Everest.

I knew there was a possibility of seeing the mountain that day, but only if the sky remained cloudless. After only an hour's easy walking, from the lodge skirting the side of a valley, I rounded a corner to arrive at a sublime viewpoint. There, laid out before me, were several peaks all glistening under a brilliant blue, cloudless sky. One particular peak immediately grabbed my attention.

With its summit just poking out, almost hidden by the other mountains dominating the foreground and a snow plume billowing away to the right, there was no mistaking the mountain I was looking at: Everest – the highest mountain on the planet.

Everest had fascinated and intoxicated me for over ten years and finally I was viewing it with my own eyes. At that precise moment, it went from being something I had fantasised about in the pages of books and magazines to something very real.

A few days later, still buzzing with the adrenaline of seeing the mountain, I arrived in Namche, the true gateway to Everest. On the steep forest path up to the town I got a further glimpse of the mountain, this time a bit closer.

Namche was a world away from most of the places we had stayed over the past seven days. With its internet café, bakeries and various shops, it was the last major settlement before reaching Everest.

After spending a week trekking, I had well and truly embraced the Nepali culture. Stupas dotted the trail at regular intervals, some with the all-seeing eyes of Buddha painted intricately into the structure. Prayer wheels and complex carved Mani stone walls were around every corner. Prayer flags flapped in the wind almost everywhere. Printed with mantras, these multi-coloured cloths greet you the minute you land in Kathmandu. Used to promote peace, compassion, strength and wisdom, the general principle is that they carry prayers to the gods. Tibetans, however, believe that the mantras on the cloths are blown by the wind to travel the world, bringing benefit to all.

Either way, it is a beautiful message of peace and wisdom. I do not know a single person who hasn't been moved by what they experience on the trail to Everest. It was certainly moving me on my first visit to Nepal.

In six days' time, I would reach Everest Base Camp and my trek's destination. But before that, there was the most spectacular scenery to trek through.

All the worries and anxieties that I had experienced in the past few months, on the run up to this trip, eased away with each day's trekking. As I got closer to Everest, I was becoming fitter with every step. I was missing my son so much, but the days in Nepal so far had done exactly what I had hoped they would.

The trip certainly took my mind off my broken marriage. Taking in the incredible scenery melted everything else away. At times, I could go an hour without passing a living soul on the trail. It felt like I had the mountains and landscape all to myself. It was divine in its splendour and I eagerly soaked it all up.

Tengboche, with its impressive monastery, offered a tantalising view of Everest, peeking from behind the Lhotse-Nupste wall. The mighty Ama Dablam stole the show, however, with its sharp summit pyramid and large snowcap. It was easy to see why Edmund Hillary once called it unclimbable.

On day eleven I ascended Chukhung Ri with Monica, the Canadian girl. It was the first time in my life that I had been over 5,000m in altitude – and also the first time on the trip I experienced a headache for my efforts. A quick descent down to Dingboche soon cured it, though. After a further rest in Dingboche the next day, we trekked for a few hours to Lobuche, my penultimate overnight stay, before reaching Everest.

It wasn't the prettiest village on the trek. In fact, it was positively filthy, with used toilet rolls strewn around the nearby hillside. The following morning I was keen to leave and hiked out with an American trekker called Tim, whom I had met in the lodge the previous night.

Our aim was to reach Gorak Shep (the last settlement before the head of the Khumbu Glacier and Everest Base Camp), have some light lunch and then ascend Kala Patthar. From the top of this classic viewpoint, I would get a real look at the upper slopes of Everest and the infamous Khumbu Icefall.

It took us both just under two hours to reach Gorak Shep. After vegetable fried rice and a lemon tea in the first lodge we came to, we began the trek up Kala Patthar.

Years dreaming of seeing Everest and the Icefall were about to come true. Nuptse and Pumori both dominated the morning walk and looked mighty impressive as we made our way across the Gorak Shep flats. A little over an hour later, I reached the top after the lung-busting hike to the prayer flags fluttering in the breeze. I wish I could say that tears filled my eyes as I stared across the valley at Everest and Nuptse, but the second I reached the top I came down with an excruciating headache.

I had probably raced up too quickly in my eagerness to see Everest. I was now paying the price for my haste. All I could think about on top of Kala Patthar was descending back down. I did manage to have my picture taken with Everest over my right shoulder, and I was able to crack a small smile, but stayed at the top for no more than a few minutes before skipping and running all the way back down to the lodge. Once at lower elevations my headache instantly dwindled.

Ellis feeling ill on Kala Pathar in 2000

This wasn't how I had imagined my first good look at Everest, but at altitude you take what you can get.

After a night's rest back in the Snowland Lodge at Gorak Shep, I set off the following morning to trek along the glacier for a couple of hours to Everest Base Camp. Base Camp had been the target of my entire trip since leaving Milton Keynes seventeen days earlier.

There was a noticeable skip to my stride as I walked along the terminal moraine of the Khumbu Glacier. The headaches that had plagued me for the last few days showed no signs of reappearing. I felt hydrated and full of beans, and I sped along eager to finally reach a place I had only dreamed about until this point.

At 10am, Tim and I strode the last few metres in to the start of Base Camp, a sprawling 2km-long tented city that curved around the bottom of the Icefall – the gateway to the upper slopes of Everest.

Monica soon followed behind and we gave each other a huge hug before sitting down to rest on a boulder on top of the groaning glacier beneath. I took in all my surroundings and a familiar feeling started to take hold. I couldn't explain it, as I had never visited Base Camp before, but it felt like I had arrived somewhere that I knew well.

Although Base Camp was very much an alien landscape, with its towering flutes of moraine and ice sculptures, it never felt remote to me. Right then, at that exact moment in time, there was nowhere else on the planet that I would rather have been.

The three of us began exploring Base Camp together. I was conscious that most teams wouldn't want trekkers poking their heads through their tent doors, so I stayed away from most tented areas, but I was happy to wander around and in between.

Wandering around Base Camp that day, I spotted the tents of Adventure Consultants, the New Zealand guiding company which, four years before, had been at the centre of the storm that tore through the upper stretches of the mountain. Well documented in the book *Into Thin Air*, lead guide and Adventure Consultants owner, Rob Hall, was killed, along with guide Andy Harris and two clients, Yasuko Namba and Doug Hansen.

Guy Cotter, a fellow kiwi guide and good friend of Rob's, now owned and operated the company after Rob's widow, Jan Arnold, asked him to take the helm. Guy naturally obliged.

The next camp I stumbled into was a team from Nomad Expeditions. They were a Kathmandu-based operator, on Everest that season to support a Sherpa by the name of Babu Chiri in his sixteen-hour speed ascent to the summit.

Babu was a Sherpa with a legendary reputation, having reached the summit nine times. He had even spent twenty-one hours on the summit the previous year without oxygen, a staggering achievement.

I began speaking with a softly spoken Sherpa, wearing a Mountain Hardwear test team baseball cap. It was Babu Sherpa.

He gave me a lemon tea; I shook his hand and wished him well as we spoke about his attempt. His plan was to go from Base Camp to the summit in one continuous push, breaking the seventeen-hour mark. (A month later he would go on to do just that, reaching the summit for the tenth and final time, in sixteen hours and fifty-six minutes.) As I departed, he placed his cap on my head, told me to keep it and patted me on the back.

One year later, Babu Chiri returned to Everest, aiming for his eleventh summit of the mountain. On the 29th April 2001, he was up at Camp Two in the western cwm. It is believed that he was taking pictures from different areas of the camp when he fell into an unseen crevasse. His body was recovered the following day. Nepal had lost one of its greatest ever Sherpas since Tenzing Norgay.

Having visited Base Camp, I made my way happily down the valley over a leisurely four days. I then waited two further days in Lukla before I was finally able to get a flight back to Kathmandu. The flight back was every bit as exhilarating as I had been promised, as we skimmed no more than a few hundred metres above lush pine forests and rolling green hills.

Ellis at Base Camp in 2000

No sooner had I settled into the flight than we began the descent. Around forty-five minutes later, I walked across the tarmac back in Kathmandu. The hazy afternoon heat warmed me instantly. It felt good to be back in civilisation after four weeks in the mountains.

Kathmandu went by in a haze of alcohol, chocolate cake and sizzling yak steak. My international flight home wasn't for another six days, which meant I had plenty of time to soak up all the sights and sounds of Kathmandu's bustling nightlife, which I was keen to do.

Monica and I spent a few nights in Fire and Ice, and several bars with rooftop terraces, where we danced the night away to the local house band.

Trekking to Everest had been an amazing experience and I didn't regret one moment of it. However, I was beginning to really miss Aaron. I longed for home now, whatever shape or form that would turn out to be.

I had received an email from Vikki whilst on the trail. I read it one night in an internet café in Thamel. She informed me that Aaron was well and that I had received an offer of employment from the shop in the snow slope.

This was great news. It meant that I would immediately have an income upon my return, especially important as I was going to need a new place to live. I would be returning home to what would surely be a testing time but I still had a few days left in Nepal.

A few days earlier, I had wandered into a tattoo parlour in a back street in Thamel. I watched as a chap from the UK had the all-seeing eyes of Buddha etched onto his forearm. It looked impressive and I congratulated him on a nice addition to his body.

I then watched on, in horror, as he had the crest of Liverpool Football Club added.

I decided that I would come back in a day or two. On a map of Everest I had bought from a bookshop, I picked up on the Nepali word for Everest – *Sagarmatha*. Depending on which source you consulted, the general consensus was that this local word for Everest meant 'Forehead in the sky'.

Late one night back in my room at the Annapurna guesthouse, I roughly sketched an idea. Monica kept me company the morning I went back to the tatooist. I gave the young Nepali my idea, and he told me to come back in thirty minutes. After a quick coffee, he had turned my concept into a worthy piece of art, one that I would be proud to have etched on my shoulder for the rest of my life.

An hour later after it was completed I left and excitedly emailed back home to share the good news about my new Everest tattoo. Mam's response took me by surprise: "Why couldn't you have bought a T-shirt like most normal people do?"

I was proud that I now had a permanent reminder of my life's goal. T-shirts fade and wear out. This wouldn't.

Monica was so impressed that, a day later, she went back to the tattooist and had the same design added to her lower back. As far as I know, there is just me, and a Canadian girl called Monica with whom I trekked to Everest, walking around this planet with the exact same tattoo.

With just one day left in Kathmandu, I was ready for home. I had all but depleted my budget. I had run out of money a few days earlier, but managed to get a cash advance on a Visa credit card to keep me going until I flew back to England. I had sampled every fine bakery, coffee shop, bar and restaurant that the city had to offer. After buying a few gifts to take home, I had just a few dollars to my name. This was about to bite me on the backside, big time.

On the morning of departure, my guesthouse arranged for a taxi to take me to the international airport. As I left the hustle and bustle of Thamel behind, I was excited to finally be on my way home after my longest trip away from British shores.

I quickly went through security at the airport and joined the back of a large queue at the Gulf Air check-in desk, bound for Bahrain in the Persian Gulf.

When I got to the front of the counter, there was already a confrontation taking place with several irate Dutch passengers who, as I discovered, had been bumped off an already largely over-booked flight. *Poor people,* I thought, as I handed across my ticket and passport. I wouldn't wish that on anyone.

The check-in clerk jolted me back to the present by barking, "Where is your confirmation stamp?"

"My what?"

"Your stamp for confirming your flight home. You must reconfirm your flight forty-eight hours before departure. No stamp, then I am afraid no flight."

Unbeknownst to me, I should have called into the local office for Gulf Air in Kathmandu a few days prior, and informed them that I would be on my flight home. They would then stamp my ticket – that I had paid money for – to ensure a seat on the plane that I had every intention of sitting in. Surely, the fact that I had paid money for a return ticket to Kathmandu was proof enough that I planned to be present on the return leg?

I began remonstrating with the already enormously stressed-out airline clerk, who by now was trying desperately to quell a major backlash from the group of Dutch passengers growing angrier by the minute. I realised I was fighting a lost cause. It was time to pull a rabbit out of my backside, or else I was screwed.

About to be stranded in Kathmandu, I first told the guy that I had reconfirmed and that there must be a mistake. He got a colleague to frog-march me to an office where he proceeded to switch on what looked like a first-generation Apple Macintosh computer from the 1980s. We waited for what felt like a fortnight for it to boot up. By which point, the plane – and my seat on it that we were debating over – was probably already in the air.

The young Nepali opened what must have been the reconfirmation list for my flight, to prove there was no tick next to my name. He could have been showing me his list of favourite Rolling Stones songs, for all I knew; yet still I persisted.

"I couldn't care less what your computer tells you," I said. "I *did* reconfirm." He wasn't buying it, though.

Back at the Gulf Air check-in desk, things were turning from hectic to desperate all-out warfare, with the passengers from Holland leading the charge.

The situation nosedived further, and deteriorated into an almost tribal flight-or-fight mentality, when the actual captain of the plane approached the desk. "I have just five seats left on the plane," he shouted over the din of the mob. "Please, first ones here in front of me."

A predictable stampede of passengers ensued, fighting their way through to the front, taking no prisoners as they went. Arms and legs flailed everywhere. My faith in humanity was seriously being tested at that moment – especially seeing the terrified look on a little Dutch girl's face, who couldn't have been more than seven years old. I picked her up in my arms as her parents argued their case for flying to the plane's captain, but it was to no avail. The five chosen passengers and their bags disappeared through to the gate with the captain.

Having no flight home was bad enough, but now I was faced with the alarming prospect of being stranded in an airport in a third-world city, with no money, no way of contacting home and no way to book a new flight. I had to act, and fast.

To this day, I do not know what possibly possessed me to do what I did that day. I stood on my trolley, so I was as high as I could be, and over the noise of all the disgruntled passengers, I stated my case loud and clear:

"Hey everyone," I began. "My name is Ellis. I am from England and in three days' time I am due to get married."

As the words left my lips, I secretly cringed at this enormous lie I was announcing to an airport full of shocked onlookers.

"I need to get back home, or else I am in a world of trouble with my fiancée," I further embellished.

In fact I was going home to a divorce, not a wedding, but I figured that desperate circumstances called for desperate action. I knew that just drifting away quietly into the night was not going to do me any favours.

"I have no flight home, no money to phone home and no way to get home. Can anyone help me please?" I finished.

No sooner had I jumped down from the trolley than an American lady approached, offering me $20 to make a phone call. A few of the Dutch families, who had been making the biggest protest of all, looked equally concerned and said they would help me in any way they could. With one last desperate attempt to convince the Gulf Air check-in clerk to put me on the next flight home, I pleaded my case and expanded on the whole 'getting married' story.

One Dutch family, who had taken me under their wing, informed me that they were being taken to a hotel on the outskirts of Kathmandu whilst they waited for a new flight home. For all their protests and arguing with representatives of Gulf Air, I did feel sorry for them, despite my own predicament. They had reconfirmed and were still kicked off the flight. I didn't really have a leg to stand on.

I looked directly at the chap on the desk. With big rabbit eyes, I implored him to let me on the bus to the hotel and catch the next available flight home. I told him that I accepted that I wouldn't be flying home that night, but at least if I could get back to the hotel and let everyone back home know the situation, then the damage would be minimal.

"I might still miss my wedding," I added, "but at least we could delay until my return."

"Get on the bus."

"Thank you sir," I whimpered. I was one lucky so-and-so, albeit a lying and amoral so-and-so.

The bus took us to the lavish Everest Hotel on the outskirts of Kathmandu. As we checked in and collected room keys, the Dutch were still grumbling about the injustice of it all. I kept quiet. We were informed that each of us could have three minutes of free international telephone calls daily during our stay.

The lady from the family, who seemed most concerned about me, offered me everyone else's free minutes so I could sort out the mess they thought I was in. I felt terrible, but I couldn't back out now and admit it was all a lie. I had to keep the pretence up, in case I lost my place on a new flight home. Every time someone offered me some assistance, I graciously accepted, but secretly died a little inside.

We had been informed that all meals and drinks would be free during our stay, but we would have to pay for alcohol. This, once again, did not go down well with the Dutch. I kept my head down during the ensuing melee in the reception area, trying to distance myself from the verbal scrap.

When I finally went up to the reception desk to collect my voucher for telephone calls, the manager enquired if I was the English chap who needed to be home for his marriage.

"That's me," I said, trying to look sad and forlorn.

"For you, free bar," she said.

Could this gratuity towards me get any worse? Over the next few days, the answer to that was a resounding *yes*.

The biggest lie I had ever told had bought me a short stay in a nice hotel. I had also now been given a new flight home, but it wasn't for three more days. There was nothing to do other than rest, read, eat, drink and lounge around the pool. After the trek to Everest, this was a real holiday.

Throughout my time at the hotel, I tried to keep my head down as much as possible. If I caught someone's eye, I would have to speak to them, which generally meant elaborating on my deceitful wedding story. I felt guilty enough as it was without having to embellish further.

I read Anatoli Boukreev's *The Climb* from cover to cover during my time in the hotel. This strengthened my resolve to climb Everest, and kept my mind off the fictional wedding.

When the day of my new flight came, I exchanged email addresses with some of the Dutch people, who were keen to hear how things developed back home. I realised my little indiscretion was going to keep me feeling guilty for a while longer yet.

Check-in went smoothly this time around. When I got to the check-in counter, I handed across my passport and was presented with a business-class boarding pass. The airline must have felt genuinely bad that I had missed my initial flight (and wedding). To avoid a possible lawsuit, they were determined to make it up to me. Flying me home business-class was definitely a step in the right direction. *If only they knew the truth,* I thought. The cabin crew gave me champagne and dinner served on fine crockery – and this was only my third international flight! On the way to Bahrain, I reclined my seat flat and drifted off to sleep. Who says lying doesn't pay?

If I thought business class was lavish, this was nothing compared to what I had in store on the flight back to Heathrow. For the last leg of the journey home, Gulf Air upgraded me yet again. I was shown to a seat in the first-class part of the plane. There I was in my shorts, flip-flops and scruffy red T-shirt, when most of the other passengers in first-class were suitably attired in business dress. They must have assumed that I was either just some rich traveller or in the wrong seat. I glanced back down the plane into economy, revelling in the fortune that lady luck had bestowed upon me.

I allowed myself to enjoy the luxury while it lasted. I knew that, once I landed, I would be arriving home to a different future. It was a future in which I would be a single father to a three-year-old child, and a divorcee, not newly married as my dishonesty had stated. But this dishonesty had got me home.

I hoped at some point that my future would include a return back to Nepal – maybe even to attempt Everest one day, not just walk to the bottom. For now, though, I needed to sort my life out. I was returning home to a sea of unrest, not the wedding I had so eloquently invented and lived on for my last three days in Nepal.

When I returned home from Everest, seven months of the most testing year of my life to date still remained. I had just completed the best part of the year, in finally seeing Everest. That meant the worst was still to come – and come it would.

Within days of arriving home, I needed a new place to live. I had tentatively agreed to sign the family home across to Vikki before I left for Nepal, and she was keen to see me keep my promise. Besides, I had no intention of dragging this break-up on and on.

Luckily, I did not have long to wait before an opportunity became available. A cousin of mine, who lived in Stevenage, offered me a room to rent in his house. This was great news – it meant I could accept the job offer at the snow slope shop, and still live close enough to see Aaron through the week and at weekends.

I started the job at the beginning of June and purchased a small car on hire finance, so I could commute the one-hour daily journey from Stevenage to Milton Keynes.

Once again, I was back working in an outdoor equipment shop, only this shop was more dedicated to the ski and snowboard scene rather than climbing and trekking. The shop was located inside Xscape, a newly opened indoor snow slope in the centre of Milton Keynes. As jobs went, this one was a keeper. I was paid reasonably well to stand around all day, looking like God's gift to snowboarding and skiing, of which I had done neither.

I spent the summer of 2000 learning to be a snowboarder and partying like I was one too – but I was twenty-seven and had a son to think about. This kept me reasonably grounded.

The rest of the shop staff were in their early twenties. I was seen as the granddad of the bunch and I was happy with that, as they knew my boundaries. As the floor manager, I had to keep a level of professionalism to our relationship, even if that meant all getting drunk together occasionally.

Although this all sounds like great fun, the reality was that I was desperately unhappy. I was living in a spare bedroom in my cousins house, only seeing Aaron every other weekend and some weekdays. I missed him desperately and I began to feel like a failure as a parent.

One day Vikki called into the shop on her lunch break.

"How are you doing?" she opened with.

I couldn't keep the sarcasm out of my response. "Never better."

"Do you know your son has been ill for a week now?"

"No, I didn't know," I replied.

"Well I did text and leave you a voicemail, days ago." The next thing she said broke my heart. "He has been asking for his daddy for days."

Aaron had a bad ear infection and had been very poorly with it. While I had been living as carefree as possible, my son had needed me, and I wasn't there for him. This really stung. I needed to step up to the mark and become a responsible parent. Somewhere along the way I had forgotten to be. This was the kick up the backside I needed to get back on track.

To take my mind off this feeling of incompetence, I sought refuge in my Everest books. I had now seen the mountain and I knew for certain that I could, at the very least, reach Base Camp on an attempted climb. I knew that putting 'trekking to Base Camp' on a prospective Everest expedition application form was hardly going to give the green light to an attempt. My climbing CV was incredibly lacking and I knew it.

Throughout my research, I realised that before tackling Everest, or any other high-altitude peak, climbers would spend time getting to grips with summits of lesser difficulty and height. This made perfect sense. I knew I would need to get some serious altitude under my belt before I could even consider going to Everest.

From the outset, it was apparent that I could not spare the time or money to disappear off for a year of adventure, climbing all across the planet as I went. Nor did I want to. I didn't want to leave Aaron any longer than necessary. But, I began to hatch a plan that I hoped would get me into a prime position to tackle Everest.

They say that some of the best ideas are born from inebriated nights in the local pub. One November evening, after a session on the slopes snowboarding and several beers, I announced to some of my shop colleagues that I was off to climb Aconcagua, the highest mountain in South America. It was quickly dismissed as drunken banter, but I was serious. I really was going to climb Aconcagua – in just two months' time, in fact.

I had identified two mountains that, if I climbed them, would prepare me for Everest. Aconcagua, at 6,961m, was to be the first of these mountains. Cho Oyu, at 8,201m in Tibet – the planet's sixth highest peak – would be the other.

I hoped climbing these two mountains would equip me with the skills and resources I would need to attempt Everest. I wasn't exactly setting out to climb the North Ridge of K2. It was well documented that Everest was nothing more difficult than a long and extended easy snow climb, but at extreme attitude, in harsh conditions. These were the real difficulties in climbing the mountain. If I could climb to over 8,000m, I knew I would be well on my way with my plans for Everest.

I came up with the rather imaginative heading of *Between Heaven and Earth – Climbing the World's Highest Mountains* as the title for my endeavours. Having decided that Aconcagua was to be my first real mountain, I needed to decide who to go with. The mountain was no pushover. A quick glance at the statistics revealed it could also be deadly, with vicious winds a constant threat.

As one of the fabled Seven Summits, the list of mountains made popular by Dick Bass twenty-five years previously, it was quite rightly a significant challenge on the road to Everest.

Having read *Into Thin Air* repeatedly over the previous few years, I was very aware of Adventure Consultants, the New-Zealand-based guiding company. Despite the tragic events on Everest almost five years previously, they seemed to be flourishing under the leadership of Guy Cotter. I sent him an email, after viewing the company's impressive-looking website.

'Climb Everest for $65,000 USD with the world's best', proclaimed a scrolling banner. I didn't have $65,000 USD, but I was confident that I could get together the $4,400 USD that it would cost to climb Aconcagua. If they are the best in the world on Everest, then the same logic must apply to all other mountains.

There were other, cheaper outfitters I could have chosen to go with. Hell, I even considered doing it all off my own back, the same way I had done when I trekked to Everest. I looked at the impressive success rate of UK-based Himalayan

Kingdoms and a small start-up guiding company from Cumbria called Adventure Peaks. But, ultimately I wanted my first experience of a climbing expedition to have as much chance of success as possible. By signing up with Adventure Consultants, I felt I would be giving myself that possibility.

As it happened, Adventure Consultants had never run a trip to Aconcagua before. The 2001 expedition would be their first ever climb of the mountain. Guy Cotter himself – the CEO, and also a mountain and ski guide – would be personally running the trip. At the time Guy had summited Everest twice, most recently in 1997, a year after Rob Hall, the co-founder of the company, had died high on Everest.

One day in late December, I received a telephone call from an overseas number I didn't recognise.

"Hey, Ellis mate, how's it going?" announced a Kiwi accent. It was Guy on the phone, responding to my email. "So you want to climb Aconcagua with us do you?" he added. I spent ten minutes enthusing to Guy all about my credentials to climb the mountain, and then Cho Oyu, and then Everest. "Steady on," Guy said, "One step at a time, mate."

The climb was planned for February the following year, just five short weeks away. If I signed on to the expedition, Guy wanted me to meet him in Mendoza, South America, on the 28th January. Mendoza was a beautiful city in north-west Argentina, on the eastern side of the Andes mountain range. Mendoza was to Aconcagua what Kathmandu was to Everest. Almost all teams attempting to climb Aconcagua would fly into, and out of, the city.

"I'm in," I proudly and enthusiastically announced down the phone.

"No worries, sweet as," Guy remarked back. He enquired how fit I currently was. I told him I was fit enough to attempt Everest now, let alone Aconcagua. This was a blatant lie. I was becoming very good at lying lately. "Send me a copy of your passport and I will get you added to the expedition list," Guy finished.

This was really happening and I realised I would be taking a giant leap towards Everest if I could pull this off. Guy told me that the route we would be tackling was the Polish Glacier Direct. This was quite an ambitious target, given that the climb involved negotiating a steep glacier covered with seracs on a 45 to 50-degree slope.

There was an easier way to the top, namely the Falso De Los Polacos, otherwise known as the normal route, on account of the fact that it was the preferred way – nothing more than a tough hike, albeit at high altitude. The route we would attempt was more technical, necessitating the use of a short rope, crampons and an ice axe.

If I was going to climb this mountain, then it may as well be by a more challenging route, I told myself. Better preparation for Everest.

When I put the phone down, I immediately became aware of four major hurdles that could stop me before I even began. Firstly, I didn't have the $4,400 USD that the trip would cost. Secondly, I was nowhere near as fit as I had made out. Thirdly, but perhaps more alarmingly, I had never used crampons and an ice axe before. And lastly did I mention that I didn't have $4,400 USD? I didn't have $4.

The money would have to be found, but when it came to fitness and lack of experience with technical equipment, I would just have to wing it. I had a few nights' layover in the hotel in Mendoza with which to get to grips with my crampons. Not ideal preparation before attempting the highest mountain in the world outside of Asia, but it was all I had. I had talked myself into this climb with the leader of what was probably the best-known mountain guiding company in the world, all thanks to that book. I now needed to walk the walk my mouth had talked me into, and climb to the top of the western hemisphere's highest point.

I had a little over four weeks till departure and in that time I had so much to do. I had decided to hand in my notice at Xscape and would work up until the expedition started.

As for my fitness, I wasn't in bad shape. Since coming home from the Everest trek earlier that year, I had remained active. I had a mountain bike, which I regularly rode around the Milton Keynes cycle network, and I was also a member of the gym in the snow slope. I would work out two to three evenings per week, mainly on the indoor rowing ergo, which I was very strong on. This was a throwback to my Dragon Boating days. It served me well back then, so I continued to train on the ergo whenever I could. I also ran a few days a week. So all in all, I felt able to take on the challenge of Aconcagua, confident that I wouldn't show myself up.

I was in no way Everest fit, but then this was only a three-week trip and I didn't need to be. *Remember, small steps, Ellis.*

I didn't have the money to pay for the trip, and nor was I likely to earn that much in such a short period of time. So with that said, I did what all people in my situation would do: I borrowed the cash from my bank. Obviously I didn't inform them that I had just quit my job to travel halfway round the world to climb a mountain. On the application form, when asked why I needed the money, I stated 'debt consolidation'.

Thanks to a combination of using my contacts in the outdoor equipment industry, and by borrowing what I couldn't blag, I managed to get all the clothing and equipment together on my kit list. It all came together nicely. I wasn't going to be a walking billboard for one particular brand on the mountain that was for sure – I was more of an entire brochure from various outdoor brands. But I didn't care. I was on my way and that was all that counted.

I spent the night before departure with Aaron, my mam and my Aunty Pam, who had travelled down from the North-East. I think, at the time, Mam thought my dream to scale Everest was just a passing fad that would go away in time. The fact that I was now about to jet off to Argentina, to attempt to climb a mountain we both struggled to pronounce, perhaps altered her perspective a little.

I was to fly from Heathrow once again, but this time with the Italian airline Alitalia, via Milan and Buenos Aries before arriving in Mendoza. As I checked in, I made a mental note: *I must remember to reconfirm on my way home.*

PART FOUR: BETWEEN HEAVEN AND EARTH

Anything I've ever done that ultimately was worthwhile… initially scared me to death. – Betty Bender.

After twenty-seven hours of travelling, I finally arrived in Mendoza at 3.30pm on Sunday 28th January 2001. In all that time I slept for just two hours. Landing in Buenos Aries, I then had to find a taxi to take me across the city to the Jorge Newbury Aeroparque, in a neighbourhood called Palermo.

Throughout the journey, the taxi driver regaled me with his knowledge of England and its culture. He didn't speak much English, but I did pick up on one or two words through his Spanish. It appeared as though Eric Clapton, The Beatles and David Beckham were the de rigueur celebrities of choice for Argentines. I concluded this after the waiter in the airport cafeteria said the same names to me upon discovering I was English.

After a short flight, a driver picked me up at the airport in Mendoza and took me to a hotel in the centre of the town, where Guy Cotter and the rest of the Adventure Consultants 2001 Aconcagua Expedition were staying. To say I was excited would be an understatement.

I checked in to my room and threw my stuff all over the bed. I was desperate to get in it, but knew I needed to stay awake to meet my team members, and get the introductions out of the way. Not more than a minute later, there was a knock at the door. I opened it to be greeted by a lean athletic-looking chap, wearing a black Adventure Consultants cap.

"Hi Ellis, Guy. Pleased to meet you, mate. How was your flight?" he asked.

"Tiring," I replied.

We spent ten minutes chatting and getting to know one another a little. Guy informed me that only three of us were on the trip. As well as Guy and myself, a 59-year-old architect from Switzerland, called Arnold Witzig, would join us. Guy informed me that Arnold also wanted to climb Everest, which he had planned for the following year. Unlike me, though, Arnold had the money to make it happen. I just had the ambition, without the actual resources to cash in on the dream.

The fact that we were a small team could only be a good thing, as it meant we could all share just one tent. I could really get to know Guy and tap in to his vast Everest knowledge – which, I figured, he would be willing to share with a potential future Everest client.

On the flip side, there was the possibility that, in such a small team, any mistakes I made would be immediately exposed, highlighting my weaknesses. The same would apply for Arnold too, though.

I met Arnold later that evening, after I had showered and slept a little. All three of us went to a restaurant, not far from the hotel, that served a buffet of predominantly beef. Argentina prides itself on its beef and it was easy to see why. For just $8, you could eat as much as you liked.

Fresh from a recent ascent of Vinson Massif, the highest mountain in Antarctica, it was obvious that Arnold was on the Seven Summits journey, of which Aconcagua was the South American tick. He was an amiable fella and I warmed to him fairly quickly, as I had done Guy.

We spent the evening drinking Cervezas and eating enough Carne de Vaca to make a T-rex proud. By the end of the night, I felt I had got to know my two new team members fairly well. It was critical we bonded, as we would be sharing the close confinements of a three-man dome tent.

The following day, we visited the tourist information centre, where we collected our permits to climb Aconcagua. The mountain is situated in Aconcagua Provincial Park and you need a permit just to be able to visit the surrounding area, the same way you do in Nepal if you wish to visit Everest.

As neither Guy nor Arnold had ever climbed the mountain before, it felt like I was part of a group of friends stepping into the unknown, rather than a member of a commercial expedition.

Before we left for the mountain I had just enough time to call into the local Alitalia airline office. I showed my passport and ticket and said that, unless I died on the mountain in the next few weeks, I had every intention of being on the plane on the way home, so could they please not resell my seat?

We had a journey of around 113 miles by bus to reach a small town called Puente Del Inca, at an altitude of 2,720m in the Horcones Valley. This was the main approach used to access both the normal route and the Polish Glacier Direct.

The drive into Puente Del Inca was impressive. As we drove higher, through some dramatic rocky scenery with clear blue skies, it suddenly dawned on me what I was here to do. Technically speaking, the only mountains I could claim to have climbed at this point were Ben Nevis and Scafell Pike back home.

That evening the reality of the climb sank in after chatting to an Australian climber who had just come down from the mountain – the only one to reach the summit out of a team of eleven climbers. This wasn't what I wanted to hear on my way to the mountain. Out of my small team of three, I was the one with the least experience. Arnold was fresh from climbing in Antarctica and Guy had climbed extensively all over the world, including on Everest twice. If any of us would fall short of the goal, it would be me. The writing was all over the wall.

The next three days of trekking were a joy. I threw myself into it, just as enthusiastically as I had in Nepal trekking to Everest. We had to gain almost 1,500m in elevation to reach our base camp at Plaza Argentina.

On the first day, we followed a well-defined trail alongside the Rio de Las Vascas river for seven miles. We made good time and arrived at a primitive settlement called La Lena Shelter for 3.00pm.

Along the trail on the first day, we passed a team of four climbers on their way out and Guy commented on how spent they looked. In passing conversation, one of the members informed us that their guide had come down with high-altitude pulmonary edema (HAPE) and that their climb had to be abandoned. They also mentioned that it was very cold and windy on the mountain, and that climbers were dropping like flies with frostbite. The seeds of doubt began eating away at me once again.

Day two of the trek began as day one had ended. We passed another team on their way down, who again informed us that the mountain, or rather the wind, had defeated them. I began to wonder if anyone actually climbed this mountain at all! Even the national park ranger who checked our permits commented that a lot of teams were retreating off the mountain. "Good luck," he told us, before adding it was now windy season and our chance of success was small to say the least.

We reached Casa De Piedra Shelter at 3,200m on this day, located along the east bank of the river that we had skirted for the first few days. From this vantage point we had our first view of Aconcagua and could see the whole of the Polish Glacier that we intended to climb. The mountain looked much more impressive when viewed for real. Even though we were still one day away from reaching Base Camp, it looked intimidating and steep. I gulped at the enormity of the climb I had set myself.

Crossing the Rio De Las Vacas river became a highlight of the trek. This looked more difficult than it actually ended up being. We removed our boots and socks and simply waded into the shallows, treading carefully as we went. The icy water instantly froze my feet and I had to vigorously rub life back into them once on the other side.

The six-mile hike to Base Camp would take us six to eight hours more, according to the guidebook I carried.

For the third day in a row, I felt strong. I was soon trekking on my own ahead of Guy. Our team leader was waiting back for Arnold, who seemed to be having a bad day. Before long I was completely on my own, with not a soul to be seen. It was obvious which direction I ought to be heading; Aconcagua dominated the head of the valley.

For three days, I kept hydrated and looked after myself as best I could. I hadn't suffered a single headache and I had barely noticed a change in altitude. *Perhaps I am suited to high-altitude environments,* I began to think to myself. Still, this was far to early in the trip to be getting ahead of myself. There was still a long way to go before I could truly test that theory out; almost another 3,800m, in fact, before reaching the top of the mountain.

Base Camp was a desolate, windswept place, yet it was luxury, comfort and rest compared to what life would be like higher up the mountain. The mountain seemed to create its own weather system, and I got an immediate glimpse into how quickly things could change.

Less than thirty minutes earlier, I had been gazing up at this perfect mountain, framed in the clearest blue sky. Yet now the summit ridge was completely covered in cloud. An ominous weather system quickly blew in and the wind picked up dramatically. *Welcome to Aconcagua,* I thought to myself, *one of the windiest mountains in the world.*

The following day was a rest day, but the day after that, we would carry tents and food up to Camp One.

After a morning of sorting all the food we would need for our time on the mountain, I was sitting around in Base Camp when I heard a helicopter circle and land. A climber from another team got in and was promptly whisked away down the valley. This must have been fairly serious if he was unable to walk.

Guy said it was probably common to come down with altitude sickness on this mountain, as the height gain was quite substantial in such a short space of time.

We later discovered that the evacuated climber had reached Camp One and immediately collapsed, struggling for breath. It turned out he was suffering from high-altitude pulmonary edema (HAPE), a potentially fatal condition in which the lungs fill with fluid. Ultimately, if left untreated, it leads to respiratory failure.

This sharpened my senses to the fact that we were not messing around here. This was the real deal. If we didn't acclimatise sensibly and slowly, we too could find ourselves being flown down in a helicopter. Altitude was an invisible deadly killer and demanded all of our respect and attention.

Walking around Base Camp that afternoon, I found a British Army team on the mountain. The team consisted of ten climbers, two of whom had already left the expedition due to pulmonary edema.

In just three days, I had witnessed far more people going down than I had going up. I began to allow negative thoughts to cross my mind. Had we left it too late? Should we have been here two weeks earlier? All the signs hinted that it would remain windy and cold for the remainder of the season. The harsh wind and altitude were taking their toll on battered and bruised climbers, who appeared to be dropping like flies.

A strong wind kicked up from nowhere and battered our tents for the rest of the day.

The following day, the winds had eased, so I packed early and was ready for the climb to Camp One at 5,000m.

I started off fine with no problems. However, just two hours in, I became increasingly aware of a violent headache forming, which seemed to get worse whenever I stood still. I soon fell well behind Guy and Arnold, and was a good half an hour behind them, when I finally reached Camp One.

The terrain was terrible – loose scree up 35-degree slopes. With each step, I slid back two or three. I was mighty relieved to see the tents of Camp One come into view at the top of this scree slope.

I ditched my pack and collapsed in a heap, my head violently throbbing. I wanted to see how long I could endure it before telling Guy. After only ten minutes, I started down. I didn't want to worsen my headache. I was distressed that, after just one sortie to 5,000m, I had succumbed to symptoms of acute mountain sickness (AMS).

On the way down to Base Camp, I cursed myself over and over for what I thought could be the end of my climb. Luckily, Guy changed our plans to allow us another rest day down at Base Camp, instead of going back up to Camp One with more equipment.

This was the first day, since being out here, that I realised just how important climbing this mountain had become to me. The thought of failure worried me enough not to mention my headache to Guy, in case he removed me from the trip. What would I tell everyone back home about my failure at coping with the altitude? I could just say it was due to an event outside my control. But to be beaten by altitude sickness, on my first big peak, would surely sound the death knell on my aspirations to climb Everest.

I had one more chance to prove I deserved to be there. In two days we would be going back up the mountain. I immediately began taking on more fluids, thinking that dehydration might have been the culprit. I also told myself I would move more slowly. I recognised that if I failed on Aconcagua, then Everest would be out of my life almost before it had entered it. Another of my big life dreams would be shattered. I was frightened of facing a future without Everest as a guiding force.

During our rest day, I spoke to an American climber who had just come down from Camp Two, but he couldn't go any further due to a chronic headache, which kept knocking him sick. Three times he had been up to Camp Two and on each occasion the same thing happened to him. He had decided enough was enough, and was on his way down. What was it with this bloody mountain and descending climbers with headaches? I began to think it would only be a matter of time before we descended too.

After our full day's rest, I felt much better in both my headspace and how my body was feeling. I was fit and raring to go. The following day, it was time to find out just how ready I was.

After packing up our tents at Base Camp, and sorting all of our personal belongings, it was time to head up the mountain. The next time we would be back in Base Camp would be after the summit attempt.

Setting off back to Camp One in the mid-day sun, I felt the weight of my pack immediately. I knew the day would be a test of my fitness and mental resolve. On a big Himalayan peak Sherpas help with the load carrying of equipment and tents, but on Aconcagua we had no such luxury. We had to personally carry everything we would need to be self-sufficient on the mountain. This included tent, sleeping bag, personal clothing plus gear, equipment and food.

The climb up to Camp One with a heavy pack was far more gruelling than anything I had experienced trekking in Nepal the previous year. Guy and Arnold had left Base Camp after me, but soon caught me up at a large area of penitentes. These strange but natural snow and ice formations are only found at high altitude, and the lower slopes of Aconcagua were covered in them.

This area of tall thin blades of hardened snow provided my first respite from the relentless uphill slog. From here I began the torturous ascent of the scree slopes that led up to Camp One. It was an absolute killer and brought me to my knees on more than one occasion. I finally dragged my weary body over the lip of the scree, and into Camp One, a good five hours after leaving Base Camp. The other day this same journey only took me three and a half hours. The difference on this day was that, although equally tired, I didn't have any headaches and didn't appear to be suffering the effects of the altitude.

All three of us spent our first night together crammed into a tent that Guy had carried up. I slept blissfully, which was a great sign for the nights to come.

Moving up to Camp Two on Aconcagua

We spent the next five days on the mountain resting and ferrying loads up to Camp Two, which on Aconcagua is the high camp from which climbers launch their summit bids.

On the 7th February we rested at Camp One, adjusting to the altitude of 5,000m. Throughout the night there had been a commotion outside our tent. Guy went out to see what was happening. A Polish climber was delirious, making no sense whatsoever; it became obvious that he was suffering an episode of HAPE, or perhaps another serious condition, high-altitude cerebral edema (*HACE*). Luckily, his team recognised this and began to evacuate the unfortunate climber down off the mountain, where a few days later we discovered he had made a full recovery. He was just another victim of a mountain so far showing no signs of yielding to its visitors.

At just short of 6,000m, Camp Two would be the highest point so far on my journey to the summit. I knew that if I couldn't reach the camp, my adventure in South America would be over, and with it my dream to climb the highest mountain in the world. In fact, from here on in, every day was critical. One slip up and it could be all over.

I had found a pace that worked well for me on my journey up to Camp One, and I called on it again for the journey up to Camp Two. Guy and Arnold quickly moved out in front, as expected, but I just concerned myself with my own slowly-slowly pace. The climb was arduous and every bit as energy sapping as the climb up to Camp One. When we made it to Camp Two in around four hours of climbing I had a slight headache, but nothing that a quick gulp of water didn't cure. I felt surprisingly well, considering how high I now was.

The summit seemed so tantalisingly close from this new vantage point.

We found a good spot and pitched a tent at the base of the Polish Glacier, the route we intended to climb, and then began the descent all the way back down to Camp One. This was one of the annoying things about having to acclimatise. All that effort and energy expended in reaching a higher altitude had to be instantly undone.

What had taken four hours to climb took just forty-five minutes to descend. Guy set off down at lightning pace and I think was a tad surprised to find me still on his heels when we reached our tent at Camp One. This summit became all-encompassing for me and I was relieved to still be in the hunt after tagging almost 6,000m.

The winds had picked up through the night and we woke to a fierce gale whipping straight into the tents of Camp One. If at any point the winds died down, we would pack up and leave for Camp Two. If not, we would wait another night, which turned out to be the case.

The following day we were finally able to reach Camp Two, after the winds that had pinned us down and battered us for the past thirty-six hours dissipated. We climbed with a glorious sunny backdrop and the odd gust of wind, but nothing too serious.

I passed a large English group on their way up the mountain and felt full of zip as I breezed by. Guy was a complete machine at altitude and moved as fast at 6,000m as he did down at 3,500m. I had resigned myself to the fact that there was no way I could keep up with him, so I didn't even try. My pace allowed me to go past most of the slower groups up ahead, and that was fine with me. As long as I was still moving up, I was still in the game.

Upon reaching Camp Two, my head was once again pounding. Tension flared up for the first time when I collapsed flat on my back, whilst Guy and Arnold flailed around trying to erect the tent in strong winds. "Get off your arse and get over here," Guy barked at me. Once the tent was up, I collapsed inside feeling totally spent.

I was now just 1,000 vertical metres beneath the trip's objective, the summit of Aconcagua. As I lay in my tent at almost 6,000m peering up at the summit, Guy informed me that there had been a change of plan. We wouldn't be tackling the Polish Glacier any more. Instead, we would be using the normal route, also known as the Falso De Los Polacos. We would traverse around the bottom of the glacier and join the normal route at an obvious ridgeline. I think the decision to change our route was down to a number of reasons, but most significantly I felt it was down to me.

I hadn't moved well up to Camp Two and I knew it. Guy would have been keeping a keen eye on me. The Polish Glacier was stripped bear of snow, exposing sheer blue ice. This would have made the climb more strenuous than it normally would have been. Arnold also questioned the technicality of the route; he just wanted to reach the summit and he didn't care which route he took. I guess I felt the same way. This was my first mountaineering trip and I was happy to just play the 'yes man', bowing down to Guy's knowledge.

From Camp Two, the summit of the mountain by the Polish Glacier was a punishing 10-15-hour climb. If we traversed onto the normal route, the summit was a mere 7-9 hours away. So, the normal route it was.

The expedition to Aconcagua had made one thing glaringly obvious: I wasn't as fit as I thought I was, and nowhere near as fit as I would need to be for an 8,000m peak. Which was next on my grand plan. I knew that if I managed to summit this mountain, there would be a lot of physical work needed to get myself ready for part two of my plan to reach Everest.

We spent two days and nights resting at Camp Two, waiting and hoping for a weather window. I had spoken with plenty of climbers lower down who had given up on their own climbs because the winds never let up. Climbing mountains meant you were at the mercy of the weather most of the time, and success often came down to being in the right place at the right time when the weather cleared.

On the evening of the 11th February at 6.30pm, we climbed into our sleeping bags and tried to get some much-needed sleep. But sleep would not come for me, due to the infernal racket caused by the relentless winds. No matter which position I contorted my body into, I could not get comfortable. With Guy on one side and Arnold on the other, I tried to lie as still as I could, but clearly I was failing miserably.

Guy sat bolt upright. "Lay the fuck still!"

Eventually, after what seemed like a good few hours of lying awake listening to the winds howling around outside, I must have succumbed to sleep. The next thing I remember was the *beep, beep, beep* from my watch at 2.30am. Arnold was already sorting through his gear. Like me, he also had a restless night and had been awake a good hour before my alarm went off. Guy slept the best of the three of us, which was evident when at 2.48am I had to nudge him awake – several times – before he finally stirred.

"What do you think?" I asked Guy hopefully. "Are we going?"

We sat in complete silence for a few seconds, before Guy asked, "Do you hear that?"

"Here what?"

"Exactly! Pack your stuff, we are going for it."

The winds that had battered us for the past day and a half were no more. It was eerily silent.

We left the tent at 3.40am, after boiling up some water for our bottles and eating a quick breakfast of porridge and jam. Although the wind had stopped, I immediately became aware of how cold it was. A thin layer of frost covered the inside of the tent and showered down onto us whenever anyone moved. When we left and began our climb to the top, my feet instantly felt cold, even inside my four-season winter mountaineering boots. We set off by the light of our head torches, skirting the base of the Polish Glacier. Staring up at the ice, it looked steep, cold and foreboding. I was glad Guy decided to avoid it.

As we linked up with the normal trail via a diagonal traverse at the base of the glacier, I began to slow. My whole body was shivering, and to make matters worse, I felt nauseous and had a mild headache coming on. I looked at my altimeter watch. We had only been on the go for 45 minutes, and had climbed just 60m higher. I remember thinking, *For fuck's sake, how am I going to keep this up for another seven to ten hours if I feel like this now?*

After just ten more minutes I needed to answer a call of nature. I shouted up to Guy ahead to hold up, so I could address the situation. "Already?" he barked back. "Hurry up, man – it's freezing." If someone who had been to the summit of Everest twice was saying it was cold, then it must have been cold.

I apologised and began the process of undressing, so I could squat and empty the contents of my digestive system onto the side of the mountain. I was wearing a pair of salopettes, which required undoing my whole bottom half and exposing my bare bottom to the freezing air. It wasn't so much the cold on my exposed cheeks that I was worried about, though. I was seriously concerned for my little fella! As I gazed down in that general direction, I couldn't even see it. *Where's it gone?* I thought. It must be true what they say about the cold affecting its size.

I sorted myself out and got back on the trail. I took a huge gulp of water and motioned to Guy that I was good to go. The second I began climbing again, I felt better. However my fingers still felt every bit as cold as my toes did inside my useless boots. *Four seasons my arse,* I thought – although to be fair, I was at an altitude of 6,100m, at four in the morning, on the side of one of the coldest mountains on the planet. I stopped to swap gloves for mitts and this made all the difference, as I massaged some warmth back into my fingers.

For the next several hours I plodded on behind Guy and Arnold, not really saying much, just keeping my head down and monotonously placing one foot in front of the other.

We moved through a large snowfield at roughly 6,150m. I had my axe with me, but it felt somewhat redundant; I used it more as a walking stick, prodding and poking it into the snow for grip. When we came to the other side of the snow, the sun was beginning to very slowly infiltrate the night sky. This immediately lifted my spirits and as I climbed higher and higher the sky became ever so slowly lighter and brighter.

We kept moving up and saying very little to each other. After every ten to fifteen paces I would lean down on my ice axe, resting my head on my arm. After thirty seconds or so of heavy breathing, trying desperately to get some air into my lungs, I would begin moving again. This process went on for hour after hour. The sky kept getting lighter, but I could not yet feel the warmth that the sun would surely bring.

Just as the sun broke into the sky, we reached a ridge we had been aiming for since leaving the comfort of our tent. I turned my head torch off and allowed the sun to warm my tired, frozen body. My feet had become a huge concern and I could hardly feel them. I checked the temperature on my watch and was astonished to see that it was -20°C. It is no exaggeration to say that it was the coldest I had ever been in my life.

After a quick rest stop, taking on some water and a few jelly babies, we pressed on. We passed 6,200m, then 6,500m. I was setting a new personal altitude record with each step. The climbing was over some of the most horrendously loose rock and scree I had ever experienced. It was torturous. The whole mountain appeared to be one giant pile of shifting rocks and boulders, easy to dislodge and send hurtling downhill.

At roughly 6,650m, Guy called a halt and told us that we would rest for thirty minutes. This was incredibly welcome news. With the sun now high in the sky, I contemplated taking my boots off to massage some warmth back into my lifeless toes. Guy agreed with my way of thinking, and joined me in doing the same. As we rested and rubbed our feet, an American climber caught up to us and we had a brief chat.

It turned out this was his third attempt on the mountain, and the highest he had reached so far. I wished him good luck as he continued on. After another ten minutes or so, we were also on our way, with Guy out front setting the pace. For once, Arnold and I were moving at a similar speed. For the first time since leaving Camp Two, I allowed myself the feeling that I was going to pull this off.

Soon we reached the most notorious section of the normal route to the top. A 400m, 33° chute called the Canaleta, filled with disagreeably loose rocks, was all that barred the way to the roof of South America. This section became the most frustrating and downright painful climbing of the entire trip – a fitting final objective, as well as a psychological hurdle.

The guidebook described the challenge of the Canaleta as nothing to do with technical climbing, but rather superior mental and physical stamina. For every two metres of progress, you would slip back one. I would only read this upon my return to Base Camp. At the time, I had no idea I was on such a lacklustre and energy-sapping area of the mountain.

We were sitting, drinking water and resting when a shout of joy shattered the silence. "Yes!" We all heard it as clear as day. I looked straight up to the ridge ahead and could see the American climber, with his hands held triumphantly above his head. "Christ alive," Guy said. "That must be the top."

Everything hinged on the next hour of my life. *Slip up here*, I said to myself, *and you may as well have no life.* Everest meant everything to me, and in that moment in time, so did reaching the summit of Aconcagua. If I could reach the top, I would be firmly cementing my credentials for a shot at Everest. I knew it and so did Guy.

Guy told us to crack on and he would catch us up. I thought this was a selfless thing to do; I assumed he wanted his clients to reach the top before he did. The weather was perfect. There wasn't a cloud in the sky as I stood up from the rock I had been perched on in the Canaleta. I took off my outer windproof layer, stuffed it into my pack and I was off. I was like a man possessed huffing and puffing up the final section to the summit. I also started to become emotional as I realised I was about to stand on top of the mountain; despite the earlier scares of altitude sickness and lack of fitness, my determination had won through. I had battled as best I could and was about to be rewarded with a view from almost 7,000m.

Time and time again I stumbled as I inched higher to the magic altitude of 6,961m: the summit of Aconcagua.

I welled up, thinking about where I had come from, and what this would mean on my path to Everest.

With the God-awful Canaleta now a thing of the past, the final 50m towards the famous cross that marked the summit went by in a blur. I could not tell you a single thing about the terrain I was moving across. It could have been red-hot coals for all I knew. I was a man on a mission and I had the summit immediately in my radar.

I touched the summit cross and then collapsed flat on my back. I had done it. Aconcagua was climbed. Guy was the first one over to congratulate me. He helped me to my feet and gave me a huge bear hug. Arnold joined in and the three of us patted each other on the back, as we began to take in the view from the highest point in the western hemisphere. To say I was elated was an understatement. "Knew you would bloody do it," Guy said. "You're on the road to Everest now, mate," he added.

At 1.50pm on the 12th February 2001, Guy Cotter (Adventure Consultants' CEO and lead guide), Arnold Witzig (a 59-year-old millionaire architect from Switzerland), and Ellis Stewart (a scruffy 28-year-old shop worker from a Northern English seaside town) shared a unique moment in time, on top of one of the planet's iconic mountains. It was a magical moment in my life. I spent forty-five minutes on the top, lost in my own thoughts. Other than the American climber, who was there with us, we had the whole summit to ourselves. It was sublime.

Aconcagua summit – Ellis, Arnold & Guy

As I spent time on the roof of South America, I wondered whether I would ever reach the top of Everest, and if so, when that would be. For my two climbing companions that day, the answer would come a lot sooner.

Guy had already reached that illustrious pinnacle twice before, including guiding for Adventure Consultants alongside Rob Hall in 1992. After Aconcagua, later the same year, he would climb Makalu, the planet's fifth highest mountain. In 2006, he would climb Everest for the third time, again in a guiding capacity for Adventure Consultants.

For Arnold Witzig, his summit of Everest came the following year, in 2002. He is such an unassuming man that, if you search for him online, there is no mention of his Everest climb and his seven summits. In future years, Arnold and his wife used profits from the sale of his company in Switzerland to set up an annual prize fund of $1 million to help finance research into issues affecting the Arctic. This Arctic Inspiration Prize is akin to a Nobel Prize for Arctic researchers. Recently, Arnold was asked in an interview how long he could keep financing the prize. "Forever," he replied. This became Arnold's real Everest.

My own Everest dream would take a lot longer to materialise, but I never lost sight of my goal. Reaching the top of Aconcagua, as glorious as it was, was really just the start of a long and winding road. If I had known back then just how long that road would be, I might not have continued along it.

After having our photos taken together at the top, we began to get ready for the descent. I had noticed some threatening clouds rolling in across a nearby mountaintop. Guy noticed them too and motioned for us to head down. I knew that in all likelihood I would never set foot here again, so I gave the summit one last long look and thanked whoever had looked after me and given me the strength to climb the mountain.

Although I am not devout in any form of religion, I do believe that there is something, or somebody, looking out for us. Perhaps it's a sensation caused by a lack of oxygen to the brain, leading to a hypoxic altered state of consciousness. That would be the rational scientific explanation. I prefer the alternative theory: that we all have someone watching our backs. The first time this happened to me was on my descent from Aconcagua's summit.

Having put everything into reaching the top, I didn't leave enough in the tank to descend. The first half an hour or so, coming down from the summit, was very scary. My legs constantly collapsed from underneath my tired body and I was struggling to stay upright. Guy, concerned, stood in front of me and told me to follow him down. We stopped every few metres for me to rest and take a sip of water. Every time I stopped, it took a herculean effort to begin moving again. I was in a state of complete exhaustion, having been on the go for almost twelve hours.

After an hour of descending, we came upon a climber heading up who, like me, was having a bad time. It was late in the day, with the weather closing in fast, and this chap was still heading up to the summit. It would take him another four hours to get there. Guy recognised that this individual was in more need than I was, and immediately switched his attentions towards him. "What is your name?" Guy asked. He received a garbled, incoherent response. "Where is your high camp?" The climber pointed to the sky. Realising he was in serious trouble, Guy tied a short rope around his waist and began to slowly escort him down the mountain. Each time he slipped, Guy would hold him upright with the rope. Considering this climber wasn't part of our team, Guy's actions ultimately saved this person's life.

This should be the unbroken rule of any mountain-climbing trip. If you see someone in trouble, you should do whatever you can to assist, even if that means giving up on your own summit. This is an often-mentioned moral dilemma on Everest, where the chances of encountering someone in trouble are very high.

Guy kept glancing back, enquiring how I was doing. Something rather weird had begun to happen. I no longer felt exhausted and could feel my energy levels returning. I had this sensation that there was someone there with me, by my side, who kept telling me that I was going to be fine and to believe in myself. This feeling stayed with me for no more than ten minutes, after which I was back to being as strong as an ox. Guy had given me one of his trekking poles when he realised I was struggling; I packed it away now, much to his astonishment. I can't explain what happened, or where I found the energy to descend that day, but as I breezed back into Camp Two, I felt like a mountain god. Almost fourteen hours after leaving my tent, I collapsed onto my sleeping bag.

Guy and Arnold followed an hour later. The climber, whom Guy had assisted down, was able to locate his team's tents. Guy went across and scolded the team leader, recommending immediate evacuation off the mountain. Luckily, they listened and, less than an hour later, the entire team packed up and began to descend.

As we descended from the summit, it was alarming to see several teams still heading up at such a late time of the day. The weather had taken a turn for the worse, yet climbers were still moving up, seemingly oblivious. The mountain guide inside of Guy kicked in and he turned several teams back, informing them it was too late to reach the summit. We even witnessed one girl being physically pushed up the mountain by her guide. This was wrong on so many levels. Guy begged them to turn around, but the guide wouldn't listen and carried on up the mountain. "Unbelievable!" I heard Guy say.

In my mountaineering career, I have come to realise that mountains can bring out the best in people. But they can also bring out the worst, as I discovered on Aconcagua that day.

Climbing Aconcagua gave me a glimpse into an intoxicating world, one that I was now eager to experience more of. I arrived home in the UK a completely different person from the one who had left just four weeks previously. I was still Ellis, twenty-eight years old, drifting from job to job, with a three-year-old child. However, I was now Ellis, the chap from Hartlepool who had been somewhere that none of his immediate circle of friends and contemporaries had ever been, or would ever be likely to go. This made me feel very special and unique. For the first few weeks of being home, my feet never touched the ground. Everest was now upfront and central, burning bright in my immediate radar, and it wouldn't be long before I would take that next step on my journey to the mountain.

During my final few days in Argentina, Guy asked me what my future climbing plans were. I told him that I was considering travelling to Tibet to attempt Cho Oyu, the planet's sixth highest peak.

At over 8,200m, Cho Oyu would be more than 1,200m higher than I had been on Aconcagua. However, I realised that the experience of climbing an 8,000m peak in the Himalayas would be priceless in my plan to scale Everest.

I knew that Adventure Consultants were running a trip to the mountain later the same year, and Guy was very interested in getting me to sign on. Guy wouldn't be running the trip himself, as he would be climbing Makalu in the spring. But he assured me I would be in good hands with one of his International Federation of Mountain Guide Associations

(IFMGA) certified guides – the highest seal of approval a guide can acquire.

I had no doubts I would be in very good hands, but there was a huge stumbling block that ultimately prevented me from signing up: the cost. Adventure Consultants were charging $16,000 USD in 2001 to attempt Cho Oyu. They described it as the ideal first 8,000m peak to climb, and the perfect preparation for an Everest attempt. This price included the use of oxygen, which would be required as the mountain poked into the Death Zone – above 8,000m, the altitude above which human life can no longer be sustained. Climbers start to deteriorate the longer they remain above this point.

It was now mid-February. The Cho Oyu climb was in September/October. Unless I was prepared to rob a bank, there was no way I would be able to raise that much money, which amounted to £11,000 GBP, in seven months. However, a UK guiding company that I had considered for Aconcagua were offering a climb of Cho Oyu at the same time. Adventure Peaks, relatively new in mountain-guiding circles, charged just £6,000 for the chance to climb the mountain. There was one caveat, though: this price didn't include oxygen.

They said it wasn't required, as the mountain was only just over 8,000m. You could basically rush up the sixth highest mountain in the world, tag the summit and get the hell out of there before the altitude had a chance to kick your backside. That's how I read their brochure anyway. When I say brochure, what I really mean is a few pieces of A4 paper stapled together – a far cry from Adventure Consultants' impressive full-colour, glossy magazine offering.

Still, a few sheets of word-processed information or not, Adventure Peaks were cheaper by several thousand pounds, and that was my number-one priority. Sadly, loyalty had no place in the life of a nomadic, part-time shop worker. If money were no object, then it is fair to say I would have gone to Cho Oyu in the autumn of 2001 with Adventure Consultants. But it was, so Adventure Peaks it had to be.

I informed Guy that, much as I would love to climb Cho Oyu on an Adventure Consultants team, unless he could drop his price by £5,000, I couldn't possibly contemplate it. He was naturally disappointed, but he fully understood. We parted company in Buenos Aires and he wished me the very best.

I learnt a lot from Guy and my time with him on Aconcagua. Having the expertise of someone so wealthy in mountaineering knowledge was worth the cost of the trip alone. Climbers spend upwards of $65,000 to sign on to an Adventure Consultants Everest climb. They don't spend anywhere near the amount of time I had climbing with Guy, and I only paid $4,400 for the privilege.

When we parted that day, never in my wildest dreams did I think that the next time I would see Guy Cotter we would both be caught up in a life-or-death situation. But that is sadly what happened. Life moves in mysterious ways indeed.

I would go on to spend a tumultuous and unpredictable few months upon my return from Aconcagua. Still living in Milton Keynes with my cousin and his wife meant I could keep my relationship going with my son Aaron. We'd now been living apart for almost a year.

I struggled to get a foothold into anything of note since coming home, and I was desperate to get stuck into something. Climbing mountains sure was a whole lot of fun, but it didn't pay the bills. If I didn't find something, and soon, there would be no further fun in the mountains and I could most certainly kiss goodbye to Cho Oyu, not to mention Everest.

Before going to Argentina I had tentatively applied for a job with Columbia Sportswear, the large US outdoor clothing manufacturer. This was for a position based in Chiswick, West London, as a Visual Merchandiser. The job would entail travelling around the UK, once again staying in hotels. I had forgotten all about my job application when, one morning, a letter landed on the doormat, inviting me to London for an interview. Bingo! I was back in business.

I attended the interview and charmed the backside off the national sales director and Kate, the very pretty young marketing manager, whom I would be working directly alongside. I got to work, impressing her with my tales of high climbing in Argentina.

I left the office after the interview and they said they still had people to see, but they would be in touch. No more than five minutes later, as I walked through the reception area, Kate ran out of the lift and asked me to go back up to the office. They had changed their minds and decided to offer me the job on the spot, without even seeing any of the remaining candidates.

A week later I travelled into London, ready to begin my new role as the Columbia Visual Merchandiser. I received an Audi car, a laptop, mobile phone and a salary of £25,000 – a marked improvement on the £7,750 I began my outdoor career on, only three and a half years earlier in the Outdoor Shop.

I was determined that this time I would make this job work. I needed the stability of a career, which had so far eluded all my efforts. I needed to know that my time with Páramo, a year earlier, had come to an abrupt end because of the emotional turmoil I was experiencing in my marriage at the time.

I was on borrowed time and I wouldn't be given many more chances within the outdoor clothing trade to prove that I wasn't a 'fly by the seat of his pants' chancer. I was deeply worried that I was fast becoming just that.

For six weeks, I drove the three-hour round trip to Chiswick and back from Milton Keynes, trying desperately to settle in to a corporate lifestyle.

Outside of work, I began to up my training, preparing myself for what I hoped was soon to be another climb on my journey to Everest. Cho Oyu dominated my every waking moment and unfortunately this dreaming began to affect my work. I didn't want to be in an office in West London, learning about the benefits of outdoor clothing. I wanted to be *wearing* the outdoor clothing, outdoors, preferably on a mountain. The feelings that took over and consumed me when I worked for Páramo, a few years earlier, had returned. And this time they would become much, much worse. I now knew one thing – maybe I wasn't cut out for the corporate world after all.

Less than two months into my new role, my doctor signed me off sick with stress and anxiety. Once again, the demons descended and took control of my mind. I felt like a failure again, just as I had when I quit my position with Páramo. But unlike then, I didn't have anyone to answer to this time other than myself. It was myself I was letting down, and I knew it. They say what doesn't kill you makes you stronger, but at the time, I couldn't see how any of these career failures would do that. Once again I had been found wanting, and it deeply hurt.

Knowing I was letting others down hurt the most. What was wrong with me? Why couldn't I hold down a job? The longest continual employment I had in my life to date was my time in the Outdoor Shop, which amounted to around seventeen months. I was at Páramo for four months at best and Trekkit Mountain Sports, the shop at the snow slope, for less than a year. And once again here I was, about to throw another perfectly good career opportunity into the gutter.

I wasn't in a good place. I needed to find that place, but I needed to do it myself. No one could guide the way for me.

In the space of a year my mam had seen me split up from my wife, sign away my family home, become a part-time dad to my son, fly off to Nepal on a whim, and get drunk with snowboarders several years younger than me every night for eight months. To add to that, I had then jetted off to Argentina to climb a mountain she had never even heard of (and couldn't pronounce).

Once again, I was about to add some more steaming dung to the pile of festering crap that was my life, by walking out on a perfectly good job. I was certainly putting my nearest and dearest through the mill, and I bet my mam could not have been any prouder of me. Was Everest really worth all of this?

Having resigned from Columbia, I was at an all-time low. From the euphoria of reaching the summit of Aconcagua only a few months earlier, I was now rock-bottom again. I just couldn't seem to find my place in life, and this was starting to become a real worry, not only to myself but to all those around me.

I mulled around for several weeks, keeping myself occupied with long runs and bike rides. I found time on my bike, and pounding the streets running was my escape from the real world. I would engage in either activity as often as I could. At least I was becoming incredibly fit from my efforts.

In just three short months my life path had changed dramatically once again. Granted this was all my own doing this time, and I had no one to blame but myself for the predicament I found myself in.

In early July, things reached a head. I had run out of money and could not pay my way any more. My rent was due to my cousin Ian for the room I was occupying in his house, and bills were beginning to mount up. Cho Oyu was a little more than ten weeks away and I had timidly shown interest in the Adventure Peaks trip. They had been in touch on a regular basis for a few months and were obviously keen to know if I was a definite for the trip.

As much as I wanted to commit, I simply could not do so until I was in a much better place mentally, and had some means of financing the climb. As a result, I kept stalling them on my decision, offering up some pathetic excuse or another as to why I couldn't say yes just yet.

The inevitable happened by mid-July. I packed up my small Vauxhall with all my worldly belongings – which wasn't much – and drove the 230 miles north to my hometown of Hartlepool.

I coasted into town on fumes, as I did not have enough money to pay for fuel. How I didn't crash my car on that journey home I will never know. My mind was a whirl of emotions and I struggled to concentrate.

I may have avoided crashing my car, but at that moment in time, my life was a metaphorical car crash, and I knew it. By going home to Hartlepool, I had hit the very bottom. But from the bottom, there is only one place you can go. I just needed time to regroup and a goal to aim for. Cho Oyu became that immediate focus, much to everyone else's chagrin.

Mam welcomed me with open arms. Of course she would, as I was her son and I needed the respite that home could bring. At just a few years shy of turning thirty, I found myself back living in my mam's house, staying in the attic bedroom I had spent most of my childhood in. My immediate concern was finding some work. I was now living almost four hours away from Aaron, and I had every intention of being in his life – a job would give me the money to travel to see him. It would also go some way to restore my self-respect and self-worth. I hadn't had much of either since leaving Columbia.

Having proven myself on Aconcagua, Adventure Peaks persisted in getting me to sign up to the Cho Oyu trip. Besides, if I committed, it would give me some much-needed focus over the next several weeks.

There is a quote by the Scottish mountaineer and writer WH Murray, which a good friend of mine quoted to me before I left for Aconcagua. It was very relevant to my present predicament:

Until one is committed, there is hesitancy, the chance to draw back, always ineffectiveness. Concerning all acts of initiative (and creation), there is one elementary truth that ignorance of which kills countless ideas and splendid plans: that the moment one definitely commits oneself, then providence moves too. All sorts of things occur to help one that would never otherwise have occurred. A whole stream of events issues from the decision, raising in one's favor all manner of unforeseen incidents and meetings and material assistance, which no man could have dreamed would have come his way. Whatever you can do, or dream you can do, begin it. Boldness has genius, power, and magic in it. Begin it now.

I signed on to the trip and agreed to pay an initial deposit as soon as I could. The rest of the balance would be due ten days before departure. I did not know how I was going to pay for the climb, but I knew that somehow I had to find a way. Having now committed, I knew I definitely needed a job to tide me over till the climb, but also to put some money back in my pocket. The only thing I really knew how to do was work in outdoor retail shops. That became my immediate target. I looked to see which shops around me might be recruiting.

As luck would have it, a store in Newcastle upon Tyne was looking for part-time staff. Part-time work wasn't as good as full-time, but it would be a start. The LD Mountain Centre was a North-East England institution. It was the birthplace of the iconic British outdoor brand Berghaus, and I was offered 16 hours a week at £4.50 an hour, working in the shop's climbing department.

I had lost touch with some of my friends back home, but one evening I reacquainted myself with a guy called Ian, with whom I had worked as a DJ all those years ago. We went to the Whitehouse, a popular pub in Hartlepool, where you could guarantee to bump into people you hadn't seen for ages. I saw several people from my past that night who came over to talk to me. Surprisingly, they knew all about my Aconcagua climb and my plans to climb Everest. Unbeknownst to me a local newspaper, the *Hartlepool Mail*, ran a feature on me a month or so ago, when I was still living in Milton Keynes.

I had a great night in the pub, and one too many drinks to be honest, but it was much needed after everything I had recently been through. As we left the pub and waited outside in the car park for our taxi, we began arguing with a group of girls about whose taxi had just arrived.

One of the girls in the group was louder and oozed confidence as she forced her way through her friends to the front. "Hi," she said. "I'm Tamara. What's your name?"

"Err, Ellis, pleased to meet you."

"We are going to a club, would you like to come?"

I left my friend Ian, and went to the town with this Tamara girl and a few of her friends. I wasn't allowed into the club as I had trainers on, but when I left to go home I had Tamara's phone number. "Call or text me," she said.

I was instantly attracted to Tamara, with her dark hair and foreign looks. She reminded me of Winnie, from the American TV drama *The Wonder Years*, albeit an older version, I must add. Little did I realise that I had just met someone who would change my life.

Fifteen years later that bold confident girl, who stole my taxi and whisked me away to a club, is now my wife, and has been for almost ten years. We also have two daughters – Lara born in 2008, and Isla who came along a year later.

Straight away, Tamara knew what she was getting with me. She hadn't met Ellis, a career professional who liked to keep fit and play squash at weekends. She met a guy who was rebuilding the pieces of a broken life, living in his mam's attic room, working part-time in a shop. But this guy was also going to climb Everest one day. This was made abundantly clear from the beginning of our blossoming relationship. What Tamara saw in me, God only knows. I wasn't much of a catch it has to be said.

Fresh from graduating university with a degree in computing, the world was Tamara's oyster. At twenty-two years old, her parents must have been pretty devastated when she announced she had met a twenty-eight-year-old divorcee, with a four-year-old son, who didn't have a career and wanted to climb mountains. They say love is blind. That was never more true than when the daughter of an orthopedic surgeon from Palestine decided to take a chance on a seemingly no-good loser, who was on a devastating collision course with the world's highest mountain.

Now that I had found some work a few days a week, I was starting to feel slightly more content. I could feel my self-loathing beginning to lift and spending time with Tamara certainly helped that. From the moment we met, Tamara and I had become inseparable.

We would spend most of our spare time together. She accepted everything about me, including this wacky plan to climb Everest. I spent many an evening educating her about high-altitude mountaineering and the thrill to be had from the mountains. She would listen intently and then announce, "Nope, still don't get it!" She understood the appeal, but was never able to fully grasp the sheer passion and dedication required to go off and climb a mountain. Nor did she wish to join me in that pursuit either.

With Tamara I had someone who was happy to go to the Lake District walking for the weekend. But she was never going to be my tent companion on the side of a mountain, and nor did I want her to be. My love of mountaineering was my 'me time', and I was perfectly happy keeping it that way.

With just five weeks to go till departure for Cho Oyu, I still did not have a penny towards the cost of the trip. How on earth was I going to raise over £6,000 in the remaining time? This conundrum kept me awake every night. I would also need some decent kit for the climb. What I had used on Aconcagua wouldn't do the job on an 8,000m peak, and I knew I needed a whole new wardrobe of technical kit and gear. For Aconcagua, I had managed to persuade the outdoor gear manufacturer Mountain Hardwear to loan me a down jacket, sleeping bag and tent. I would need a lot more than this for Cho Oyu.

The local hospice in town had read my Aconcagua article in the newspaper, and contacted me one day saying how impressed they were that someone from Hartlepool was aiming to climb Mount Everest. They asked whether I would consider supporting a local charity through my exploits. If I pledged to support them they could offer me PR and a media manager, who would help me try to attract corporate sponsorship. I was intrigued by this and welcomed any help I could get. I agreed to do what I could to help raise money and awareness for the charity. This was much easier said than done, though, as I would come to discover.

I now faced a double challenge: to raise money not only to pay for my climbing fees, but also to hand across to the hospice. Either of these tasks on its own was difficult; combined together it became almost impossible to convince people to loosen the purse strings.

I have always been uncomfortable with the notion of asking for corporate assistance. Don't get me wrong; if it came my way I would have gladly accepted it. But what didn't sit comfortably on my shoulders was asking organisations for money so I could fly off to some far-flung destination and have the adventure of a lifetime. Why would anyone want to pay a complete stranger to achieve a personal ambition?

This was something I struggled to comprehend throughout my entire journey to Everest. I was never at ease picking up the phone, calling around local companies, asking to be put through to their marketing directors. I also felt that my story wasn't compelling enough. From what I had read and witnessed, sponsorship always went to those with a Unique Selling Point (USP). What was my USP? Did I even have one?

I certainly didn't have any angles that I could call upon. I wasn't going to be the youngest, the oldest, the fattest or the thinnest. I couldn't lay claim to a single record-breaking attempt to bolster my chances. *Because I deserve it* was never going to make company directors rush for their chequebooks. I needed to get creative and think outside the box, and fast. Why would anyone want to be associated with me? What would they get from such a relationship? What would I be expected to offer in return? These, and more questions like them, gave me many a headache. I simply didn't have answers that were good enough.

With the clock ticking, my mam's brother, Uncle Tony, said he would construct a website for me, which might help with the appeal to any potential backers. As an IT manager at an offshore oil and gas engineering company, he was able to put together a basic but attractive site, which we called Between Heaven and Earth (BHAE), the collective name for my attempts on Aconcagua, Cho Oyu and hopefully Everest.

I added several images from Aconcagua and gave a detailed account of the climb. I used a few of the other pages to talk about my plans for Cho Oyu and Everest. I now had my very own space online, which Tony assured me wouldn't do me any harm with my hunt for sponsors. I joked that his company could become my first sponsor for Cho Oyu. "That's not as daft as it sounds," he said, before adding, "Leave it with me."

A few days later I attended a meeting at Heerema Fabrication Group, the Dutch company my uncle worked for. I extolled the virtues of my proposed Cho Oyu climb to the site manager, explaining how it would be an epic adventure to be involved in. To my knowledge, no one from my hometown had ever climbed the mountain before, which I was keen to stress. I was trying to imply that it was some kind of a first. It was a tenuous attempt at best. There are lots of things that people from Hartlepool have never done, and are never likely to. I am probably safe in the assumption that no one from the town has ever ridden a unicycle naked along the Great Wall of China, or wrestled with a bear whilst wearing a pink tutu.

My climb of a distant Himalayan peak, which the site manager for Heerema Hartlepool had never even heard of until I sat down in front of him, was no more worthy of sponsorship than either of the above examples. I was clutching at straws, but it was all I had to bring to the table. Everyone and their dog had heard of Everest – it would have been a much easier sell, with instantly recognisable value to the company. But it wasn't Everest, it was Cho Oyu.

I wasn't expecting anything to come from the meeting, and my uncle had already warned me not to get carried away. He advised me to treat it purely as practice for further pitches I would hopefully make over the coming weeks. Therefore, I was pleasantly surprised when they agreed to cover my deposit for the climb, which was 10% of the total trip cost. It wasn't the full 100% I required, but it was a start – and in my first meeting with an organisation about Cho Oyu I had persuaded them to part with some cash. *Wow, this is easy,* I remember thinking. How wrong I was!

With the deposit secured, I was able to finally contact Adventure Peaks and arrange to transfer some money their way. It made Cho Oyu more real. *£650 paid, only another £5,850 to find,* I recall thinking. I was quietly confident that I might have a chance after my first meeting had gone so well.

The hospice had arranged for a free fitness membership for me to use at the local gym. Other than running outside and going for bike rides, I now had the opportunity for some strength training. My fitness began to improve dramatically and I was training in some capacity every day. Even though it wasn't a given that I would be heading back out to the Himalayas, I trained as if it were. I couldn't just kick back and relax, waiting for the money to come in. I would never have forgiven myself if the opportunity to go to Cho Oyu came along and I wasn't ready because I wasn't expecting to go.

My relationship with Tamara was going from strength to strength and we really hit it off. After university in Leeds, Tamara had moved back home to her parents' house in Hartlepool. We really got to know one another that summer and we were soon living in each other's pockets. After the break-up of my marriage the previous year I was now officially in a new relationship. I didn't know where it would lead at the time, and neither did she. We were both happy to see where it would take us, though.

Now that the hospice was beginning to promote my involvement with the charity, press coverage began to increase. The local newspaper printed an article with the headline: 'CLIMBER AT HIS PEAK'. Most of the main facts reported were accurate and they announced Heerema's involvement as one of my sponsors, although they used the word 'principal' before the word 'sponsor'.

In 1975 when Chris Bonington led his crack team of British alpinists up Everest's South-West Face, he was able to do so because of an obscenely large injection of cash from Barclays Bank. They paid for the privilege of being the principal sponsor for a groundbreaking world first on Everest. I hardly think the £650 Heerema gave me justified being referred to as my principal sponsor. A supporter would have been a better description.

As I read further I came across the following paragraph, which almost made me spit out the mouthful of cereal I was eating: *'Ellis's quest is all the more remarkable after suffering a marriage breakdown and the loss of several jobs.'*

What the hell is wrong with this paper, I thought. The following day I was about to call through and let the reporter know what I thought of him and his bloody newspaper, when my phone rang. I answered to a lady who introduced herself as Audrey Cotson. She had read the newspaper article and contacted the paper to ask for my contact details.

"Have you packed for China yet?" she asked.

What an odd question, I thought. "No I haven't."

"Well you had better start, as you are going," she said back.

Audrey had read my story and, as an avid armchair mountaineer, was thrilled to see someone from her hometown want to climb Everest. If going to Cho Oyu first would help with that, then she wanted to make sure it happened. She offered me £3,000 cash towards the cost of the trip. *Good old newspaper,* I thought. This was amazing news, and I could not believe what I was hearing.

This was really happening. I immediately thanked her and, of course, I accepted. I had been thrust up onto a cloud and for the remainder of that day my feet would not touch the ground. Tamara and my mam were thrilled for me, and I began to accept that I would now be heading back to Nepal in just five weeks' time. I still had just short of £3,000 to find, but I was confident I would find that from further sponsors. What I had discovered was that Cho Oyu by itself was not a big enough pull, but dangling the carrot of Everest as the end goal made it seem more enticing. I immediately changed my battle plan. Cho Oyu became my pre-Everest climb. It was time to reel in some sponsors. The battle had just begun, and I was now in the mood for the fight.

I had to do some soul searching when I discovered that my generous benefactor, Audrey, was a 76-year-old retired grandmother. What was I thinking? I couldn't possibly accept her donation knowing this.

Once again, the newspaper was up to its old tricks by reporting incorrectly on my climb. Only this time they really went for the jugular: *IT'S GO FOR CHO AFTER DONATION FROM PENSIONER'* screamed the headline. Further in was a picture of a frail-looking Audrey holding a picture of me. The whole article really stung. It made it appear that I was taking money from a vulnerable little old lady's pension pot to fund my dream trip to the Himalayas. The truth was so far removed from that.

Only days earlier I had met Audrey in her home, and I found a very warm and compassionate person with a genuine, deep interest in climbing. She reminded me of Elizabeth Hawley, the famous lady of Kathmandu who is renowned for the up-to-date mountaineering records she has chronicled for over four decades. Audrey impressed me with her knowledge of climbers and routes on mountains. It was clear she wanted to help me with my climbing goals, and she said she would have been offended had I not accepted.

This put my mind at ease, but I still wasn't happy with the way it was being reported. Everyone close to me who mattered told me to accept her offer and ignore any negative press. I would have to, or else I certainly wouldn't have been over halfway towards my target.

One day whilst working at LD, the outdoor shop in Newcastle, I was fitting a customer with a pair of walking boots when we began discussing Everest. I mentioned that I was hoping to climb the mountain and that I would be climbing Cho Oyu as part of my preparation. The chap (who was called Tom) mentioned that he had attempted Shishapangma, an 8,000m peak in Tibet, only a few years back. He never reached the summit due to illness, but we immediately recognised the common ground between us.

We spent the next thirty minutes discussing all things big-mountain related. "Have you got all your gear?" Tom asked me. I replied that I hadn't. "Ah, it's your lucky day! What do you need?" It turned out that Tom was a good friend of the British mountaineer Alan Hinkes. Alan had given him a lot of his clothing and equipment from his climb of K2.

"Tell you what," Tom said, "I'll bring in what I have and you can take what you need."

Once again, the stars had aligned and things were working in my favour. "Thanks very much. You have no idea how grateful I am."

A few days later, true to his word, Tom left a huge Berghaus duffel bag in the shop. Within the bag was an expedition-weight down jacket, which would come in handy for the colder temperatures higher up the mountain. Also in the bag was a one-piece yellow windproof suit, which I immediately recognised from pictures I had seen of Hinkes on K2's summit. It was branded with large Berghaus logos and a Challenge 8,000 badge, which was the title of Alan's quest to scale all the 8,000m peaks. I found lots of other things that would come in handy, and overall it was quite the haul. I couldn't believe that a chap whom I had only met briefly in the shop had given me all this gear.

With just four weeks to go until the departure date for Cho Oyu, I was still over £2,500 short of what I needed to pay. I produced a basic sponsorship proposal and printed out fifty copies, which I distributed to local town businesses. I walked into each and every business and asked to speak to the manager. This brought in several more donations, varying from £50 to £100.

My mam had kindly offered to cover my international flights, which meant I could just concentrate on trying to get the money for Adventure Peaks, who kept a regular check on my fundraising. "It's getting there," I would always answer. It *was* getting there, but I was running out of time. Dave, the director of Adventure Peaks, had made it clear than unless the full balance was paid in full before departure, I would not be able to join the expedition.

I relentlessly carried on with my hunt for the money in the remaining time I had. When I wasn't working in the shop, I'd spend days working flat out, emailing and calling companies.

In the evenings I would train and then spend time with Tamara. Rejection letters and emails rained in on a daily basis.

With forty-eight hours to go till departure I still did not know whether I would be going. I needed to find just £1,500 and transfer it to Adventure Peaks. I had exhausted all avenues and my efforts at securing full sponsorship had fallen short. I was now out of options. Two days before I was due to go away for seven weeks, and attempt to climb one of the planet's highest mountains, I hadn't packed a single thing.

I became despondent, thinking there was no point any more. My passport was ready; I had tickets for a flight and I had kit and clothing. What I didn't have was £1,500. My mobile rang constantly throughout the day. It was Adventure Peaks. They undoubtedly wanted an answer. Am I going to be on the plane in two days' time or not? I couldn't bring myself to talk to them. I didn't want to have to say: "No I won't be."

But that is exactly the response that was poised on the tip of my tongue. I went to bed that night praying for a miracle.

The following morning, Wednesday 5th September, I woke knowing what I had to do. At that moment in time, I had only paid the initial deposit, which was the money I had secured from Heerema. As it turned out, it was the only donation I was able to muster from a large corporate company. All my other micro donations came from local coffee shops, hairdressers and the like, of which I had around fifteen. They had given me donations, not sponsorship, as they didn't require anything in return. *It will be easy to refund them all,* I thought.

I informed my mam and Tamara of my decision and they were clearly upset for me. There was only one thing left to do, and that was to call Paul Noble, the expedition guide, and inform him that I was out. For weeks he had been a great source of guidance when I would call him to ask for advice: Would a certain piece of equipment be suitable? Would £300 be enough spending money for three weeks? How many film rolls should I take? I simply dreaded what I was about to do.

My Everest dream was imploding around me and I was about to pull the pin out of the grenade signalling the end. I was in the kitchen with Tamara and my mam, so I left to go into the sitting room where I could make the call in private. It took five minutes.

I went back into the kitchen and Tamara asked me: "How did he take the news?"

"Not very well," I said and burst out crying.

The truth was, I hadn't called. I couldn't bring myself to call it off. Every ounce of me wanted to go. I had worked so hard for this, and I really believed that it was my destiny – why else would I have trekked to Everest to begin this journey, and why had I climbed Aconcagua? This was the path I was meant to be on, so why was it being denied to me now? It hurt deeply. Surely to God I could find £1,500, even if I had to steal it.

For the rest of the day I moped around. I was inconsolable. Tamara, assuming I had cancelled my expedition earlier in the day, was being as supportive as a new girlfriend could be. Everything was in place, except the money. This would become the story of my life in the quest for Everest.

The one thing you don't necessarily take into account when deciding to climb mountains is the cost involved. It is no coincidence that you rub shoulders with some extremely wealthy individuals high on mountainsides, but I was coming into this at the opposite end of that spectrum. The day before I was meant to be leaving for Tibet, I literally didn't have two pennies to rub together. And that was the crux of my entire problem.

I once again evaded all efforts to be contacted by the outside world. The newspaper and Adventure Peaks had been calling me all day. There were several other calls and numerous emails flooding in too, to which I turned a blind eye. I wanted to curl up in a ball and blank out real life as much as possible.

The flight to Tibet was scheduled for the following evening. I was due to go from London Heathrow to Doha in

Qatar and then on to Kathmandu, arriving the morning after. With less than twenty-four hours until that flight, I still did not know if I would be on it.

That evening, I spent time with Tamara in her parents' house. She was trying to console me as best she could, but she could see how much this meant and how deeply I was hurting.

"There is nothing more you could have done," she said, adding that as I had told them that I wouldn't be going now anyway, in all probability they wouldn't be expecting me to show up tomorrow.

"That's not strictly true," I added. I told Tamara that I couldn't bring myself to give up on my dream, and therefore I hadn't informed anyone I wouldn't be going.

"So as far as Adventure Peaks are concerned, you will be on that flight tomorrow?" Tamara asked.

"Yep, what a mess."

"No, not at all. We just need to make sure you are on that flight, then."

Tamara had only been my girlfriend for a short time, but at 2.00am the night before departure for Cho Oyu, she made a gesture that would keep the fires of my dream alive. She gave me £500. I was just £1,000 short now.

At three in the morning I raced home to my mam's house and began to pack my bags. This was not ideal preparation for a seven-week trip away from home, but these things are sent to test us. At the eleventh hour everything had finally come together. I was on my way to climb Cho Oyu. At 6.00am I finally collapsed into bed, and at 7.30am my alarm woke me.

"Come on, Mam" I said. "We are off to the airport."

Even though I was still £1,000 short I figured I would worry about that later. Adventure Peaks were not going to deny me a place on account of being short by £1,000.

I had done tremendously well to raise what I had in such a short amount of time and I was determined not to let this chance go begging. The outdoor shop worker was now on his way to attempt his second big mountain in the same calendar year. Somehow, I had pulled a rabbit out of a hat.

I sent a quick email to Paul Noble, telling him I would see him that evening in the airport. He was obviously up and busy, as he immediately responded. "Fab news," he said. "There is nothing like taking it to the wire, eh." He told me Dave Pritt from the Adventure Peaks office would be in touch later to sort out the remaining balance. *A minor detail,* I thought.

The date was 6th September 2001, and thanks to all manner of people and events coming together, I was about to set off for the second leg of a remarkable journey. Other than feeling emotionally drained and extremely tired, I was as ready as I would ever be. A nervous excitement swept over me. This was it. I was now on my way to tackle an altogether different proposition. Cho Oyu was a *real* mountain in every sense of the word. And it would go on to test me in ways that I couldn't have imagined.

During the five-hour drive from Hartlepool to London Heathrow, we planned to stop off in Milton Keynes so I could spend some with Aaron. I would be out of the country for seven weeks and I was keen to see him, however briefly, before I departed. I had planned on getting the coach down, but Tamara wanted to drive and I was more than happy to let her. My mam wanted to come along with us. I think she sensed the seriousness of what I was about to go off and attempt to do.

Since returning from Aconcagua seven months earlier, it is fair to say that I had been through enough upheaval and turmoil to last a lifetime. Driving down to London that day, crammed into Tamara's Vauxhall Corsa, all my troubles felt well behind me. With the three of us and all my kit, there was hardly any room to move. I opened the car window a little, revelled in the breeze and allowed my mind to wander to the challenge ahead.

Cho Oyu was not a technically difficult climb. It was nothing more than a steep walk up some easy-angled snow slopes, with the odd steeper section (which required abseiling back down) thrown in for good measure. However, like all 8,000m peaks, the altitude and objective dangers such as avalanches, hidden crevasses, falling and exposure were the real challenges.

The North-West Face of the mountain was our intended route to the top, using three camps along the way: Camp One at 6,400m, Camp Two at 7,100m and then finally Camp Three at 7,500m. From Camp Three the summit was only six to nine hours away, depending on fitness. We would need to overcome a 50m steep ice wall along the way, which presented the most technical climbing on the route.

In Milton Keynes we took Aaron out for lunch and I tried to explain to him all about what daddy would be doing, and why he wouldn't see me for a while. I knew he didn't understand, but it meant the world to me to see him before I left.

From Milton Keynes, I boarded the coach to Heathrow from the bus station. This meant that Tamara and my mam could get home at a reasonable time without having to drive in and out of one of the world's busiest airports late at night.

We shared a very emotional send-off and my mam was in floods of tears when I gave her a cuddle. Tamara gave me a kiss on the cheek and told me that she would make sure my mam was OK. We had only been dating for around seven weeks when I left for the Cho Oyu climb, but we had grown incredibly close in that time. "Look after yourself," she said to me, and then made me promise her that I would come home. I assured her I would. I wanted to climb mountains to live, not die.

On the coach on the way to Heathrow something caught my eye in the newspaper I was reading. It was by a chap called John Green and was one of those inspirational quotes that you might see on the wall of a gym or in some famous movie. It said:

What is the point of being alive if you don't at least try to do something remarkable?

I couldn't agree more, I thought, as the bus pulled into the central bus station at Heathrow. For the next several weeks I would be attempting to achieve 'the remarkable' on a mountain that until a year earlier I had never heard of.

At the Qatar Airlines check-in desk I met up with Paul Noble, the expedition leader employed by Adventure Peaks, and three other members of my team. As well as Paul, there was Geir Jenssen, a professional musician from Norway, plus John Michael Dowd and Patricia McGuirk, a middle-aged couple from Ireland who were also hoping to eventually climb Everest. The sixth and final member of our team, a Brit like me by the name of Stephen Hunt, would be meeting us in Kathmandu. We made our introductions, went through the formalities of checking in and had a few hours to relax and shop before the flight to Doha in Qatar.

I was the youngest member of the team, and although I had the recent experience of the climb up Aconcagua, on paper I was possibly the least experienced. Paul instantly struck me as an able leader with a warm, humorous disposition. In his mid-thirties and from Scotland I appreciated his down-to-earth demeanour.

Being back in Kathmandu, for the first time since my trek to Everest the previous year, felt amazing. Those who have been to Kathmandu on multiple occasions describe it as being like a home from home. On just my second visit to the place, that is exactly how I felt. It was so familiar and inviting, and I felt very lucky to be back there again so soon. It had taken me almost 27 years to visit for the first time and now, just 17 months later, I was back for my second visit – albeit a transient one as we passed through on our way to Tibet.

For two days we stayed at the Gaun Shankar Hotel, where we sorted last-minute gear and met up with our climbing Sherpa, Krishna, who would be accompanying us on the mountain. We appeared to be a competent bunch. The Kathmandu-based operator Asian Trekking organised logistics for the climb and we looked to be in capable hands as we left the hustle and bustle of Kathmandu and headed for the Tibetan border.

With a yellow silk khata scarf – a traditional ceremonial scarf in Tibetan Buddhism, given to me by Asian Trekking – around my neck, I felt spiritually safe as the minibus lurched and skidded round the back lanes and dirt tracks of Kathmandu, which became a hazy blur through the rear-view mirror.

The monsoon rains still showed no signs of letting up. It was raining hard as we made the journey to Kodari, a Nepalese border-crossing town and gateway to Tibet. At one point on our journey, a large section of the road had been wiped out by a landslide caused by the relentless rainwater. We had to get out of the jeeps and give our bags to porters, who fought over who got to carry what. The porters carried everything we needed for the climb across the slippage in the road until we got to the other side, where a new bus was waiting for us to continue on our way. This was a minor inconvenience although one I could have done without, as it cost me 500 rupees. I didn't have pots of money on this trip and had to be extremely careful.

Kodari was the exit point from Nepal for all those climbers heading up to climb Cho Oyu, Shishapangma and even Everest by the North Ridge route. To reach Chinese-occupied Tibet you crossed the Sino-Nepal Friendship Bridge, a large modern concrete bridge spanning the Sun Kosi River. On one side was Kodari in Nepal, on the other Zhangmu in Tibet. A red line in the middle of the bridge marked the border.

The passport-control building and bridge were very militarised. I can't say I enjoyed the experience of being there, waiting to cross into Tibet. Whilst we waited at Kodari some rather distressing news made its way down to us. An experienced Korean climber had died on Cho Oyu a few days earlier. Apparently, he had slipped and fallen into a crevasse lower down on the mountain. This sent shudders up my spine, and made me feel uneasy. This guy was experienced and still came a cropper. Just what was I letting myself in for? If I didn't know already that this *wasn't* a weekend's excursion in the English Lake District, I certainly knew now.

We didn't need to wait long for the sombre mood to be ratcheted up a notch when, later that evening, the body of the Korean climber came through Kodari. I watched as he was placed into the back of a truck, wrapped in his own sleeping bag pulled tight around his head. Nepali children swarmed all around the truck, with the body of the climber now inside. This was the one thing that unsettled me most about the whole spectacle. Sadly, these children were probably used to seeing climbers brought down from Tibet's mountains in this manner.

Tensions were still high in Nepal with the Maoist uprising in full swing. Armed foot soldiers patrolled up and down the border town, giving the whole place a menacing and intimidating feel. That night, as I lay in my sleeping bag, I felt a million miles away from home. So far this didn't feel like the trip of a lifetime to climb a Himalayan mountain. I felt afraid, not only of the mountain, but also of the political and civil unrest in rural Nepal.

After finally being allowed to cross into Tibet, we made the short drive in our land cruisers to the town of Zhangmu, the customs town and entry point into Tibet proper. At the modest altitude of 2,300m, the whole area was lush with green vegetation. A further land slippage had wiped out another section of road shortly after the friendship bridge. Once again we had to walk past the worst of the mud and rubble. Porters again scrambled for the largest of our packs: the heavier the load, the bigger the pay cheque. This trip was already costing me a small fortune, one that I hadn't anticipated so early in the expedition.

After lunch, along with the rest of the team, we decided to step out and explore Zhangmu. Once more the heavens opened and the sloping concrete streets became gushing waterfalls. We retreated back to the dryness of our hotel.

That afternoon I struck up a conversation with Steven Hunt, one of my team members. Back home he was a supply teacher, which meant that he would get to work in whatever school needed a teacher to cover for a short period of time. He would work enough days to be able to afford to pay for a climbing trip and then he would be off. It sounded like a dream job to me – one with no binding contracts. We started to discuss our climb of Cho Oyu and we both came to the conclusion that we had signed on to a budget climb. The price we had paid certainly reflected that. Adventure Consultants had been charging double what I had agreed to pay Adventure Peaks.

Our climb of Cho Oyu had been advertised as a 'non-guided ascent of the world's sixth highest mountain'. This really meant that, should the shit hit the fan, you were on your own. We had to do all of our own load carrying; we didn't have any oxygen and we didn't have a personal climbing Sherpa. These things are taken for granted on a guided commercial climb of Everest. I was happy with this arrangement, as it had ultimately saved me a lot of money I didn't have. Deep down I secretly told myself that, if I could climb this mountain with minimal support, I knew I would be giving myself the best possible crack at Everest.

As much as these trips were adventures in their own right, I had done them mainly to get ready for an ascent of Everest.

From the outset, I had become what I referred to as a 'lazy mountaineer'. I didn't have the time, money or inclination to spend a lengthy apprenticeship in the mountains, gradually climbing higher and higher peaks. I signed on to do the bare minimum to get ready for a shot at Everest. For me, that was to climb Aconcagua, then Cho Oyu and then train like hell on my fitness. I am in no way endorsing my attitude and my plan of attack for Everest. It is actually not the way I would recommend anyone to approach a climb of the mountain. By a direct comparison, if I were a heavyweight boxer starting out on my career, then what I was attempting to do was to have just two professional fights and then get in the ring with Mike Tyson. Not ideal in anyone's book. But fifteen years ago, with my limited resources, it was the best and quickest method to reach Everest that I could come up with.

After leaving Zhangmu behind we drove steadily higher until we reached a town called Nyalam at 3,750m. Here we would spend two days resting and walking. The night before we departed for Nyalam I shared a room with Geir, the Norwegian member of our team, who was older than me at thirty-eight. Back home in Norway, he was famous as a music producer. In the Himalayas it didn't matter what you did or who you were. All that mattered were the skills you brought and how well you could integrate into the team. Geir kept himself to himself and from the beginning it appeared as though he preferred his own company, drifting off to places on his own, recording sounds on his minidisc recorder. One particular evening we were both idly listening to the BBC World Service broadcast on Geir's radio, writing in our journals and generally just chilling out. It became more and more obvious that what we had both assumed was a radio play about a terrorist attack on America was in fact real news.

When you ask most people about 9-11, they will always remember where they were the day America came under attack. I was in Tibet, on my way to climb a mountain, when the terrible news reached us.

I carried on listening for an hour or so, before sleep finally consumed me. I was conscious that I would be waking up to a whole new world landscape; one in which a team of highly trained terrorists could hijack our own civilian aircraft and use them against us as weapons.

As we made our way to Nyalam the following day, we hardly said a word to one another. We were all lost in our own thoughts at the events of the previous day. Our shock was further compounded when we finally saw the footage on TV in our hotel. I spent the rest of the day writing furiously in my journal about all I had just witnessed.

For the next few days we tried to focus on what we were there to do, and that was to climb a mountain. Paul didn't see any reason why these events, as tragic as they were, needed to alter our plans. I was inclined to agree with him, as were the other four members of the team. American climbers turned around and left in their droves, especially those with direct ties to New York. We carried on and, eventually, after four more days and nights, reached Chinese Base Camp (CBC). This was the point where we finally ditched the vehicles and began trekking towards the mountain. It was a welcome relief for us all to be under canvas.

On the way to CBC we stayed in a town called Tingri, high on the Tibetan plateau. This was a small community at just over 4,300m – a soulless place and incredibly bleak. It reminded me of the sort of town that Clint Eastwood would have strolled into in a cowboy movie. We spent two full days and nights there, where I became ill thanks to some food I had eaten that hadn't agreed with me. My lasting memory of Tingri is having to constantly go outside to the rooftop toilet in the dead of night. The night sky was incredible by all accounts but I can honestly say that, in my delicate and fragile condition, I didn't notice a single star. Before I became ill, one of the highlights of arriving in Tingri was seeing the North Face of Everest on the horizon. It was still a good distance away, but it looked entrancing even from this far out.

The horrors of Tingri were firmly behind me by the time we reached CBC. The expedition moved into a different phase and I could sense the urgency in the rest of my teammates for the climbing to begin.

We spent a few days resting at CBC, settling in to our new surroundings. At 4,900m, we felt every sudden movement and were certainly aware of our high altitude. The weather had been abysmal since arriving and we didn't get a decent glimpse of Cho Oyu during the time we spent there.

On day 13 of the trip we left CBC and spent a long day trekking up to an intermediate camp at 5,300m, where we would spend a night, before pushing further up the glacier on our way to Advanced Base Camp (ABC).

I left that morning with Steve, Pat and John. A few minutes out of camp we hit a fork in the path.

"Which way?" I asked.

The general consensus was that none of us had a clue. "Let's just take this path," Steve said. "They are both heading up the valley so either way we can't go too far wrong."

We trekked along a raging river which scarred the landscape for at least a couple of hours before I realised we were no longer in the same valley we had set out in.

"I think we have gone wrong," I stated to the group, dejected. "We can either continue or turn back."

We turned back. As we trudged back to the fork in the path I cursed the fact that we didn't know the route. Krishna, our climbing Sherpa, had already been up at the intermediate camp for a day and started to become concerned when nobody arrived at the expected time in the afternoon.

It was almost dusk by the time we finally plodded into camp. Krishna came out to meet us with a hot flask of tea. He took one look at me and tried to take my pack from me. "Here, sir, let me help."

"I'm fine," I scolded. "I can carry it myself."

My frustration at the day's events was spilling over into anger. I immediately apologised. Steve chimed in: "We are all just as tired. We'll be fine after a rest."

154

The following morning the clouds parted and I had my first full, close-up view of the mountain we would be ascending. It looked terribly steep and nothing like the pre-trip literature had described. Ice cliffs and seracs covered the face and it was hard to see where the route went. I gulped hard and felt a bout of nervous trepidation begin to take hold. At midday we packed up and trekked further towards our Advanced Base Camp. We still had another night to spend on the glacier before finally reaching our home for the next five weeks. I felt very strong as I trekked and listened to the music blaring out of my Walkman.

That night – the first of many on the mountain – I shared a tent with Geir. He finally relaxed a little and we shared a nice evening chatting about our lives back home. While I was a humble shop worker, Geir had released a number of ambient electronic music albums back home in his native Norway, under the name of Biosphere. Mountains brought people from all walks of life together, and we certainly proved that theory, as we talked long into the night about my life in Hartlepool and his in Tomso within the Arctic Circle.

The following day, I put in another strong trekking performance and after two hours I arrived at 5,700m – the site of Advanced Base Camp.

For the next few days we adjusted to the relatively high altitude. ABC was situated at the very base of the mountain and, using binoculars, you could see the entire climbing route. For two days we rested and I sorted out my new living space. I spent a lot of that time peering through my binoculars, watching climbers strung out between Camps One and Two. It still looked steep, but not as steep as it had appeared a few days previously. I still gulped, but this time not as hard.

As I was now at 5,700m above sea level, I began drinking continually to remain hydrated. Headaches appeared from time to time. They weren't too bad, though, and I tried not to worry about them.

On one of my rest days at ABC, I went for a wander to see the various other teams on the mountain, but the thorny stares made me realise my presence wasn't welcome. I soon departed back to my tent.

I expressed my concerns to Paul that evening and he told me it was better if we didn't do too much socialising with the other teams. As an individual who thrived on being social, I just didn't get this. We were all climbers with the common goal of reaching the top of the mountain; surely we would have a better chance if we looked out for one another? That night, as I lay in my tent, I drifted off to sleep thinking I had better not become a liability high on the mountain. I would be on my own if that happened.

As one of the very few teams on the mountain that wouldn't be using supplementary oxygen, I realised our chances of success would be slight. Most of the other teams were planning to use it. This just made me more determined to do well and go as high as I was able.

Later that afternoon I spoke with Tamara on the team satellite phone. It was 3pm back home, which meant she was still at work. We didn't speak for long – just long enough for

me to say that I was doing well and that I was looking forward
to starting the real climbing now.

Camp One on Cho Oyu

The next day was our first push up to Camp One.
Perched on a snow ridge at 6,400m, from here we would
launch all of our forays up the mountain.

The move up to this camp was soul destroying. A steep scree slope guarded the passage all the way. It was reminiscent of the Canaleta on Aconcagua as I heaved and toiled my way slowly upward, resting on my trekking pole every few paces.

Camp One offered a glimpse to the route ahead. From my tent door I could see the route up to Camp Two and beyond. Camp One was the start of the fixed ropes on Cho Oyu and it was here the real climb of the mountain began.

Every day on the mountain saw climbers aborting summit attempts because of the high winds. This was a similar pattern to how things had been early on Aconcagua. Once again, climbers in their droves were leaving the mountain, just as they had on Aconcagua. A few climbers had also been spooked by events a week earlier in New York and had not been able to get their heads focused enough to complete the climb. Either way, it was disheartening to see so many people leaving the mountain. My mind began to wander to home and I found myself homesick on several occasions.

Over the course of the next week, I began the process of acclimatising to higher altitudes. I would climb up to Camp One, spend the night, then descend all the way back down to Advanced Base Camp for a few days' rest. Camp Two was at an altitude of 7,100m and involved climbing a steep 60m ice wall. Being clipped in made this relatively straightforward, albeit a little unnerving. The first time I came to this ice wall, I climbed to the top and immediately abseiled back down, retreating to Camp One.

Camp Two was over 150m higher than the summit of Aconcagua. Other than a slight cold and feeling light-headed, I suffered from no major altitude symptoms. With just over 1,100m to go to the summit, I felt good and allowed a little optimism to creep in – but over the next few days this completely unravelled and came crashing down around me.

I was spending a rest day at Camp Two when the radio burst into life.

"Camp Two, come in."

Geir responded. "This is Geir and Ellis, everything OK here."

After a few seconds the radio spluttered again. "Hi guys, it's Paul. I have some bad news. Pat and John have decided to call it a day." I knew John had been struggling to acclimatise, but Paul went on to say that after an aborted attempt to reach Camp Two, he had decided enough was enough. "I am going to accompany them both down to CBC," he added. "I need you guys to sit tight."

I took the radio from Geir. "Why is Pat leaving?" I enquired. I knew that Pat was very close to John, and I was almost certain it had something to do with the fact that John had decided to return home.

I wasn't expecting the answer, however. "Pat felt hopelessly out of her depth," Paul added. "She reached the headwall and turned back." Pat had hopes to go on to Everest so the fact that she had been spooked on this mountain rattled me. She had been one of the fittest members of the group, and out of all of us she was the one that I would have put money on reaching the top.

As I lay restless in my tent that evening, I worried about the same thing happening to me. *What if I hit a wall and freeze?*

After a restless night's sleep at Camp Two, the plan was for Geir and me to retreat back down to ABC. Here, we would spend a few days recuperating with Paul and Steve before we would all begin our summit bid together. However, as is often the case in the mountains, the weather had other ideas. For the next two days, heavy snowfall and incredibly strong winds pinned us down at Camp Two. On the third day, the weather was glorious and finally we were able to descend down to ABC. There we found Paul having a hard time. He had pushed himself by trekking out to Chinese Base Camp, with Pat and John, before then racing back to ABC. This had left him completely exhausted. More worryingly, he had picked up the most horrendous cough. A few days later, when we finally began our summit attempts, Paul's condition rapidly deteriorated. As soon as we reached Camp One, he collapsed into his tent with his debilitating cough tearing into him.

After spending a night at Camp One, I began the move up to Camp Two once more. This time I would rest and rehydrate before pushing higher up to Camp Three. With our climbing Sherpa Krishna leading the way, Geir, Steve and I reached Camp Two after just five hours. The summit was now within touching distance.

After resting up for several hours, we were due to strike out for the summit that evening, leaving Camp Three at around midnight. The best-laid plans of mice and men often go awry, as they say. After a relatively calm night, hunkered down at Camp Two, the next day dawned with a piercing blue sky and not a cloud in sight. We could not have been granted a more perfect day for our attempt to reach 7,500m, the height of our tents at Camp Three. There was just one small problem: I had woken feeling awful. I began shivering uncontrollably and shortly afterwards I vomited my blueberry porridge into the snow outside my tent door. Geir didn't seem impressed as he kitted up for the move up the mountain with Steve and Krishna.

It became obvious that I was going nowhere that day. I was demoralised and despondent when the three of them patted me on the back before clipping into the fixed line, snaking away in the distance. "Tough luck," Steve said with sympathy as he began the climb.

This was tough to take. I knew I would not have the energy for our summit attempt later that night. The realisation dawned on me that, unless I could rid my body of this bug, my attempt on the world's sixth highest mountain was as good as over.

As I lay sweating in my sleeping bag, I prayed for a miracle. As quick as I drank, my body would reject it and this left me dangerously dehydrated. At over 7,000m in altitude, I needed all the fluids I had, but I was getting rid of far more than I was able to keep in.

That day, stuck in my tent on Cho Oyu, was one of the longest in my life. I spoke on the radio to our support team down at Base Camp to inform them that the others had left, but I was ill so had wisely decided to stay. Paul heard my conversation and told me to remain where I was and see if I was able to improve. "You still have time to do this," he told me. All the signs pointed towards a few days of good weather up high, so we needed to be in a position to take advantage. I reasoned with myself that if I were able to continue, then I would do so. I had plenty of food and gas and Cho Oyu wasn't over for me just yet.

However, the horrible realisation set in that, if I were to reach the summit, I would be doing so completely alone. If that weren't bad enough, I would also be climbing without oxygen. On only my second major mountaineering expedition, I was hopelessly out of my depth, with only a walk to the top of South America on my climbing résumé. I had so far performed well enough, but now was the time when it all mattered. As I lay in my tent that night, I told myself that I certainly didn't do things by halves.

Ellis on Cho Oyu

On the day I struck out for Camp Three, Paul felt well enough to move up to Camp Two, putting himself back in business for a summit bid. My condition had improved and luckily it appeared to have been a short-lived 24-hour illness. Shortly after 9.00am I was up on my feet outside my tent, ready to push higher than I had ever been. At Camp One I had discovered a stash of goodies that were left by Pat and John, and as I left Camp Two that day, I felt extremely grateful to them both as I shoved a handful of jelly babies into both pockets of my Gore-Tex jacket.

For the first hour or so, I ascended a wide, moderately angled snow slope out of Camp Two and found the going fairly easy. The wind began to pick up, but nothing gave me cause for concern until half an hour or so later, when the wind began to really increase. I could feel my fingers beginning to freeze under my mitts.

A few hours after leaving my tent, at an altitude of around 7,300m, I rested on the rope and drank from my water bottle. I tried to radio Paul down at Camp Two, but the batteries on my radio were dead. I was now faced with a dilemma that my frozen brain found difficult to comprehend. The wind that was whipping across the face of Cho Oyu had become ferocious – if I hadn't been clipped in to the safety line, I would have been picked up and blown clean off the mountain. I trudged on for another fifteen minutes or so to reach an anchor point. This meant unclipping my jumar from the rope and swapping it to the other side of the ice screw anchor. Detaching my jumar was a struggle in my big mitts, so

I made the foolish mistake of removing them. I had thin liner gloves on, but they afforded no protection against the bitter cold, made worse by the wind.

I carried on struggling upwards for what seemed like another 100m, but when I glanced at my altimeter watch I was downhearted to see that I had only climbed a further 15m since the last anchor point. With no one else on the mountain that day moving up or down, I was totally alone, in mind, body and spirit. I felt fine enough in myself, but I was deeply concerned about my fingers and now my toes, which felt frozen solid in the rented plastic boots. The time had come to make a decision. In a talk, I had once heard Alan Hinkes say 'no mountain is worth a digit'. With that thought racing in my head, at approximately 12.10pm at an altitude of 7,365m, I turned my back on the summit pyramid of Cho Oyu and retreated back down to my tent at Camp Two. My fingers throbbed with intense pain the whole way down.

They say never to let failure get to your heart, but as I descended the mountain my soul was torn in two. I knew I had made the right call. You live or die based on the choices you make, and I made the choice to live to see another day. I had come within 800m of the summit. Back home this would have been a stiff two-hour climb to the top of a Lakeland fell. At over 7,300m on the world's sixth highest mountain, along with rapidly freezing fingers and toes and no supplementary oxygen, it was quite simply a bridge too far.

In time I would begin to see this failure as a success in progress, but at the time it deeply hurt and I questioned whether I should continue on my path to Everest. How could I climb Everest when I couldn't climb a mountain 650m lower? These thoughts would haunt me for a good few months after my return to the UK.

When I began to analyse why I had failed on the mountain, I immediately saw that I was being a little harsh on myself. In the autumn season of 2001, very few climbers reached the summit of Cho Oyu. Fewer still did so without oxygen. On what was one of the windiest seasons on record, most of the big-name guiding companies returned empty-handed, including Adventure Consultants. Even Arnold Witzig, now with Alpine Ascents, fared no better. I could lay no blame on Adventure Peaks. I knew what I was letting myself in for when I signed up, and that was a non-guided, no-oxygen ascent of the mountain. That is exactly what I got.

For the record, Geir Jenssen was the only member of our team of six climbers to reach the summit. He did so alongside Krishna, our climbing Sherpa, after Steve Hunt made the decision to turn around at an altitude of 7,600m, again citing the cold as the main reason for turning back. Having struggled lower down on the mountain, Geir found his mountain legs the higher he went and was rewarded with our team's only summit that season. I began to take some positives from this. Out of the six of us, only Geir and Steve went higher than me. Steve was a competent alpine mountaineer with eighteen years of experience under his belt, and Geir lived in the middle of the Arctic Circle. Maybe the boy from Hartlepool didn't do so badly after all in reaching 7,365m.

Paul Noble had just been unlucky getting a dry hacking cough. He was incredibly strong on the mountain and although this was his first experience guiding on an 8,000m peak, it certainly wouldn't be his last. Over the next 15 years, he would go on to summit Everest, in a guiding capacity, on several occasions from the North.

On reaching Kathmandu, I discovered that I was out of money. I did the only thing that I knew how to do, and that was to sell stuff to people. I sold all my technical kit to Shona's, a store in Thamel and I sold my Berghaus Gore-Tex jacket to Steve.

I spent my last night in Kathmandu at the famous 'Rum Doodle 40,000½ Feet' bar and restaurant. The place was named after the 1956 short novel *The Ascent of Rum Doodle*, a parody of a mountaineering expedition set in the fictional land of Yogistan.

Everest summiteers get to sign a foot-shaped beer mat, which is then stuck to the walls and ceiling. They were quite literally everywhere. As I stared up at the walls, I wondered if I would ever return one day and get to sign my own foot-shaped beer mat. I envied the owners of all the signatures I could see, for doing what I had dreamed so long about doing myself. But at that moment in time, I had failed on my most recent attempt to get closer to Everest, and the mountain seemed further away than ever. With no summit of Cho Oyu to add to my summit of Aconcagua, I couldn't see how I would be considered for an Everest climb by any of the leading guiding teams. Aconcagua by itself was hardly going to green-light my way to the mountain. I could feel my Everest aspirations slipping away from me as I sipped from my Everest beer, cursing my misfortune. Failing on Cho Oyu had stopped my dream dead before it had really got going.

For the next thirteen years, the intense fire that had been burning brightly within me to climb Everest would be extinguished to a small flickering flame. But it was a flame that never completely went out. Ten years after my attempt to climb Cho Oyu, that flame began to burn brighter again. And this time, nothing was going to stop my date with destiny.

PART FIVE: A DECADE TO DREAM AGAIN

Set a goal so big you can't achieve it, until you grow into the person who can – Anonymous

When I returned home from Cho Oyu, I spent the first few weeks hopelessly depressed. Not for the first time in my life, I felt lost and I needed to find myself again. At that moment all seemed futile. Everest was as good as gone. When I returned from Aconcagua earlier in the year, I had arrived home to a life of uncertainty, not even sure where I would be sleeping from one week to the next.

Although everything in my life still had uncertainty surrounding it, one thing I was sure of was my feelings for Tamara, which had grown stronger during our separation. Tamara would become the constant in my life over the next few years that I desperately needed. I just didn't realise it at the time.

I immediately returned to work at the LD Mountain Centre in Newcastle upon Tyne and this saw me through the remainder of the year. "So why didn't you reach the top of the mountain?" became a question I would hear repeatedly from shop customers. As the monotony of the question (and my answer) began to wear thin, I found myself embellishing slightly, depending on whom I was speaking to. If it was someone who didn't have much knowledge about mountains and altitude, I would add in a little drama: "I had severe frostbite on my toes, but fortunately we were able to save them." Or "The wind must have been close to seventy knots when I was forced to turn back." The looks of awe and wonderment made me feel special, if only for just a fleeting moment. I basked in my deceitful storytelling, certain that no one knew I was bending the truth somewhat.

In early 2002, I took a job in a call centre in Hartlepool. It was silly to continue driving to Newcastle – a distance of thirty miles – for what amounted to a pittance in pay and which barely covered my fuel costs. There was, however, another more depressing reason why I took a job closer to home.

Whilst I was away in Tibet, on the day the world watched the twin towers collapse, there had been a knock at my mam's front door. Two formally attired gentlemen introduced themselves as being from a debt management company and that they had orders to repossess my car. My mam had no choice but to hand over the keys as she was informed I had missed the last three monthly payments. I knew that I was one month in arrears, but in the last-minute rush of going to Cho Oyu, I had completely forgotten to make sure I had enough money to cover the car payments.

On the journey home from Heathrow, Mam whispered to me that my car had been taken away whilst I had been gone. I didn't care. They had done me a favour by taking it. I was struggling to keep up with the payments anyway and it meant this was one less thing to worry about. I told Tamara that I had sold it, rather than face up to the truth. I didn't want her to think she was getting involved with someone whose finances were all over the place. I didn't have the money to pay my way, let alone climb mountains. Yet I had made it happen. Even if that meant that I got myself into an awful mess with money.

For the rest of 2002 I remained in the call centre job, as a target for middle-management hostility. Representing a major telecommunications company, I took around fifty phone calls a day from business users across the UK. Around 95% of the calls were from people who were angry that they were still being billed, despite cancelling their accounts. I learnt to take the abuse, apologise profusely and then agree to issue a refund, which I would pass on to another department. It was a soul-destroying, thankless job, for which being a verbal punch bag earned me just over £9,000 a year. The call centre was one of the main employers in my hometown and it employed people from all ages and backgrounds. At my desk I could be sitting next to a 16-year-old fresh out of school one week, and then a 55-year-old who had just been made redundant from a previous role the next; such was the diversity. We were all cogs in a wheel, in which the only winners were the directors.

When I wasn't on the phone listening to the abuse being hurled at me, I spent my time on mountaineering websites and forums. By far the most popular site of the time was the US-based Everest News. Long before Alan Arnette began blogging about all things Everest, this was the go-to source of information if you wanted to discover what was happening on the mountain. In the spring of 2002 I spent hours glued to the site, following all the drama of that year's Everest attempts. The incredible jealousy I felt inside was too much to bear.

Since Cho Oyu I had wallowed in self-pity and a small amount of loathing towards myself. This feeling of being a failure wouldn't go away. I was once again facing up to living a life that I didn't want to live. I felt trapped in a place, in a role that wasn't for me. Apart from my relationship with Tamara, everything else had turned to shit. Once again, depression was beginning to take hold at an alarming rate.

My life showed no signs of improving. I know that my mam sensed how fed up and miserable I was. One day, after finishing a shift in the call centre, I walked to the end of a pier near the marina where I worked. I crossed a metal fence, which had been erected to warn of danger from high seas and waves on the other side. I sat there for forty minutes, reflecting on my life to date and whether I wanted to continue living or not. I knew that if I jumped, I would be committing the most selfish act that a person could do to the loved ones left behind. My mam would be heartbroken, I would be leaving a child without his father, and my new girlfriend, of less than a year, would be pretty grieved too. Luckily, I wasn't the only person on the end of the pier that day. A solitary fisherman had been sitting less than five metres away from me the whole time I was there with my head in my hands. Other than a small nod to acknowledge each other's presence, we hadn't spoken a word to each other. I was jolted back to reality when he spoke to me.

"Don't do it, fella. Whatever you are going through, just think that there are people going through far worse."

Of course, I knew he was right. I knew that I was being completely irrational by even contemplating ending it all. "Oh I am not going to jump. I am just watching the waves," I pathetically added.

"Whatever," he said back to me, before adding once again for me not to do it.

We spoke for a short while more and I opened up to him about how despondent I had become with everything. I gave the poor chap my life story, condensed into ten minutes. He listened as sympathetically as a stranger can do, I guess. I immediately felt better for offloading like this, and I knew I was no longer going to do what I had thought about doing. I said my goodbye to him and think he was just relieved to see me climb back across the fence to safety. Just as I was about to leave I thanked him for listening to me, and at the exact moment he got a bite on his fishing line. As I watched him reel in a large cod from the depths, he said something that has stayed with me ever since:

"Ellis, if this mountain of yours means that much to you, it will not pass you by."

I walked home feeling slightly better about things. This would become a pivotal moment in my quest to climb Everest and I often think back to that day on the end of the pier, and the fisherman I encountered. My one regret is that I never asked his name, so he will forever be 'the fisherman' to me. I hope he reads this book and realises the part he played in helping me to step back from disaster. After all, you could say I owe him my life.

He wasn't the only one who helped me to recover and refocus back on my Everest dream. Sensing just how down I had become, Tamara gave me a card depicting a scene from a Tolkien landscape with spectacular mountains and a full moon in the sky. Inside she wrote:

There is no doubt in my mind that you will get to Everest's summit! Just take care and come back to me and Aaron in one piece.

It meant everything to know that I meant everything to Tamara. I knew she was planning on being in this for the long ride. She was supportive of my attempts to reach Everest from the moment we met.

That day on the pier would be the last day of my old life. I vowed from that moment on that I would begin to truly live my life, and stop moping around blaming everybody but myself for my lack of success.

Fresh with new energy, I got through the rest of the year as a brand new version of myself. I restarted my training and I worked on becoming mentally tough.

At the end of the year, I quit the call centre and focused everything I had on Everest. The year 2003 was the 50th anniversary of the very first ascent by Edmund Hillary and Sherpa Tenzing Norgay. Surely there was an angle there I could exploit.

With just Aconcagua and a failed attempt on Cho Oyu to call upon, I began working towards being a member of an Everest team for the spring of 2003. My lack of experience was just petty semantics and I was determined I could overcome it once I was on the mountain. I stopped referring to my attempt on Cho Oyu as a failure and began to see it for what it was. I had reached well over 7,000m. In fact, I had reached the point where, if I had been on Everest, I would have used oxygen. I was only stopped in my attempt because my fingers and toes were freezing cold. Plus, climbing alone, I didn't feel I had the necessary reasoning skills to decide whether or not to continue. I needed to stop being so hard on myself. All things considered, I had done bloody well. There would be people going to Everest who had not climbed anywhere near as high as me. This new way of looking at things gave me the necessary motivation to launch my attempt at Everest, and over the next few months I tackled it with enthusiastic rigour.

The hospice, which I was still keen to work with, had put me in touch with the head of my local shopping centre, after mentioning my aim to reach Everest. Cormac Hamilton, the manager of Middleton Grange Shopping Centre, was an ex-Royal Marine captain, so I knew straight away that he would appreciate what I was attempting to achieve. I went along to the centre early in January for a meeting and to see if there was anything he could do to help my cause. I was keen to climb

Everest by almost any means necessary, and I was willing to champion any brand or business – within reason – that wished to be involved.

Cormac explained that a large company, which managed many shopping centres as part of its portfolio, managed Middleton Grange. As a non-local company, he knew they wouldn't stump up the cash, but said that he would personally help in any way possible. This was certainly a step in the right direction. Since leaving for Cho Oyu, I had not convinced a single company or individual to get behind my Everest dream. I was a realist and knew I had nothing of note to offer a potential sponsor. With no golden carrot to dangle, I pinned my hope on the year being the historic 50th anniversary of the first climb of the mountain. With the press coverage that such an auspicious year would surely bring, this became the focal point of my attempt to reach Everest later that year.

Cormac offered me an interesting proposition: the use of the shopping centre on a busy Saturday to put on a fundraising event. I jumped at the chance and began to think about what I could do that would be both a spectacle and raise awareness for my attempt to reach Everest.

In the gym where I trained there was a Versa Climber machine. I had used it, but not that often on account of it being incredibly difficult. This vertical contraption allowed you to place your feet into two pedals, which you then moved up and down, alternating each foot as you went. With two handles to hold onto it was easy to slot into a rhythm, but far from easy to do for any prolonged period of time. Next to it, on the wall of the gym, there was a poster showing various landmarks with their respective heights in feet. I realised that it was to motivate anyone using the Versa Climber to climb the height of Nelson's Column in London, or the Eiffel Tower in Paris, for example. The chart increased in height and landmarks, finishing with Ben Nevis, Britain's highest mountain.

On one of the first times I used it in the gym, I climbed the equivalent height of Ben Nevis in just over an hour. That was 1,344m of climbing in a simulated environment. I recall stepping off, drenched in sweat and with every muscle screaming. As I thought back to that day, I wondered if anyone had ever climbed the equivalent height of Everest on one. After some quick online research, I discovered that it was a popular challenge, but it was tough and not for the faint hearted. It was seen as the ultimate challenge on the machine. I quickly worked out that as it had taken me an hour to climb over 1,344m, to climb the full 8,848m of Everest would theoretically take around seven hours – but of course I wouldn't be able to keep that pace going for the full duration, so I would aim for around ten hours.

I called Cormac to inform him of my ambitious plan. He loved it. "Sounds bloody epic. Are you sure you can do it?"

I wasn't sure at all, but I would give it a go. "Of course I can do it," I boldly announced. "It will be a piece of cake."

As I was putting the phone down, I heard Cormac say: "Rather you than me, mate."

I hoped I wouldn't regret what I had just agreed to take on.

So with the idea cemented, I needed to pick a date and begin to advertise the challenge. However, there was one minor problem with the whole plan. Where the hell was I going to get a Versa Climber from for the day? Corus, a steel manufacturer near Redcar, had one in their gymnasium and said that, if I could dismantle it and take it with me, I was welcome to borrow it for the day. "Besides," the chap on the phone added, "no one uses it anyway – it's too bloody tough." He asked me what I intended to use it for. My answer resulted in a stunned silence for a second or two, after which he said the exact same thing as Cormac: "Rather you than me." I was beginning to think they might have a point.

With the Versa Climber in place, the date was set. In just two weeks' time I would finally get to achieve my life's dream of climbing Everest. The only difference was that I would be on a stage in front of Woolworths, in a shopping centre.

I used the remaining time until the day to train on the thing in the gym as much as I could. As it was the one piece of equipment overlooked by most members, I didn't think they would object to me hogging it for several hours at a time. Most gym-goers looked at me as if I were mad as I spent hour upon hour stepping up and down. After two weeks I had climbed thousands of feet, probably equalling the height of Everest, but I hadn't done it non-stop. The most I had managed to do so far without stopping had been four hours – and that had been incredibly tough. How the hell was I going to be able to do another six hours on top of that? I must be honest, I did think about calling the whole thing off, but soon remembered why I was doing it in the first place: to get some money together so I could hopefully climb the real Everest.

I knew that climbing the height of Everest in a shopping centre was going to be nothing like the real climb. For a start, there was a serious lack of snow, crevasses and avalanches to contend with. Also, I wouldn't be battling some of the coldest, harshest conditions known to man. On Everest I wouldn't be able to unclip and step into Woolworths for some pick-and-mix sweets. But what I would be doing was pushing my body non-stop for up to ten hours, and the challenge that this presented was enticing. I wanted to see if I could do it. On the real summit day on Everest, I would be moving for a lot longer than ten hours straight.

The day I would climb Everest in the shopping centre would be, I hoped, the start of an avalanche of donations towards my attempt. Getting myself out there and noticed would surely help with this. As is often the case in my life, I was to be proved wrong in this assumption. Still, on the eve of the challenge, I was excited, ready and willing. *Bring it on,* I thought.

For the attempt, my mam, one of my aunts and Tamara offered to walk around the shopping centre holding collection buckets. A few days earlier I had drawn a rather crude mountain against which my progress could be measured. As I stepped through the day the chart was updated to reflect my current position on the mountain. On the stage, alongside the Versa Climber, I pitched the Mountain Hardwear tent that I had used on Cho Oyu. Outside that, I placed a cook set with a pan on it. Arnold Witzig, my climbing companion from Aconcagua a few years earlier, agreed to loan me his down suit, which he had used successfully on Everest the previous spring. I got in touch with him a month earlier to ask if I could borrow it, in case I made it to Everest. He willingly obliged and agreed to freight it across from Canada. I had to pay around $90 in custom duties upon receipt, but it was still a lot cheaper than paying for a brand new suit, which I simply could not afford. I placed the suit on a mannequin, with goggles and a backpack. Strung from the top of the Versa Climber I tied a set of prayer flags, which I stretched out across to the other side of the stage. The whole setup certainly looked the part, and gave off the desired look of a Himalayan scene. The *pièce de résistance,* though, hung behind me above the whole stage.

Cormac had agreed to foot the bill for a five-metre-long yellow vinyl banner, emblazoned with the words: *'GETTING TO THE TOP – Help Ellis achieve his dream and raise money for charity'.* This was followed with: *'FIRST HARTLEPOOL MAN TO THE TOP OF EVEREST'.*

Wearing a black T-shirt designed especially for my attempt, I began stepping my way to the top of Everest at 9.00am and soon slotted into a steady rhythm. An hour in and I had already soared past Scafell Pike, the highest mountain in England. I had marked off various landmarks on the progress chart to give the whole thing a sense of scale. Tamara would come up to me every so often and update me on donations. For the first few hours, donations were few and far between. Old dears would stop and look in bemusement, then shake their heads and walk off, muttering disapproval as they went. I began thinking that the whole attempt was going to backfire on me and I would be left looking a right wally, with just £23 in the collection buckets to show for my effort.

As the day wore on, though, more and more people began to donate. They would stop and watch for five minutes before speaking with Tamara, who was at the front of the stage handing out flyers. The flyer would give all the details as to why some chap was on a strange exercise machine, huffing and puffing away, on a busy Saturday afternoon in a shopping centre. The flyer seemed to do the trick and most people donated after reading it. From time to time, people spoke to me personally, saying how well I was doing and they hoped I achieved my dream. "This town needs more people like you," one older chap said to me, as he put a £5 note in the bucket at my feet.

I kept a water bottle near me, from which I would sip several times an hour. I didn't want to drink vast amounts, as I didn't want to stop and use the toilet. This was a non-stop attempt to achieve the height of Everest, and I didn't plan to step off the climber until I had done so. I also had a bunch of bananas and several energy bars, which would be my nutrition throughout the day.

By late afternoon, I was really beginning to tire as I passed the 6,000m barrier. With just over 2,800m to go, I was hanging in there through gritted teeth. Everyone warned me this would be a tough challenge and I was finding out just how tough as I stepped slowly up and down. Each and every step was agony and I constantly stared up at the large clock above Woolworths. Time seemed to have slowed down.

Slowly but surely, I ground down the distance and 6,000m soon became 7,000m, which soon became 8,000m. During those last few hours, as I closed in on the summit of Everest, I wasn't even aware of my surroundings any more. I vaguely registered an announcement going out over the centre PA system, stating that I was getting close to completing my epic challenge. I hit 8,200m – the height of Cho Oyu, – on the Versa Climber, which was the penultimate milestone before the magic figure of 8,848m. At 5.00pm, after stepping since 9.00am without a break, the summit of Everest bore down on me. I knew I was going to complete the challenge. I tried to force a banana down, but instantly my body rejected it and I spat its contents into a bucket.

At 6.00pm I took the final few steps until the readout on the contraption, which I had clung to for the past nine hours, clocked 8,850m. It actually stopped at 8,852m, so technically I was now floating a few metres in the air above the summit. As I stepped off the climber, I genuinely was floating in the air as I was hit by the magnitude of the challenge and what I had just done. I collapsed onto my back to a round of applause from those shoppers who had stayed to see me across the finish line. As I rose wearily to my feet, a teenage girl came up to me and thrust a McDonald's fry in my face.

"Want a chip?" she said.

I began to laugh. A photographer from the local newspaper thought this would be a great photo, so I was asked to step back onto the climber and pose whilst the girl handed me the fry. It's the only image I still have of that day.

A few minutes after I had climbed Everest, Tamara passed her mobile phone to me. It was a presenter at the local BBC radio station, who interviewed me live on air about the challenge and why I had chosen to do it.

"Why climb Everest in a shopping centre?" he asked.

I answered: "Because I had to." I had made the decision to take this challenge on, and everything had come together to enable it to happen. "I never back out of a challenge," I added. "Once I say I am going to do something, then I do it." I finished with: "Bring on the real Everest."

As the interview came to an end, I heard the presenter announce: "That was Ellis Stewart speaking to us there, fresh from climbing Mount Everest today outside Woolworths and Boots the Chemist." The irony was evident in his words.

All told, my climb of Everest on the Versa Climber raised a total of just over £500, which Cormac told me was great for a shopping centre collection. I was deeply disappointed. I knew I was never going to walk (or limp) away that day with £18,000, but I was hoping for a lot more than just £500. Charities could raise that just by standing there with a bucket doing nothing. I had climbed Everest for goodness' sake. The day was a success in that I achieved what I had set out to, but it was disappointing in that it got me no closer to the financial target – which I desperately needed to hit in a matter of weeks.

A few days later, once I had time to take stock, I handed across a cheque to the hospice with proceeds from the day. *The money would be better used by the hospice,* I thought. After all, it wasn't going to send me to the real Everest. I was still £17,400 short, and with only weeks to go until the Everest 2003 climbing season kicked off, things looked bleak. So far, I had been unable to attract any sponsorship towards an attempt on Everest for 2003. With just eight weeks until a potential departure, I wasn't hopeful of bucking that trend.

Versa Climber Everest challenge

Sadly, after all my efforts, 2003 on Everest came and went and I played no part in it.

For a while I had been mulling over the idea of returning to full-time education. I told myself that if I didn't go to Everest, I would give my education some serious scrutiny. I told Tamara that I was thinking seriously about it. Knowing she would support my decision, she enthusiastically gave me her blessing and told me to go for it. If I wasn't meant to achieve one dream, then maybe I could achieve another.

"What would you study?" she asked me.

I wasn't sure, but knew I was keen to enrol on a full-time degree course. "Online business seems to be the future," I said. "I'll see if I can do a course in that."

Failing miserably in my school education was a huge blot on my résumé and no amount of sugar-coating could cover that up. In my interview with Páramo several years previously, the sales director on the interviewing panel had even said: "We can see that education is not one of your strong points." I wanted to correct that, and now was the time to do so. I opted to do a BA in e-Business at Teesside University.

At last, I had some structure to my life and for the next three years I threw myself into the role of a full-time mature student with conviction. In the autumn of 2003, I began studying for my degree. I didn't know which job or career I was aiming for just yet, but I didn't care. The fact was, I was putting my future first for a change, and 'that mountain' was about to take a back seat.

I would graduate in the summer of 2006. I realised this meant Everest was out of the picture for a while.

During this three-year period of my life, a lot of change occurred. The following spring, after I had started my degree course, Tamara bought her own house. Although technically it was Tamara's house, she made it clear that she wanted me there with her. I was elated at this, as it finally meant I could leave my mam's attic room. Living at home when you are thirty years old can knock your confidence hard, and I was grateful that I could now move on from this episode of my life. Slowly but surely, I was beginning to put the pieces of my life back together and Tamara helped me a great deal with this.

Something else happened during this three-year period that once more would turn my world upside down. I was now officially divorced from Aaron's mum and like me she had also moved on. She had been in a relationship for a few years with a guy called Scott from Australia, who was living and working in the UK.

Vikki called one night for a chat.

"Hey Ellis, so I have been thinking about the best way to tell you this," she started. "Scott wants to go back to Australia to help his father take care of his sick mother." I waited for the bombshell, but I knew it was coming. "He has asked if I will go with him."

There it was.

I knew this meant Vikki taking my son Aaron to the other side of the world. My heart sank. She couldn't take him without my permission so I had an incredibly difficult decision to make. All I could think to say was, "I'll think about it." I put the phone down and sobbed. If I said no then she would stay and her partner would have to go anyway.

After a few weeks I began to see that Aaron would have a better life living in Australia. It came down to choosing where it would be better for Aaron to grow up: Milton Keynes or Melbourne? I put aside my own feelings and thought about what was best for my son, even if that meant he would now be living thousands of miles away. I would be lucky to see him once a year. When I eventually gave my permission for him to go, it was one of the hardest decisions in my life.

Once I had adjusted to this new transition, life carried on as normal. In June 2006, I sat the final exams for the business course I had been studying for three years. The time had gone by in a blur, and I had assiduously stuck to the task. I emerged from my degree course with three things: a first-class honours in e-Business, the highest classification it was possible to achieve; a new sense of pride and self-worth; and a new friend called Steve McCarthy.

I met Steve on the first day at university, three years earlier. We were both mature students, me rather more so than him, and we hit it off immediately. From Liverpool originally, Steve had an easy-going nature and his humour gelled very well with my own. He had that most noble of skills: being able to poke fun at himself. This humility, which he had in abundance, made him enjoyable to be around. Trying to describe Steve's appearance would be unfair of me, so I will let him do it. He once told me that, in an interview for his first job, he was asked how others would describe him. His answer of 'fat and ginger' sums him up perfectly, in more ways than one.

In the last year of my studies, I stumbled upon a website which was picking up worldwide interest for its creator, along with making him a millionaire in the process. The Million Dollar Homepage was created by a young student from England, who came up with the clever idea of selling the available screen pixels on a single web page for advertising space. The page consisted of a million pixels, which he sold to potential advertisers for $1 per pixel in a 10 x 10 block. The site became an internet sensation and spawned a thousand copycats hoping to cash in on the pixel-selling craze. Sadly, I became one such copycat.

Working with one of the university's web design teams, I had a site built called the Everest Pixel Dream. The idea was simple: I would sell advertising space on an image of the North Face of Mount Everest. Starting at the bottom of the mountain, advertising would be cheapest, but then the higher up you went, the more you would pay. The space under the summit would sell for the highest amount. It was a clever concept, but I had attempted to rip off the Million Dollar Homepage. I had worked out the costs of each pixel so I would have enough money to pay for an Everest climb if I sold all the space on the Everest image. Bizarrely my idea was picked up on the popular Everest News site that ran a feature on me. There, amongst all the stories of real climbers on Everest, was my story about selling advertising space to reach the mountain.

Within a few months of launch, I had only sold about £100 in advertising, and I knew that my idea was not going to reap the rewards I hoped for. If the site had sold out and achieved the target, then the plan was to go to Everest in the spring of 2007. I was still hell bent on the north side of the mountain, as this offered my only realistic chance of going to Everest, due to it being considerably cheaper than the way from the south.

It was, however, all irrelevant. Even if the climb cost merely £5,000, I still wouldn't have the money. Repaying debts from my previous climbs meant that the only way I would go to Everest was if I won the lottery, inherited some cash or was able to attract some serious sponsorship. The first two were never going to happen. My only way to Everest was sponsorship and I knew it.

Having now failed convincingly to reach Everest in both 2003 and again in 2007 with my pixel advertising disaster, I once again allowed life to drift in and take control. I wouldn't try for Everest again for several more years, but not a day passed when I didn't think about it.

As the Everest climbing season in 2007 passed by, my focus switched to Tamara. We had been together for six years and I knew I was planning on spending many more years to come by her side. The previous winter, I got down on one knee and asked her to marry me in the exact spot where we had met, all those years ago – the car park of our local pub. Granted, not the most romantic of settings, but I knew Tamara would appreciate the sentiment. She said yes and told me to get up.

Tamara came from a family where the correct thing to do was to ask her father for her hand in marriage, and that is exactly what I did a few weeks prior to popping the question. I wasn't looking forward to the moment, because I knew I wasn't the person her parents had in mind for their daughter. I was six years older and a divorcee. If that weren't bad enough, I also had a son from my previous marriage, and hadn't held down a full-time job for more than sixteen months. I wasn't what you would call marriage material. I knew it, and so did Lynne and Maas, Tamara's parents. In fact, the only person who didn't seem to know it was Tamara herself. Plenty of tears flowed that night as I asked Tamara's folks for their daughter's hand in marriage – perhaps none of them tears of joy. Tamara's father told me that as long as Tamara was happy, that was all that counted. With me he could see that she was happy, so he gave me his blessing. I told him I wouldn't let him down.

We married in July and honeymooned in Thailand. I had asked an old school friend and sergeant major in the army, Paul, to be my best man. Paul and I had been estranged for several years when I lived in Milton Keynes and it was nice when we finally reunited. He did a great job as my best man, and impeccably walked the line he had been told not to cross. Tamara and I married in a marquee in the grounds of her parents' house, and the guest list consisted of plenty of doctors and surgeons, all pre-eminent in their fields. I felt a pang of unworthiness at my own wedding, but I disguised it very well.

When we returned home from our honeymoon a few weeks later, we brought home a little more than we bargained on; but we would have to wait nine months to fully feel the effects.

My daughter Lara was born on 29th February 2008. Far from being a normal birth, Lara was born by emergency caesarean section after a routine scan had shown she was in distress. At just short of thirty-two weeks, she was born eight weeks early and was kept in the hospital incubator for the first three weeks of her life. She has thrived every day since. Now, at almost nine years old, she is one of the tallest girls in her class. There are no signs that she was a premature baby at all. I am rather fond of Lara's birth date, 29.02.08 – or, as I prefer to see it, 29,028ft, the generally accepted height of Everest (until 1999, when it was re-measured and had several feet added). If this wasn't a sign, I don't know what could have been.

We didn't have to wait too long for our family to be complete. Around seventeen months after we had Lara, her sister Isla was born, again by a caesarean section, after the previous scar had ruptured. When the medical team went to deliver Isla, she couldn't wait to get into the world, and was already half out of the womb. Tamara remained in hospital for two weeks, where she had several operations and a few blood transfusions. You could say I have vivid memories of the two births– sadly not all good ones, but we are fortunate that Tamara had given birth to two healthy girls.

By the end of summer 2009, my family was complete. In the eight years since I had dragged my sorry self back to Hartlepool, after the disappointment of Cho Oyu and near-destitution afterwards, I now had a home again, an education, a caring wife and two healthy daughters. What I didn't have, though, was a summit of Everest, and I still desperately wanted it. It was the number-one item on my life's bucket list and had occupied the top spot ever since I had learned what a bucket list was.

I think everyone around me assumed that Everest was one of those life dreams that we all have, but will never achieve. It was viewed as being unobtainable. I never bought into this, though. Over the next five years, I never let go of the belief that I was meant to climb this mountain. It was written in the stars, as well my first daughter's date of birth. That was all the sign I needed.

Another aspect of my life that still wasn't sorted was my career. I have never had what you might call a conventional career, but rather a highly unorthodox way of existence. Having tried the corporate machine on several occasions, and falling flat on my face each time, I began to look elsewhere to find my place in working life.

After returning from my honeymoon, I started my own business called Planet Adventure. This was a website of T-shirt designs, which I had either created myself, or hired someone else to do. I had just unwittingly sown the seeds of a business, which I would run full-time from an office in my house. The business would change direction over the next several years and I eventually became the sole director of a setup providing merchandise for sporting events.

As a father to two young girls and a teenage son in Australia, I had commitments that needed honouring, and I knew I needed to be around to do that. Working from home gave me the work/life balance I needed. Tamara worked out of town, as a teacher of computing. One of us needed to be around to take the girls to school and pick them up, and my life dictated that role to me. Working the business from home also meant I was able to just drop everything and do a seven-mile run if I so wished.

My life carried on this way for several years. I took to the role of family man with ease and I loved nothing more than spending time with my family. For anyone on the outside looking in, we were the perfect family unit. In 2011 we moved out of the old semi-detached property that Tamara had bought several years earlier, and bought our own much larger house in a new housing estate on the edge of town. Outwardly, things could not have been any better. However, this picture was playing out slightly differently in my head.

In all the years that had passed since Aconcagua and Cho Oyu, I had longed for another mountain adventure. I still had my sights set firmly on Everest, but any mountain would have done. Realistically, it wasn't going to be Everest any time soon. At the beginning of 2011, I was out of shape and hadn't been to any significant altitude for ten years. I figured that, as far as getting myself ready for another shot at Everest was concerned, I might as well have been starting from scratch. Even if the money came in tomorrow, no guiding company would seriously look at me as an Everest client, having done nothing at all for a decade. It's all well and good having the desire to do something, but you must have a proven track record to back up that desire. I once had it, but in 2011 I felt it was long gone.

I had trained sporadically over the interim years, but mostly just to keep the weight off. I wasn't massively out of shape, but I was a shadow of the person who stood on top of Aconcagua ten years earlier. I took a long hard look at myself and decided to get back to how I used to be. I joined a gym and began training three times a week. The weight soon started to come off, and in no time at all, I went from around 14½ stone down to 13. My confidence began to increase and so too did the thought of maybe, just maybe, looking at Everest once again.

One night I was idly watching the Discovery Channel when a programme about Everest came on. It was called *Everest – Beyond the Limit*, and was concerned with Russell Brice and his Himalayan Experience (Himex) guiding company, which focused on the north side of the mountain.

The programme featured a British climber and self-made millionaire businessman called David Tait who had already climbed Everest, but was returning to climb the mountain again. As a trustee of the National Society for the Prevention of Cruelty to Children (NSPCC), Tait had raised thousands of pounds for this charity, using Everest as the catalyst.

I watched the entire series with interest and came to the conclusion that I was going to try for Everest again. The flame was already flickering away. It just needed turning up a tad. *One last chance,* I told myself, not having the first clue how I was going to achieve it. I hadn't got anywhere near raising enough money to fund an Everest attempt previously, so heaven only knew why I thought this time would be any different. Once more the dream had reared its head. And for the first time since my half-hearted attempt five years earlier, I felt the pull of the mountain, stronger than ever.

The first thing I did was contact David Tait. I was keen to know how he got himself in such a peak form of fitness for his Everest attempts. I looked him up online and found an email address for his place of work. I introduced myself as an aspiring Everest climber, and that I was keen to know how he trained for his (at the time) four summits. Not really holding out much hope for a response, I was amazed when an email reply came through a few days later. It included a full training schedule, week by week and month by month in the run up to his climbs. My immediate thought was that it looked bloody tough.

I thanked him for being so upfront with me and told him I was deeply inspired by what he had achieved, both on the mountain and off with his fundraising endeavours.

For a few years, I had dipped in and out of social media, using both Twitter and Facebook when the mood took me. All that changed in 2011, when I began to use both channels regularly to talk about my dream to climb Everest. I created a page on Facebook called Everest Dream. For most of 2011, I connected with just 90 people – and most of them were friends and family. Still, I enjoyed sharing all my thoughts and desires when it came to the mountain, and as the year progressed, I began to connect with some influential people who had a link to Everest.

One of these was an Australian realtor called Stephen Bock. In 2010 Bock achieved his life dream of summiting the mountain. In December I contacted him through Facebook, introducing myself and my Everest goal. As a highly successful businessman in his field, he is one of the most positive people I have ever had the fortune to meet. He has delivered training to some top corporate organisations, transforming his experiences on Everest into the boardroom. By way of a talk – which he calls *Lessons from 29,000ft* – Steve oozes confidence and charisma and delivers his speech with passion, charm and self-assurance.

For most of the year I became fixated on reaching Everest. Through my newfound connections online, I spoke about my dream with likeminded individuals around the clock. My initial aim was to be on the mountain in 2012.

However, as 2011 progressed, and I was no closer to the financial sum I needed, I knew it wasn't going to happen that year. I had contacted over a hundred organisations with a sponsorship proposal I had created. Rejection followed rejection. If I didn't realise just how tough this task was before, I certainly did now. Yet it was my only way, so I kept chipping away with the proposal, leaving no stone unturned.

In the spring season on Everest in 2012, I had to endure missing out once again. I watched with amazement as several young climbers from the UK had been successful in not only climbing the mountain, but also in securing sponsorship to make it happen. Sponsorship was possible, if you had an angle to offer and the time to commit to searching for that sponsorship. These young Brits had been successful in raising the sponsorship by dangling the 'youth' carrot to potential sponsors. At 39 years old this was well and truly beyond me. I needed to get creative if I was going to make it to the mountain.

Another remarkable event occurred on Everest in 2012. I was watching news emerge that Russell Brice, of the *Everest – Beyond the Limit* TV series had decided to call off that season's attempt. Citing warm and unstable conditions, he decided the mountain was too dangerous, and that he wasn't prepared to put the lives of his clients and Sherpas at risk. There had been an unusually high amount of rockfall off the mountain and it was stripped bare of its usual deep snow coverage. Climate change was blamed. Everest was no longer normal.

One of Brice's clients that year was UK-based charity Walking With The Wounded, supporting servicemen and women injured in the line of duty. With Prince Harry as the charity's patron, the team attracted a lot of global news with their attempt. It was a brave decision for Brice to pull out, knowing the damaging PR this could bring. However, it was without question the right call. Brice was accused of jumping ship before the season really had time to settle in.

Despite facing a barrage of criticism for pulling the plug on his clients' attempts, Brice wouldn't back down. In 2012, experienced Sherpas were not just afraid of a dry mountain and the rocks hurtling down it; of more concern was the state of the Icefall. In a newsletter released explaining the reasons for pulling out, Brice expressed his concern about a large serac hanging on Everest's West Ridge, directly above the main climbing path in the Icefall. He stated that there was potential for a huge collapse, which could kill and injure a large number of people.

Brice packed up and left Everest and the season continued. The collapse didn't happen and eventually the snow arrived and people summited. It appeared as though Brice had been hasty after all and had got it wrong. It would take another four years before the climbing community would once more wonder if Brice had indeed been correct.

For the remainder of the year I began to train, following the gruelling schedule that David Tait had been kind enough to share. One thing he had said in his email that really stuck with me was that Everest was a leg mountain. 'Everything from the waist up," he said, "is just luggage." In his email he added that if I could get my legs incredibly strong, I would be most of the way there already. This became a constant in my mind as I began the most intense and gut-wrenching physical training I had done in a long time.

As well as the training, I needed to find a potential guiding company who would be willing to take me to Everest in the first place. I was conscious that I hadn't been to altitude in over ten years and that this would surely go against me. Still very much focused on the north side, I looked around at the operators who were planning trips to that side of the mountain the following spring. Adventure Peaks were still the main player and the obvious choice for a UK company guiding the north side. I was about to contact them one day when, out of the blue, I received a message on Twitter from a climbing instructor based in the Lake District by the name of Tim Mosedale. It was short and sweet but it got my attention. 'If you are serious about the big E, then let's talk,' it said.

I looked him up online and discovered that he had guided a team of five clients to the top of the mountain in 2011, boasting 100% success. Prior to that he had also reached the summit in 2005 with a bunch of friends rather than as a guide.

He had summited from both sides of the mountain, making him one of a handful of Brits to have achieved such a feat. There was no doubting his credentials and in 2013 he would be returning to the mountain once more with a team of clients. There was, however, one small issue. He ran his trips to the south side of the mountain. For the last ten years I had been sold on climbing Everest from the north. I had always seen the south side as being out of bounds due to the higher fee involved, but I knew that statistically the south side offered a better chance of reaching the top. In addition to less time spent above 8,000m on summit day, there were a whole host of other reasons why the south side was a better proposition, but only one reason why I had never considered it: the $60,000-plus price tag. Tim's website boldly stated 'Climb Everest in 2013 with two-time summiteer Tim Mosedale for just $42,000'. I decided to contact him to find out more.

From the outset, I was honest and upfront. In a long-winded email, I told him that I wasn't a climber in the true sense of the word and that I hadn't been to serious altitude since 2001, when I had reached over 7,000m on Cho Oyu. What I could offer were passion, focus and complete dedication to reach the top. Tim responded a day later saying he wouldn't have contacted me if he didn't believe I could do it. "Besides," he said, "You have been to well over 7,000m previously, and on Everest that is the point when you would start to use oxygen."

I realised that Tim was trying to recruit clients for his forthcoming trip, but I also got the impression he wouldn't consider taking someone without the necessary prerequisite experience. I appeared to tick the correct boxes for Tim, and that now meant I had a decision on my hands. Tim had sold me on the benefits of switching my attention to the south side of the mountain which, he assured me, would be my best chance of reaching the top. Especially considering that this was to be a once-in-a lifetime deal for me. Everything pointed towards the fact that there would be no coming back if I were unsuccessful with my first attempt.

I agreed to meet where we could talk about things face-to-face and spend some time on the hill. As Tim ran a Keswick based Bed and Breakfast in the Lake District when not guiding on Everest, I went across one weekend and spent a few days getting to know him. He answered every question I threw his way and we spent a day running on the fells.

When I drove back home across the Pennines, I was pretty certain I had just found my Everest guide. From now on, all my attention switched to the south side of the mountain – where, if successful in raising the money to go, I would be returning to a Base Camp I had previously visited thirteen years earlier.

With a potential guide and team in place, I now needed to switch my attention back to the training and the fundraising. For the remainder of the year I worked on each in equal measure.

I was sure that 2013 was finally going to be my year. That summer I would turn forty. Climbing Everest before my fortieth birthday became, for the next several months at least, the entire focus of my life. It had to be now or never as far as I was concerned. I had a little over five months to find out.

I contacted the NSPCC to find out whether they could offer some marketing support if I used my potential climb of Everest to raise funds for their charity. They sent a regional fundraiser to meet with me one day and we discussed how we could work together, not only raising funds for the charity, but also for my climb. With David Tait as the charity's Everest flag bearer, I knew I wouldn't be able to raise the amount of funds he had been able to, but I was sure we could achieve something.

At the start of 2013, a lady contacted me to ask if I would attend a local Women's Institute meeting to present a talk about my dream to climb Everest. I had been featured in an article in the local newspaper again recently and she had read the article, thinking I would have a great story to tell.

On the night I spoke, I accidentally launched myself as a public speaker. Having never spoken in such a capacity before, I wasn't sure what to expect. I took along a PowerPoint slideshow full of photos of myself at Everest Base Camp, Aconcagua and Cho Oyu. I interspersed these with the odd motivational quote and somehow brought it all together, telling my life story in just under an hour. A standing ovation concluded the talk, and I realised I could well be onto something. I received an overwhelming number of positive comments, and I was asked if I would consider doing a talk to a group of retired nurses.

A few weeks later I spoke to the nurses and received a similar ovation. In total I spoke to eleven groups about Everest during the year; all coming about from the very first talk I gave. Word of mouth spread like wildfire and I became the speaker of choice to have at a group meeting. I only ever took a small donation from these talks, which I then handed across to the NSPCC, the charity I was now raising money for.

I continued spreading word about my goal to climb Everest on Facebook and I began connecting with more and more people. It became apparent that a lot of people shared the same dream, and I certainly wasn't the only one harbouring a life's goal to reach the roof of our planet. Yet I was acting on the dream and trying to make it happen, whereas for most people, it was just that – a dream.

There is a famous quote by T.E. Lawrence, which I used in some of my talks. It was apt to my situation:

All men dream, but not equally. Those who dream by night in the dusty recesses of their minds wake in the day to find that it was vanity: but the dreamers of the day are dangerous men, for they may act on their dreams with open eyes, to make them possible.

As the number of likes on my Everest Dream Facebook page began to grow, I started to think whether it would be possible to turn these connections to my advantage. They had all clicked 'like' on my page because they either had an interest in Everest, or me, or both as I hoped. Would it be possible to turn these likes into cash, I wondered? Stopping short of directly asking people to send money, I needed to come up with a strategy that would make people who visited my page want to part with some cash. But they weren't likely to do this if there was nothing in it for them.

I had sold some T-shirts with climbing slogans through my T-shirt printing business, and they had always sold quite well. I began to hatch a plan to launch a brand of clothing to run side by side with the page. I threw together a few designs, featuring a silhouette of the south face of Everest above the bold word 'EVEREST' in a distressed-style font. Underneath that I added the strapline, 'One Dream One Chance One Life'. On the sleeve I added the Sagarmatha Nepali tattoo, which I had tattooed on my shoulder in Kathmandu thirteen years earlier. Because I could print these on demand using my own printing equipment, I could offer up the design in a choice of colours and styles of garment, without having to hold any stock. If I received an order for a garment with the design, I could then order that blank garment from my wholesale supplier the next day, print it, and send it out to the customer. I wasn't expecting to sell many at all, maybe one or two to a few people on the page who appeared to be as passionate about the mountain as I was, but at least it was worth a shot.

I created a basic store and added several products, consisting of T-shirts, vests and hoodies, all featuring my unique design. I posted an update announcing the launch of the Everest Dream clothing brand in early February.

The plan was to use proceeds from clothing sales to go towards the costs of climbing the mountain. Even if it only raised enough money to pay for the insurance or the flights, then it was better than nothing. From the outset sales began to come in. It would be a lie to say that they flooded in, but I was pleasantly surprised with the steady stream of orders placed for my Everest Dream clothing. As sales increased, so did the number of people who liked the page on Facebook. I went from 100 likes at the beginning of the year to 1,800 by the time the Everest 2013 climbing season got underway.

Online, my goal to climb Everest had caught people's imagination. Through the power of social media I was able to connect with people and share with them my hopes, dreams and fears. Perhaps what resonated with many was that I was just a normal bloke trying to achieve a big goal.

Clothing sales continued to grow, as did my relentless hunt for sponsors. I couldn't let another year pass me by without finally going to Everest, yet in February 2013 that is exactly what I was facing – again. I had tried to reach the mountain on three previous occasions and each time I had been defeated before I even stepped foot on the plane to Nepal. Was 2013 about to be the fourth time this had happened to me? In six weeks I had my answer.

Once more I watched the dramas of another Everest season unfold, and once more I played no part in it. This time it hurt more than ever. I just couldn't understand why it wasn't happening for me. Of course I knew the real reason: I couldn't afford it. But I felt that Everest was a fate that I was destined to live, and the fact that it wasn't happening deeply hurt. After failing to reach the mountain once again, I did not know if I had another attempt left in me. I felt empty and soul-destroyed. Could I pick myself up and go again, when once more there would be no guarantees that I would finally be rewarded for my efforts? As the strapline on my clothing range stated: One Dream, One Chance, One Life. How many chances did I need?

Having failed in several attempts to reach the mountain, I once again gave myself a short break from Everest. I kept up the pretence online that all was well, and that 2013 was once again nothing more than a minor blip on my eventual journey to the mountain.

By now, as well as a growing following on Facebook, I also had my own blog, which I updated frequently. If ever I posted anything slightly negative on my blog or social media, my friend in Australia, Stephen Bock, would chastise me for it.

"You need to get rid of all this negative energy, mate," he would say to me in a message. "You need to control the inner dialogue and stamp out any negativity whatsoever."

Of course I knew he was right, but over the next few years I still found myself writing some misplaced and downright negative updates. I would then feel his wrath as he once again brought me back from this pit of pessimism.

"You do know that, through your actions, you are inspiring thousands of people?" he once said to me.

"Of course," I shot back.

"So bloody well inspire them, don't dampen their spirits."

In 2013 an event happened on the mountain early in the season that would tarnish the general reputation of the mountain, its climbers and the Sherpas, where the ramifications ran deep.

On April 27th three renowned climbers – Ueli Steck, Simone Moro and photographer Jonathan Griffith – got into a tussle with some of the rope-fixing Sherpas, after they refused to stay off the Lhotse Face while the route was being fixed. They assured the Sherpas that they wouldn't get in their way, but they apparently dislodged ice as they climbed higher, striking the fixing Sherpas lower down. Back at Camp Two, accusations began flying around about irresponsible behaviour. The three climbers found themselves surrounded by a hundred Sherpas, all angry at the situation. Violence broke out between the European climbers and several of the Sherpas. US climber Melissa Arnot was credited with stopping the melee from erupting further, which would have had disastrous consequences for the climbing community on Everest. However, a certain amount of damage was done, and the story went out around the world. Tensions had been brewing between the Sherpas and western climbers for quite a while, and this incident made the lid finally blow off the pot.

Once again Everest was in the limelight, and it seemed that the world's press was keen to pulverise the mountain and its climbers, rather than report on the success stories that were emerging. One such story was of Kenton Cool, the British Mr Everest, who climbed the mountain for fun every year. He successfully completed an audacious attempt to climb the three peaks that made up the Everest horseshoe, consisting of Nupste, Everest and Lhotse, known as the Triple Crown. In doing so, he became the first person to scale all three peaks in the Western Cwm in one climb. His Sherpa climbing partner Dorje Gylgen ably assisted him to the top, as he had done on most of his previous Everest summits.

This – and more stories like it – should have been the real focus of the 2013 season, but sadly 'Everest-bashing' ruled the day.

In November 2013 I applied to take part in an online voting competition run by the drug manufacturer Nurofen. Called 'Big Lives', the month-long competition awarded a £1,500 prize towards an adventure or quest to live a 'Big Life'. All you needed to do to win the cash was to get your friends and family to vote for you using an app on Facebook. Whoever got the most votes from five contestants was declared the winner. It all seemed rather ingenious! I submitted a short application and then waited a few weeks, before finding out I had been selected as one of the five finalists. The competition went live in early December and ran for three weeks. The concept was simple enough, but actually getting someone to vote for you was a different matter. From the beginning it became clear that the winner was going to emerge as either me or a chap called Paul Everitt, who wanted help to fund a round-the-world adventure on a self-built 'bike car', similar to a giant car-size go-kart.

For the first few weeks of voting we were neck and neck. One day I would be ten votes ahead, and then the next day he would be. It was pretty stressful stuff, especially considering the prize on offer would pay for my flights and insurance for a possible Everest climb.

For the next three weeks, Paul and his Going Solo campaign became my public enemy number one; just as my Everest Dream campaign became the same to him. I would wake each morning to see if I was still in the lead, or if my lead had been cut. If it had, I would start messaging around all my contacts and friends asking them to vote for me if they hadn't already done so. I even asked anyone connected to Everest to vote for me, including illustrious climbers such as Stephen Venables, Chris Bonington and Kenton Cool.

I was desperate for the cash, and I was willing to take desperate measures. This was all-out war. No matter how many votes I gained, Paul Everitt kept right on my heels. In the last few days of voting, though, his resolve seemed to weaken. I sensed from some of his updates that he didn't think he could catch me. I went in for the kill and gave it one last push with all my contacts, which powered me across the finish line. Paul finished with around 980 votes, and I finished with 1,092 – and a prize of £1,500 towards my Everest pot.

Had I known three weeks earlier what I was letting myself in for then I would not have entered. It was an awful lot of work. Still, the prize fund would come in useful, and I knew I could now pay for my flights and insurance. After the competition ended I became friends with Paul through

Facebook, and he began promoting me to his followers. He is a great guy who believes that life is there to be lived. He also epitomises the spirit of human kindness. The world could do with more people like him.

Shortly before the Nurofen competition started, I contacted British Shakespearean actor Brian Blessed to ask if he would be willing to support my campaign to reach the mountain. I knew that Brian had a love for the mountain, having previously tried to reach the summit on three occasions earlier in his life. I figured that his Everest days were probably well and truly behind him, but that he might relive that passion through my dream. I wasn't sure what I wanted from such an endorsement, but with Brian Blessed in my corner, it could only be a good thing. I sent a hastily put-together email to his Facebook page, asking if he would be willing to come and speak at a charity evening I was looking to organise for the NSPCC.

Now, I realise that I could have contacted someone who had been all the way to the top of Everest for an endorsement, but one of the things I admired about Brian was his infectious passion for life and his booming larger-than-life personality. He was the perfect person to shout from the rooftops, in a way only he could: "Come on, you bastards, get behind Ellis Stewart and send the lad to Everest!" I could picture it in my head.

It was a shrewd move on my behalf; although one I didn't think would come off. I was delighted when only a day or so later I got a response. It was not the initial response I had hoped for, but I had made an impression and that was what counted.

Brian was unable to commit to any speaking engagements due to his busy schedule and his loyalty to the several animal-based charities he was a patron of. However, when it came to Everest he would be delighted to get behind my attempt. Short of asking directly for him to attend an event or talk, he was willing to share and promote any message I wanted to put out there, within reason of course. Nothing was ever too much trouble. He modelled my T-shirts and shared the photos to his legions of fans. Sales of my Everest clothing went through the roof, proceeds of which were beginning to grow towards the Everest expedition fee. As long as I didn't ask for any involvement with the NSPCC and kept things strictly Everest, the world was my oyster – or rather Brian Blessed's full media machine was.

As 2014 dawned I was optimistic about my chances of going to Everest. However, as ever, I tried to be realistic. I had failed on four previous occasions, so why would 2014 be any different? This was my best chance so far, thanks to the money I had been able to save from the sales of my Everest Dream clothing, the prize money from Nurofen and donations I received online.

Brian Blessed wearing an Everest Hoodie

I could not have been any fitter, thanks to the David Tait training schedule I had loosely followed, plus input from Ste Bock. Joe Bonington, son of legendary British mountaineer Chris Bonington, had guided Ste in his training in Sydney therefore I knew I was tapping into a vast wealth of expertise. My weekly training for the past several months would have made Superman cry in defeat. Ste once said to me that Joe would push him so hard that he would almost puke. It was at that point that Joe would then say "And now the training can start." I liked the analogy, and I applied it to my own training. I didn't have a personal trainer, but I had experienced Everest climbers to guide me on the best way to train for the mountain.

Although I hadn't done any real winter mountaineering for a while, I wasn't overly worried. Tim had organised a training week in the Cairngorm Mountains of Scotland, scheduled for February. As long as I kept working on improving my strength and cardiovascular skills, the hill skills could be honed in Scotland. I pushed myself harder than I ever thought possible those first few months of the year, and I could do things I would not have imagined I would be able to do only a year earlier. In the gym where I trained, I used the Stairmaster religiously. This revolving staircase, like a mini escalator looping round and round, became my weapon of choice for improving stamina and endurance. When I had first started using it a few years earlier, I could manage only forty-five minutes before collapsing in a sweaty heap on the floor – and that was without any weight on my back. With just three months to go before potentially leaving for Everest, I could now go for up to three hours at a time with 25kg on my back. I would also run several times a week, choosing the hilliest route I could find. As long as I didn't have any accidents or injure myself before the end of March, I was confident that I had done all I could to reach 'Everest shape'.

One of the hardest things to do is to prepare for something when there is still a good chance that it won't happen. I found myself having to deal with this situation time and time again on my path to Everest, and it applied to the early part of 2014 as much as it did to any of my previous attempts.

There is a quote by the American Motivational speaker, Tony Robbins, in which he says: "As soon as you truly commit to making something happen, the 'how' will reveal itself." In 2014 I unknowingly applied this to my drive for the mountain. With the success of the clothing sales, I was able to put enough money away to pay the deposit for the trip to Tim. I knew there was a good chance I could lose this money if I couldn't raise the remaining balance in time, but I had no choice. To secure my name on the Everest permit, Tim needed to pay a balance to the Ministry of Tourism in Kathmandu for each member of the team. I booked my international return flights and insurance for the climb with the money I received from the Nurofen competition. But with seven weeks to go until the date of departure, I still needed to find $10,000. Somehow I had managed to raise over $30,000 from selling T-shirts and hoodies, winning competitions and receiving donations from family members and friends. I had taken a massive risk in paying the deposit and booking my flights and insurance. I could be seriously out of pocket if this tactic backfired. I knew I was praying for a miracle, just as I had always done when it came to Everest.

Not knowing whether I would be going or not played havoc with my state of mind.

In late January I had a conversation with Tim on my chances of being on his 2014 Everest team.

"On a scale of one to ten, how likely is it you will be going?" he asked. "One means not this year and ten means your bags are packed."

"I am currently on a four or a five," I answered back with sadness in my voice.

"So that means there is an almost 50% chance you are coming, which is great news," was Tim's response.

I hadn't really thought about it that way. "I am determined to hit a ten this time, Tim."

I was so near now, but still so far. I meticulously played the sponsorship game in the hope of finding that one sponsor who could pick up the remaining amount outstanding. But as ever, the rejections kept raining in.

As a training exercise, I had signed up to travel down to Wales and tackle the infamous SAS Fan Dance. This was advertised as a gruelling 24km race over two sides of Pen Y Fan (the highest mountain in the Brecon Beacons) in full winter conditions, carrying 16kg plus food and water. The route had long been seen as a great indicator of SAS recruits' fitness levels during their final selection week. This was a perfect opportunity to see how far I had come with my fitness. I did the race with my friend Mark, and I fully expected to find snow a few feet deep, which I could really test myself in. I was dismayed to find conditions wet and windy instead. Still, it was a challenge nonetheless. Described as being incredibly tough, I actually found it fairly easy-going, which proved how fit I had become. I had no doubts that this was as tough a challenge as the organisers had described, but to someone on the brink of tackling Everest, it was a training hike.

In February, Tim had organised a training week in Scotland for the Everest team. This would have been a good opportunity to get some useful snow days in, and also to meet fellow potential team members. For a good few months I had been chatting online with an 18-year-old from Cheshire by the name of Alex Staniforth, who had already signed on the dotted line. Alex had been successful in acquiring sponsorship to take his place and had recently returned from an attempt to climb Baruntse, a 7,000m peak in Nepal, in preparation for Everest. I hadn't actually met him, but we had got to know one another quite well through our own respective campaigns to reach the mountain. If successful, Alex would go on to become the youngest Brit to summit Everest from Nepal. This was his USP – and one that he was able to exploit very well. He had been far more successful than I had in acquiring sponsorship, and I began to wonder what I could offer that would bring me the same successes.

Unfortunately, Tim had to pull the plug on the Cairngorms trip due to bad snow conditions and strong winds. Tim said we would spend most of our time battling to stay upright, rather than being able to learn anything of value. I was disappointed, as I had been banking on this trip to brush up on my general mountaineering skills. Without it, I would be going to Everest – if I went at all – without putting on a crampon in over thirteen years. I expressed my concerns to Tim, who agreed to get me over to Cumbria for a night and day on the fells, where he said he would help to alleviate my fears. A week later we did just that. I spent twelve valuable hours in the hills, where we moved fast up several fells in a full coat of snow. As dusk fell, Tim pulled two gas masks out of his pack and we spent the next few hours trudging slowly up Great Gable with masks in place. This was an exercise to replicate what it would feel like wearing an oxygen mask on summit night on Everest. We must have looked odd to any passing walkers, but it was now late, so we needn't have worried. As we made our way back down to the car in the dead of night, my head torch batteries packed in and I had to stumble my way back down using the torch from my iPhone. All in all Tim said he didn't have any worries, and that I would be fine on Everest. "Once a mountaineer, always a mountaineer," he said, before adding, "It's like learning to ride a bike. Once you learn this stuff, you don't forget it." I felt a lot better about things. "One thing, though – take plenty of batteries."

As February came around, everything was in place to be leaving for the mountain the following month. Everything, that was, except $10,000, which was my shortfall from the full financial target. I had been clawing in dribs and drabs from Facebook followers who felt compelled to help, and this always amazed me. I would receive messages from people asking how they could help. My answer would be: "Apart from giving me $10,000 you could buy some of the clothing." The clothing was still selling extremely well, but I was running out of time. I had thought of all manner of weird and wonderful ways to bring in the money. Some of these schemes had limited success, and some had none whatsoever; but nothing had been a runaway success and I still remained short of where I needed to be.

I had started a supporter's wall on my blog where, for a small donation, I would add an image and a message of support. This was similar to the pixel idea I had tried several years earlier, and I immediately had people wanting a piece of the action. I worked out that, if I sold all of the squares on the wall, it would bring in around $4,000. Although this wasn't enough, every little helped. In total, I raised just short of $2,000 from this single page on my website.

With the majority of the expedition fund secured, the dream simply *had* to be fulfilled this time. The cost of the climb had defeated me on all my previous attempts to reach the mountain, but this time I was so near to my target, and all I needed was a push to see me across the finish line. At the end of February, with just four weeks until departure and no sponsor in sight, I took matters into my own hands. I decided once more to take out a loan, just like I had done for Aconcagua. I couldn't let this opportunity go. After twenty years of dreaming and four previous attempts to reach the mountain, I was finally on my way to Everest. The following day, I announced as much by updating my Everest Dream Facebook page:

Finally after twenty years of dreaming and planning I can finally announce I am off to attempt to climb Everest.

Every comment I received let me know just how ecstatic people genuinely were for me, as one such comment showed:

'Absolutely well done for teaching others never to lose sight of their dreams…' – Lindy Magnussen

This time everything had come together. Surely nothing now could intervene and stop my plans? In a few weeks' time I would attempt to climb the highest mountain in the world. I couldn't believe that I had made it happen, but I had.

The day I was finally able to transfer the money across to Tim was a day I will never forget. The run up to departure was spent in a mad dash, sorting last-minute things. I was able to call in a few favours from people I knew personally in the outdoor gear trade, and managed to secure an expedition down suit from the UK outdoor brand Rab. I also secured some equipment sponsorship from Outdoor Hire. Rather than selling outdoor gear, they hired it and I was able to look through their entire stock line and choose anything I thought I would need on the mountain. Securing the down suit from Rab was a massive boost, as this one item was the most expensive single article of clothing needed for high-altitude climbing.

As well as the loan of equipment from Outdoor Hire, I also borrowed some gear from a chap I met online called Michael Buttery. Michael had introduced himself to me several months earlier through Facebook. It was immediately obvious we had a lot in common. Also from Hartlepool, Michael too harboured the Everest dream and only the previous year he summited Denali in North America, so he clearly had the ability. We became good friends. He genuinely wanted to see me succeed and it was great having him in my corner. He even donated £250 to the NSPCC page.

A few weeks before I was due to depart, Alan Arnette, the climbing blogger from the US, contacted me asking if I would be willing to give an interview for his highly popular climbing website. In 2011 he reached the summit of Everest himself on his fourth attempt. He had since become the world's most respected chronicler of Everest news, according to Outside, a popular adventure magazine in the US. I was honoured that he picked up on my goal to reach Everest and even more so when he fired across fifteen or so questions, clearly tailored to my background: 'When did your Everest dream begin?' and 'How does your family feel about your Everest ambitions?' There was also a question which got me thinking more than the others, and he asked it in a way that gave me a huge sense of pride: 'Your tenacity to climb Everest is almost unprecedented in my experience. First, let's talk about your overall drive. Have you ever pursued anything else with such fervour?'

When the interview went live on his site it triggered an enormous number of comments, the vast majority of which were all positive, wishing me the very best with my goal.

At the end of March I gave interviews to the local press, a talk to a retired men's group, and began to wind down my training. In the final days before I left, Tamara organised a going-away party for me in the local village hall. Everyone who meant something to me came, including a few people who had connected with me online. Even my university friend Steve travelled up from London for the evening. I gave a short talk about the climb and we had a raffle, with all proceeds going to the NSPCC. I took the book *Everest – Summit of Achievement* by Stephen Venables along, and everyone who was in attendance signed it with a good-luck message, which was touching. My friend Mark's comment was particular heartfelt. 'For 20 years I have had to listen to you talking about Everest, but at last it's nearly over.' He did finish by adding for me to stay safe and that he was proud of me.

I had to delay my departure by a day due to a family commitment: my cousin Sophie's wedding. The bride and groom gave me a special mention and I had a dance with Tamara and my two daughters to the song *Gravity* by Embrace. I put this song on Tamara's phone and told her to listen to it while I was away on the mountain. As I turned in for bed that night, I updated my Facebook page. *'It's not often in one's life you can say when you wake up in the morning, you are off to climb the highest mountain in the world. Tomorrow is that day!'*

PART SIX: MOUNT EVEREST 2014

You're off to Great Places! Today is your day! Your mountain is waiting, so get on your way! – Dr Seuss

30th March 2014

This was it, then. The moment I had been waiting for had finally arrived. After what felt like a lifetime, on account of the fact that it had been a lifetime, I was on my way to Everest. I told Tamara that I didn't want the send-off to be emotional. "Why get upset?" I would say. "I am off to achieve my life's dream." In the arrival lounge of Manchester Airport, I held my two daughters tight and told them both not to be sad, and that Daddy would see them both real soon. I could see tears welling up in both Tamara and my mam's eyes, but I resisted until I went through the double doors and into departures. Tears ran down both cheeks as soon as I was out of sight. I was about to spend the longest time away since either of my daughters had been born, and whether off to achieve a life's dream or not, this still tore at my heart.

I used the flight to Abu Dhabi – the first part of the journey to Kathmandu – to come to terms with what I would be attempting to do over the next several weeks. As upsetting as it was leaving the family, I knew deep down that now was my time, and I had to do this. Ever since I first saw a picture of Tenzing on top of Everest, I had known in my heart that one day I would attempt to climb the mountain. That day was here.

I switched from an emotional family man to a focused and determined climber with a job to do. And what a job it was. OK, so I wasn't being paid; far from it. It had cost me a small fortune to be here, but if I reached the summit I would be rewarded in ways far more valuable than money.

Departures Lounge – Manchester Airport

Landing in Kathmandu instantly transported me back to my first two visits over a decade earlier, and not much had changed. The place was timeless.

A representative from Himalayan Guides, the outfitter we would be using for our attempt on the mountain, picked me up from the airport. I was transported to the Manaslu Hotel in Thamel, where I met Tim and Alex, who had already spent a night there.

When I finally met Alex in the hotel lobby, I dismissed the formalities of a handshake and went in for a big bear hug, which I knew would break any immediate tension. It did the trick. It was important that I got on well with him, as the Everest team consisted of me, Alex, and two other climbers, who had bolted onto the permit but would be doing their own thing. At eighteen years old, Alex had achieved much already just by being there. When I was eighteen, all I could think about were girls, fast cars and nightclubs. I found Alex to be the most focused and switched-on teenager I had met in a long time. When he should have been getting drunk for the first time and chasing girls around rural Cheshire, he decided instead to try and become the youngest British person to climb Everest from Nepal. I admired him greatly for it.

With just one night in Kathmandu to adjust to the time difference, I found myself back at the airport the very next morning, ready to catch the short thirty-minute mountain flight to Lukla. This was the first time I would get to experience the flight into Lukla – my only previous experience of the flight was doing it in reverse, flying back to Kathmandu. I was both excited and scared witless at the same time. Nepal's aviation had a really poor safety record. Only as recently as 2013, there had been a fatal crash involving a flight to Lukla, where nineteen people were killed.

During peak season, around fifty flights a day land at the Tenzing-Hillary Airport at Lukla. When I first flew from Lukla fourteen years previously the runway was a dirt strip, but shortly afterwards it was covered in tarmac. As I stood around chatting with Alex and Tim that morning, waiting for our own flight, I thought about the unfortunate titles that had been bestowed on Lukla. Being called the 'world's most challenging airstrip' or the 'most dangerous airport in the world' did nothing to quell the fear. However, it was a necessary evil to overcome if you wanted to even see Everest, let alone climb it – either that or start from Jiri, as I had done in 2000, adding a further ten days to the approach to the mountain.

Strapped in to our Sita Air Dornier 228 that morning, we clung to the tops of the hillsides below and made our way into the mountains. The flight didn't disappoint and the exhilaration was heightened when we approached the 1,500ft-long (but just 60ft-wide) runway. On an uphill gradient of 12%, this was the point in the flight where you really hoped the pilot was a skilled one. Overshoot the runway and you crash into the steep hillside at the far end. Undershoot, and the same fate awaits as you crash into the hillside below. This is sadly what happened in 2008 to a group of German tourists, who were all killed on an approach to the runway in poor visibility.

On this occasion, though, we landed without a hitch and I collected my pack. I disembarked, dropped onto all fours and kissed the tarmac. *Thank God for that,* I thought. That was one danger over and done with that I wouldn't have to face again until I was on my way back to Kathmandu. I remember seeing a video clip of Kenton Cool, the British mountain guide, in which he admitted finding the flight into Lukla scarier than the actual climb of Everest. I wouldn't go that far, but it is certainly an experience to test the most adventurous spirit in all of us.

On the first of eighteen days on foot, moving towards the mountain, it felt amazing to be back in Nepal's mountains. Lukla was surrounded by lush green vegetation and the odd white peak thrusting upwards. The scenery was spellbinding, even this early into the approach to Everest.

We stopped off at the Paradise Lodge teahouse for a spot of breakfast and to pick up our porter team, who would accompany us on our journey to the mountain. Led by Laxman, a friendly Nepali who had a basic but understandable level of English, our porter team was invaluable on the trek. Without them we would have carried a large amount of kit and equipment, much of it surplus to requirements during the trekking. For the first few days of the trip, Tim would routinely check the weight of my pack. If he thought I was carrying too much, he would tell me to make the pack lighter by getting rid of stuff into my duffel, which the porters carried. I think initially Tim thought I was trying to be some sort of superhero, in a vain 'look at how much stuff I can carry' kind of a way. But that wasn't the case at all. The reason I carried more than I should have was that my duffel bag was jam-packed full. I simply couldn't fit another thing inside it. I didn't want to own up to the fact that my kit bag was a tad on the small side, so I learned to grin and bear the extra weight in my daypack.

We spent the first few days finding our feet and getting to know one another. Apart from a few trips across to Cumbria to visit Tim, I hadn't spent a lot of time in his company. The foundations for our companionship over the next several weeks were being established in the lower villages of the Solu-Khumbu.

Tim spent a lot of the time mentoring our small, close-knit group along the way. This would consist of the simplest of things – such as reminding us to use antibacterial gel each time we returned from the toilet or before we ate – to the more serious issues of dealing with death on the mountain, should we encounter it. This mentoring would continue for the full duration of the trek, and Tim left no stone unturned when it came to making sure he had the fittest and healthiest of teams to arrive at Everest.

Namche was our first real opportunity since leaving Lukla to send messages back home. The last time I was here, fourteen years earlier, you needed to pay to use a computer in an internet café, of which there were a couple. Now, most lodges, teahouses and bakeries all had their own Wi-Fi connection, which you paid to access for an agreed amount of time, usually an hour. Although it was nice to be able to update your Twitter feed and communicate with loved ones in real time through messaging apps, I couldn't help but feel that the smartphone revolution had killed the art of conversation. In the bakeries and teahouses everyone was preoccupied with their phones and tablets. Hardly anyone looked up when someone new walked in. Don't get me wrong – this new technology has been good overall and I have embraced every facet of it. In fact, if it hadn't been for the emergence of social media, then I would not have been in Nepal attempting to climb Everest in the first place. But it was still sad to see how it has become such an overpowering necessity that we sometimes switch off and blank out everything else around us. I was here to see the beautiful country of Nepal and hopefully climb its highest peak, not to stare at a four-inch screen for hours at a time wondering what was going on with life back home. My online time was kept to a minimum.

Early in the trek we crossed paths with other teams en masse on their way to the mountain, each following their own schedule. Most teams would take a leisurely ten days to reach Base Camp, aiming to arrive around mid-April. We planned on taking a week longer as Tim believed in a longer trekking phase, affording us the opportunity to take in two high passes both above 5,000m. This was a tactic he had adopted with clients in both 2011 and 2013, and in both those years he had clients reach the summit. All five of his clients did in 2011. I was happy to follow this schedule and it meant that I would get to see some of the Everest region that I hadn't seen before.

Tim liked to get off the beaten path and he was keen for us to avoid conversing with other tourists as much as possible. As a result, there were days in those first few weeks of trekking when we would see one or two trekkers all day, if we were lucky. I understood the logic behind it; Tim didn't want us catching a cold or some other illness while we were on our way to the mountain. A cold up there could linger a lot longer than back home and could have serious implications on our schedule and summit bids. It was more likely we would catch something from a trekker, relatively fresh from Kathmandu, than from one another. As much as I tried to respect and appreciate this, I still found it shackling; I had paid a lot of money to be out there and I didn't want to feel as though I couldn't talk to other tourists.

When I trekked to Everest in 2000, I remember being in awe of climbers who were on their way to climb the mountain. Now I was that climber and it was my turn for others to be in awe of me.

In a teahouse early in the trek I struck up a conversation with an older couple from Australia, who were here achieving a life's ambition of seeing Everest.

"So are you heading up too?" the lady asked. "We are hoping to visit Base Camp."

I took a sip from my hot lemon. "Most definitely up I hope."

Tim was busy updating his Twitter feed but I knew he had one ear on our conversation.

The chap who was with the lady joined in. "We have a friend of a friend who is actually climbing the mountain, and we are hoping to meet him. We have never met anyone climbing Everest. Have you?"

Tim shifted uncomfortably, knowing I was about to bring him into the conversation.

"Actually, yes I have. This guy here has summited four times and we are hoping to climb it again."

An impressed look filled their faces. "Wow, you guys are climbing Everest?" the lady asked.

I was about to answer but Tim chimed in: "No, we are not here to climb Everest, we are here to try and climb Everest. There is a big difference."

This instantly deflated me and brought me crashing back to earth. The Australian couple drank up and made their excuses to leave.

I had to take it on the chin and accept that I had paid money to Tim to oversee my attempt at reaching the top of Everest. If this meant following his rules – even if I didn't necessarily agree with them – then so be it, especially if it would bolster my chances of stepping onto that summit in several weeks' time.

On 8th April 2014 we crossed the Renjo La, the first of the three high passes we would tackle during the trek in. At an altitude of 5,450m it was the first stern challenge of the trek. We had hovered around the 4,000m mark for the past few days and even had a quick skirmish up to 5,000m, but this was the first time we would get some altitude equivalent to the height of Base Camp under our belts.

That morning, as Alex and I arrived in the dining room of the teahouse we had stayed at for the night in Lunde, Tim was already there having breakfast. He had told us to meet at 5.00am. We arrived at 5.05am. He wasn't happy. He looked up from his porridge with a frown.

"What time do you call this? Punctuality is critical high on the mountain."

"But we aren't on the mountain yet," I said with a bit of a smirk, but soon realised he was being serious. This was another of Tim's tests that he set for us without our knowledge, to continually assess our strengths and weaknesses.

Tim didn't return the smile. He jabbed a finger at me. "Your team mate could be freezing waiting for you to emerge from your tent. If we were at the South Col, five minutes can make a big difference."

We passed most of these secret tests, but on odd occasions, such as this, he would berate us. At the time I thought it was a little petty, but I knew that he wanted us to succeed, and changing the way we did certain things meant that we would arrive on the mountain educated, ready, and – most importantly – healthy.

As we trekked through the morning darkness, towards the ridge and the pass, I struggled to warm up my hands. I only had a thin pair of Power Stretch liner gloves; my thicker, warmer gloves were in my duffel bag on the back of a porter somewhere behind me. I cursed my stupidity as I continually pulled my fingers half out of the glove, wriggling them all back and forth to force some blood to flow. I hadn't expected it to be this cold so soon into the trip and hadn't planned my kit correctly.

So far, we had mostly trekked in the full glare of daytime sunshine. This was our first time trekking before the sun had a chance to rise. The cold penetrated every bit of my body as I trekked higher and higher. Tim was way out ahead, but I could see his tracks in the snow as we began the final climb to the ridge, and the true summit of the Renjo La pass. Alex and I stayed together most of the way up, remaining ahead of the porters and our bags. We both certainly felt the altitude and it was a very weary couple of Everest clients who finally flopped onto the ridge. Tim had already set up a tripod for his camera and was snapping away at the view. And what a view it was.

There laid out before me was one of the most spectacular mountain vistas I had ever seen in my life. A 360° view of Himalayan mountains proudly dominated my vision. Everest directly in front was unmistakeable. It looked fierce and menacing, with its famous summit plume billowing away. The most fantastic crisp blue sky was the perfect background for the show stealers in the foreground, of which Everest was very much the clear winner. The whole view was as mesmerising as it was intoxicating and we spent a good thirty minutes just soaking it all in. I didn't want to forget this view in a hurry. My camera made sure that I wouldn't have to.

Renjo La Pass with Everest beyond

As we began to descend from the pass, I could see the day's destination: the village of Gokyo nestling at the foot of a large lake, which was still completely frozen solid.

We spent two days at Gokyo at an altitude of 4,700m before heading down the valley to the village of Phortse.

The second day in Gokyo wasn't a rest day. We left the teahouse late in the morning to make the short ascent of Gokyo Ri, a famous viewpoint of Everest at 5,400m. It was a stiff climb taking just over an hour, and the altitude made itself known with every step. I stayed within a few yards of Tim all the way to the top and for the first time in the trip I felt very strong. I had struggled to keep up with Tim the day before, as we crossed the Renjo La, but my fitness returned as I reached the prayer flags at the top of Gokyo Ri, a second or so behind him.

"Well, if you can do that in a few week's time, I have high hopes for you," Tim said as I sat on a rock and reached for my camera.

Four 8,000m peaks were visible: Everest, Lhotse, Makalu and Cho Oyu, the scene of my last major mountaineering trip thirteen years earlier.

On the 12th April we arrived in Pangboche, where we stayed for one night. After this we spent two nights in the village of Dingboche, where for the first time since we began the trek thirteen days earlier we really could put our feet up and rest. This was a time to wash gear, wash ourselves with basic but effective outside showers, and generally kick back and relax. We could frequent the bakery for chocolate cake and Wi-Fi access, and all three of us had ample time to update our blogs and Twitter feeds. Tim and Alex used Twitter to spread news of how the trip was progressing, whereas as I had built up a healthy following on Facebook and therefore shared most of my updates through my Everest Dream page. I would generally add a picture or two and then accompany that with three to four paragraphs on what had been happening since my last update. I elected not to keep a journal on the trip, preferring instead to add my thoughts and feelings online through these short updates. So far it was working quite well and the feedback I received from those following back home was comforting and encouraging.

One of these well-wishers, a lady called Kate Smith from Skipton in Yorkshire, had come to mean more to me than most. When I finally left for Everest, she was probably more pleased for me than I was. I had formed a nice friendship with Kate, and she had so far shared with me every pivotal moment; not only of the two weeks trekking towards Everest, but also the few years prior when I was attempting to get the funds together. Kate was a retired teacher in her seventies, deeply passionate about the Everest scene and mountaineering in general. She would have loved to climb Everest herself in her youth, but sadly it never transpired. She now got her fix by connecting with people such as me and sharing in our climbing dramas. I was more than happy to take her along on this journey and she was always one of the very first people to respond to my trip updates.

As we left the village of Dingboche, I felt refreshed and ready for the next phase of our march to Everest. For the next two nights we stayed in tents as we moved up to the base of the Kongma La, which was our next high pass. This gave Alex and me a chance to get to know some of the staff we would be sharing Base Camp with. Pasang Temba, one of our camp cooks, began to ply us with hot lemon tea as soon as we arrived. Our first night's stay was at Dingogma, a grassy campsite next to a large boulder with impressive views of Ama Dablam, Chukhung and Island Peak. Dorje Gyalgen, one of our team of climbing Sherpas, greeted us and we sat around in the kitchen tent while Pasang kept the hot lemon tea flowing. Dorje had a solid reputation on Everest. He had accompanied

Kenton Cool on most of his summits of the mountain, including his triple crown of Everest, Nuptse and Lhotse the year before. As we got to know one another a little, I secretly hoped that he would be assigned to my side high on the mountain. He was a Sherpa with a fantastic reputation who clearly knew the mountain well. Besides, Kenton wasn't on Everest this year – Dorje was free to buddy up with another climber.

Alex had been ill since leaving Dingboche and his condition didn't improve that first night we shared a tent together. Whether it was the effects of the altitude, or a stomach bug he had picked up, was difficult to say. He was pale as the snow outside when he excused himself early from the kitchen tent to go and rest in his sleeping bag.

The following morning things didn't look any better for Alex. We moved up to the base of the pass, which we would cross the following day. The 5,500m pass was no pushover; but first we had a more challenging ascent of the nearby Pokalde Peak planned. At 5,805m Pokalde was the highest altitude we would gain before reaching Everest in a few days' time. Located just 12km from Everest, Pokalde was one of the shortest and easiest of the trekking peaks in the Everest region, and consisted of nothing more than steep walking with some sections of rock scrambling. However, when we reached Pokalde we found it covered in deep fresh snow. As we set off for the top, some 650m higher than our camp, we realised it was going to be a tricky proposition. Dorje led the way through knee-deep snow, followed by Tim, then me, with Alex bringing up the rear.

I wasn't feeling perfect myself, and before long Alex and I dropped far behind Dorje and Tim up ahead. As we gingerly plodded on through the ever-thicker snow, I was relieved when Tim finally brought a halt to proceedings. We hadn't expected conditions to be so bad on the trek and had consequently sent our ice axes and crampons ahead to Base Camp. Lightweight trekking boots and poles were not adequate. I heard Tim shout ahead to Dorje:

"We will turn back; it's too dangerous. We are here to climb Everest, not Pokalde."

Tim didn't want any mishaps on his hands, and conditions on Pokalde could easily have turned serious. Alex was out of sorts and I wasn't firing on all cylinders, so we were both relieved to turn around and retreat back to camp, where we could rest and recover for the remainder of the day.

As I lay in the tent that night, I felt disappointed that we had been defeated on a relatively easy trekking peak which thousands of people ascended each year. It was a dent to my pride more than anything else, but still I was hoping to reach as high as I could before reaching Everest. The crossing of the Kongma La pass the following day, at over 5,500m, would have to do. In two days' time we would arrive at Base Camp, where the business end of this trip could well and truly begin. I drifted off to sleep confident that this was nothing more than a minor blip. How wrong I was about to be.

18th April 2014

The day dawned with the most spectacular clear blue sky. Ama Dablam looked incredible. After an early breakfast, and a quick dismantle of the camp, I grabbed my camera and fired off some shots. Luckily I felt much better that day as I stood and gazed at Ama Dablam in a perfect sky. As I brushed my teeth, I was happy that we would finally be back on the main Everest trail later. Once we had gone over the pass, we would drop down to the village of Lobuche, just one day away from Base Camp, where we would stay for just one night before reaching Everest the following day.

We watched our tents and cooking equipment being quickly packed away and secured onto the backs of several yaks, ready to head on up to Base Camp. We waited until they had reached the top of the pass before following. I could tell I was back to my usual self as the zip in my stride returned. Alex was feeling better too. As we both merrily trekked along, lost in our own thoughts, neither of us had any idea what had just occurred lower down on Everest. Our dreams and hopes had been cruelly extinguished in an instant, but we didn't yet realise this.

After a steep descent, we rested on some boulders at the other side of the pass, and ate a picnic that Pasang Temba had prepared for us that morning. Looking back up at the pass made me grateful that we had ascended in the direction we did. This side looked incredibly steep and I spoke briefly with a few trekkers who were on their way across it. "Rather you than me," I joked.

To reach Lobuche we needed to cross the chaotic Khumbu Glacier, which fed directly down the valley from Everest itself. It wasn't immediately obvious where to go as the three of us made our way across. On a few occasions I reached a high part of the moraine with a steep drop on the other side. I then had to backtrack to find a safer and easier path. This carried on for an hour and eventually I made it across and into the village of Lobuche.

As I reached the Kala Patthar lodge, where we had planned to stay, a helicopter went hurtling past overhead in the direction of Base Camp. There was no mistaking that we were now on the main Everest trail, with the mountain just three to four hours away. It was normal to see helicopters flying up the valley to the mountain. *Probably just a tourist flight,* I told myself, *with people eager to see the highest mountain in the world.*

A minute later, another helicopter went flying past, followed a few minutes later by a third. *Whoa, it's busy up there,* I thought, as I entered the lodge and dropped my pack to the floor of the large communal dining room. This was the last lodge we would be staying in for the next six weeks. From the following day, we would be in our tents at Base Camp. To say I was excited was an understatement. We had just completed eighteen days of trekking – and although the trekking had been deeply enjoyable, I was keen to get into mountaineering mode and do what we had come here to do. I was in a confident and focused mood as I sat down next to Tim and ordered a jug of hot lemon tea to share.

Laxman, our head porter, was standing at the counter across the room, looking at us both in a very nervous and unsettling way.

"You OK?" Tim said. "Come join us for tea and biscuits."

Laxman walked across to us and sat down next to Tim. Tea and biscuits were the last things on his mind as he began to talk.

"Very bad accident at Camp One, Tim. Five, possibly six Sherpa die. Very sad," he added.

There was a stunned silence for a second or two, finally broken by Tim. "Fuck. What happened?"

"Avalanche, Tim; big avalanche," Laxman said.

Tim, who was clearly distressed, was keen to go straight to Base Camp to assess the full situation.

"I will go with you," I announced, sensing the seriousness of the disaster that had just occurred. I didn't really want to go anywhere near the mountain in these circumstances but maybe we could be useful to any rescue efforts.

Tim seemed lost for words. In the last minute his entire Everest expedition had been thrust into a cloud of uncertainty. "No, we will stay here for now and I will try to find out further news. Stay with Alex."

With that Tim stood up and went outside, the noise of another helicopter heading up the valley deafening as he opened the door.

I spent five minutes with Alex, who took the news in the same state of shock as me. He then went for a lie down. I went looking for Tim, telling Alex that I would return with news if I discovered anything further.

I found Tim in the Eco Lodge next door; he had already logged on and was messaging his wife Ali back home. I did the same thing and was alarmed to see that I had over fifty messages, all from people concerned about the avalanche on the mountain. The news had made its way home already and Tamara had woken up to messages and missed calls from friends and relatives, all concerned after hearing reports of multiple deaths on Everest. But Tamara was pretty certain that I wasn't involved – she had my itinerary and knew that we weren't due to arrive at Base Camp until the following day. This was confirmed when the news outlets reported that all the deaths were of Nepali mountain workers, load carrying up the mountain. However, Laxman's initial news of five to six deaths was sadly not all of it. It amazed me that, although I was only 10km away from the mountain when the disaster struck, my wife back home in England knew there had been a tragedy on Everest before I did.

As I read reports online that morning, I discovered that the avalanche hadn't occurred at Camp One. It had happened lower down in the Icefall, where a group of around twenty-five Sherpas were carrying loads through to the higher camps on the mountain. It seemed that the Sherpas were brought to a stop by a broken ladder, near to the area of the Icefall known as the Popcorn Field, at an altitude of 5,800m. Some had taken their packs off and were resting, waiting for the ladder to be repaired. There were over a hundred Sherpas in the ice that morning. Twenty-five were in the direct firing line when a large section of serac fractured away from Everest's west shoulder. A huge ice avalanche came crashing down directly on top of them and buried all those in its path. Sixteen Sherpas died in the disaster – not six, as initially reported to us by our porter.

It immediately became apparent that this was the worst single loss of life ever to hit the mountain. One heartbreaking and devastating accident, which lasted seconds, had just changed the history of the mountain forever.

As I gave the grim news to Alex back in our lodge, neither of us knew just what the consequences of this would mean. Would we still be climbing the mountain? Did we still want to climb the mountain? And did Tim still want to guide the mountain? All these questions, and more, hurtled around inside my head. I went to bed that night unsure about what this dream to climb the highest mountain in the world meant to me any more. Yes, people die on the mountain every year. I had been very aware of that fact before I even stepped foot on the plane, but not like this, not in such a manner. This was unprecedented in every way conceivable.

As we made our way towards Base Camp the next day, with the constant whirl of helicopter blades overhead, Tim did his best to reassure us that if we did go up onto the mountain, we would do our best to minimise going through the Icefall. Talk switched to using Pumori, a 7,000m peak near to Everest, for acclimatisation. "We could sleep at ABC on Pumori," Tim said. "It's almost as high as Camp One on Everest." Tim was very keen to keep the wheels rolling on our Everest climb. I guess in a way so was I, even if that meant having to completely alter our acclimatisation schedule. I won't deny that I was shaken to the core.

We found a pretty sombre mood when we finally arrived at Base Camp – far removed from what should have been a joyous occasion. Pasang Temba, whom I recognised from a few days earlier, showed me to our mess tent, where I found a few individuals already inside, reading and drinking tea. Henry Todd, our Base Camp manager, was somewhere around; as was Dr Rob Casserley, a guide who was there to climb the mountain with his wife Marie Kristelle and his three clients, Lucy, Dan and Nigel.

My name was just one of fifteen members on the expedition permit who would all be aiming to climb Everest that spring. Tim was listed as the expedition leader. In fact, we had three guides who would be sharing our Base Camp under the overall umbrella of Himalayan Guides and Henry Todd.

As well as Rob and his four clients, a guide called Tim Calder was also there with his client, Andy James. Tim had Alex and me as direct clients, along with another two climbers, Chris Handy and Scott Mackenzie. Scott was a strong climber who had already climbed an 8,000m peak, Broad Peak in Pakistan, without oxygen. He was here to attempt the same thing on Everest. Chris, another strong climber, would help his attempt.

Henry himself had three direct clients who had signed on to climb the mountain with no western guide, relying on just Sherpa support: Paul Valin from France; Roman Romancini from Brazil; and Ingolfur Axelsson, or Ingo as we called him, from Iceland.

Henry could be an intimidating presence around camp and you certainly didn't want to get on the wrong side of his 6ft 3in frame. In his late sixties, Henry had been organising logistics for Everest expeditions for as long as I had wanted to climb the mountain. He had a pretty decent track record at helping his clients to achieve their dreams. He also had a reputation for accepting no bullshit and I was careful to stay on his good side. Henry would drift in and out of the mess tent fleetingly over the week, and each time he did, he brought news of the situation as it developed.

When, Alex, Tim and I arrived at Base Camp, a four-day mourning period had already begun. This meant the mountain was systematically shut down for that period. No one was moving anywhere near the mountain during this time, and nor did they appear to want to either. The avalanche up in the Icefall had caused a lot of angst amongst the Sherpas, who had returned home to their families for a period of reflection and private grief. Whether they would return remained to be seen. Without the Sherpas we knew that it was game over. We couldn't climb the mountain without them. An eerie silence settled across Base Camp for days and there was nothing to do other than play cards, listen to music, play some more cards and sit tight and wait. The news we received was patchy at best, coming mainly from Alan Arnette at home in Colorado. We were there in the heart of it all, at the bottom of the mountain, yet we were relying on news from a climber thousands of miles away to ascertain whether the mountain would reopen. It was as insane as it was implausible, yet that's just the way it was.

On one of these days playing the waiting game, Alex and I trekked up nearby Kala Patthar. It was mainly to stretch our legs and get some exercise, but also to escape the tension at Base Camp, which was becoming unbearable. From the top, as I stared across at the Icefall revealing itself in all its savage glory, I wondered why the mountain I loved had been so cruel. Fourteen years earlier, when I had first stood on top of Kala Patthar, I had gazed upon the mountain in awe. But on this day, when I looked across at Everest all I felt was dread. A deep ominous fear blackened my mind.

Over the next three days, the mood at Base Camp went from one of renewed hope that the mountain would reopen, to one of complete despair when it became obvious that it wasn't going to.

On the 23rd April, five days after the disaster, we had our team puja prayer ceremony and were genuinely excited that things were about to be resolved. Our Sherpa team had returned the previous day and seemed keen to climb again, even though all around us teams were packing up and leaving the mountain in droves. Rumour had it that Sherpas and their families were being threatened with violent attacks if they continued to climb. But who was making such threats and why?

Ellis and Dorje during the 2014 Puja

Sadly, the disaster on Everest became the chief weapon in a political attack on the government. A few younger, more educated, vocal Sherpas decided to hold the government to ransom, with a list of demands they insisted must be met if they were to keep the mountain open. Top of this list was better compensation for families of the deceased Sherpas. An initial offer of just $400 per family, by the government's Ministry of Tourism and Aviation, was described as an insult.

To answer these demands, and quell the rebellion that was in full force, the Ministry sent an official representative to Base Camp by helicopter on the 24th April, with the aim of pacifying the baying mob. It didn't work. The young instigators of the mutiny were winning the war. Within a day, climbing on Everest in 2014 was as good as over. No one was prepared to run the risk of compromising the safety of their Sherpas, and Henry explained the situation to us one last time in a sombre team meeting.

"It is with a heavy heart that I must tell you this, but sadly we are all going down." As he spoke tears welled up in his eyes. "Climbing is no longer a viable or safe proposition for our team of Sherpas. I am sorry but that is just the way it is." Henry slumped down in a chair and dropped his head.

I had never seen such an imposing man look so defeated and dejected. What was happening was without precedent. Everest had never been shut down before, yet we were on the brink of that happening.

Henry had kept us informed how the situation was unfolding for the past week, as we hunkered down at Base Camp. The axe was hovering and we had been asked to play the waiting game on two occasions throughout this time. Now, though, the axe was finally being brought down, crushing all of our dreams in the process and all we could do was let it happen.

Henry rose to his feet once more, this time with anger in his eyes. "You all have every right to be pissed off, and you should be. I am."

For most of us, this was the end of the line. I had come to climb Everest and had got no higher than I had done fourteen years earlier when I last visited as a trekker. In fact, on that occasion I had gone higher by going into the Icefall. On reflection, I was glad I was going nowhere near it this time.

The realisation that the flames of a twenty-year dream had been extinguished began to sink in. As I took stock of all that was happening, an air of fate and calm acceptance began to sweep over me. After all, the Sherpas are fundamental to the success of any Everest climb and without them we could go no higher. Henry knew this, our guides knew this and now it had just been made obvious to us, the clients. Talk of trying to climb without Sherpa support was instantly dismissed, even by the stronger, more independent mountaineers amongst us. The decision had been made. There would be no climbing on Everest – on the south side at least – for 2014.

Tension in the mess tent in 2014

With the expedition officially over, there was nothing left to do other than pack up our belongings and get the hell out of there. Henry assured us that he would get our expedition kit to Kathmandu; we just needed to get ourselves to Lukla, where we would pick up the short flight back to civilisation. This was a civilisation I wasn't ready to go back to just yet though. Climbing Everest wasn't meant to end this way. All those years of dreaming and planning had resulted in nothing, apart from a very expensive trek to Base Camp. I spent the last day at Base Camp in a state of shock at what had happened. My emotions went from incredible sadness at the loss of life on the mountain to bitterness at being denied my chance to climb. I felt angry, but I wasn't sure whom my anger was directed towards – the mountain gods, perhaps, for allowing untold heartache and loss of life, or the young instigators who led the rebellion against Nepal's government and effectively forced every team to pack up and leave. People back home sent me messages saying 'at least I was one of the lucky ones who was coming home.' I completely understood that, but it did nothing to stem the feeling that I didn't get the chance to do what I came all this way to achieve. It was like running a marathon and reaching mile twenty, but then being denied the chance to run the final six miles and cross the line.

With a sad heart I left Base Camp the day after Henry gave us the news and trekked out with Tim Calder and his client Andy James. I found both to be likeable characters during the week we spent at Base Camp, and we spoke about our lives back home as we sped down the Khumbu away from Everest. In Pangboche I allowed myself a glass or two of red wine with Andy and Tim as we each spoke about our own disappointments. Tim had reached the summit of Everest previously, so it probably wasn't so much of a disappointment as it was for Andy and me. The wine certainly helped us come to terms with the premature end to our collective dreams. The following day I trekked the 30km back to Lukla along with the other team members so we could catch the only available flight back to Kathmandu for the next week.

Back in the UK, I enjoyed an emotional reunion with my two daughters, my mam and Tamara in the international arrivals hall of Manchester Airport. I found myself home four weeks early and still pretty much in a daze about what had happened up on Everest.

Ellis at Base Camp before leaving

When the avalanche hit, I just wanted to return home to my family as quickly as possible. I feared that the same thing might happen again and I had to look deep inside and find the inner resolve to keep my focus and determination strong. I have never been one to suffer from homesickness, but I certainly did for those first few days at Base Camp. I felt as detached and isolated from my loved ones as it was possible to be. For the first time ever, my dream to climb Everest no longer mattered. What counted was surviving and being there for my family when they needed me – and right at that moment I needed them desperately. As the days passed, I began to control my emotions and I soon learnt to deal with the fear that had consumed me since April 18th. By the time it was announced that the climb was off, I was back in a strong place mentally, but I will never know just how strong I would have been.

As expedition members of an Everest 2014 team, we all went through our own feelings of guilt and anxiety at the events that unfolded. No matter what else happens in my life or where I go, I will always carry around the dramatic events of that spring in Nepal. I'll always share in the sense of loss and profound sadness at what conspired to end our dreams of reaching the roof of the world. But the price was too costly. When push came to shove, I was happy to go home when I did. At the time my Everest dream had reached a sad conclusion and I assumed this would be where the journey ended. Once again, as so often proved to be the case, I was wrong in this assumption.

As a sad footnote to the events on Everest in 2014, a young Sherpa by the name of Chhewang – who had been on the mountain when disaster struck – walked four days back to his home in Nunthala. Having survived the ice avalanche without serious injury, he walked the last day in a heavy storm with hail and lightning. Only minutes from his home, he was knocked to the ground by a bolt of lightning. Another bolt hit nearby and killed him. Indirectly, Everest took its last victim of the season.

PART SEVEN: A NEW HOPE

When things go wrong as they sometimes will, and the road you're trudging seems all uphill, when the funds are low and the debts are high and you want to smile but you have to sigh, when care is pressing you down a bit, rest if you must but don't you quit. – Edgar A Guest

After returning home from Nepal, I tried not to dwell too much on Everest and the disaster, but this was proving very difficult. Everywhere I went, anyone who knew about my trip to the mountain asked me if I was going back. My page on Facebook had swelled in numbers since the disaster and I now had over 13,000 subscribers. I figured that the interest in my dream would drop off, but in fact the exact opposite happened. During the summer of 2014, not a day passed when someone didn't enquire as to whether I would be trying again. I spoke to the press and the local BBC radio studio, where I was interviewed live on air about the events on Everest. Both the newspaper and radio pushed me on whether I would be returning to the mountain for another attempt. If the decision were mine to make alone, without considering anyone else, then my answer would have been a resounding 'yes!'. This mountain was now under my skin and, whether I liked it or not, it wasn't done with me just yet. It took me just a few months of being home to realise this.

When I had first returned home from Everest, I was pretty certain that if I so much as mentioned the 'E' word to Tamara then it would signal the 'D' word. I was very careful to allow time to heal things a tad, and I also needed to be certain that I wanted to go back too. When that certainty swept over me, I began to openly discuss my feelings – not only with Tamara, but also with other family members and friends. Mam knew I wanted to go back, but she kept her distance and didn't want to become involved, knowing it was a sensitive issue.

But as I went on to explain to anyone who enquired if I was looking to return, it wasn't that simple. I now had a wall of resistance to overcome, and the person putting up the biggest defiance was the person closest to me: Tamara. She categorically stated her objection to another attempt as soon as I came home.

We spent a very thorny evening over a bottle of wine discussing the subject.

"That could have been you in the Icefall that day, so you should count your lucky stars that it wasn't," she said as she took another sip of wine, staring at me with as serious a look as I have ever seen.

"Yes, you are right, it wasn't me. In fact I was nowhere near the Icefall," I offered up in my defence. I realised I had a battle on my hands if I was going to get her to come round to my way of thinking, but still I persisted. "I didn't step foot on the mountain. I put everything into this and came home having achieved nothing."

"What! You have achieved far more than most people will in a lifetime. You just need to see that."

But I didn't see that, I didn't see that at all. I hadn't achieved what I had set out to, and through an appalling disaster and then a politically driven hijacking I was back to square one.

"You had your chance and it wasn't to be, but someone was looking out for you. As far as I am concerned you need to put all this behind you. Everest is done. Accept it."

As she spoke I could feel myself becoming angry and resentful. "I won't accept it and it is far from done." Inside I was thinking *screw you, this is my life and I will do what I want. No one tells me what I can and can't do.*

This way of thinking stopped dead in its tracks when Tamara said, through tears, "What would I have said to the girls about why Daddy wasn't coming home ever again?" I fell silent. She continued, "I don't want to be in that position again, and I think it is fucking unfair of you to ever put me in that position again." She stood up, and slammed the kitchen door behind her.

I knew in my heart that she was right. I also knew that the correct thing to do was to forget about the mountain, and throw all my efforts going forward into my family and my business. But, as the days turned into weeks, and the weeks into months, the feeling of unfinished business intensified. Selfish or not, the desire to climb the mountain had become a drug that I was heavily addicted to – even if I risked losing my family.

My immediate circle of family and friends all wanted me to move on and accept that I'd had my shot and, through circumstances outside of my control, it wasn't to be. Even the strapline on my Everest Dream clothing line stated: 'One Dream One Chance One Life'. Maybe this had been my one chance, and sadly the dream hadn't happened. But it was still my dream and I still had my life left to achieve it. I wasn't going to walk away from it all now, not when I had been so close.

Whereas family and friends tried their best to discourage me, online the picture was very different. The clothing was selling better than ever, and to keep up with demand I had recently launched a new website featuring photos of me at Everest wearing the T-shirts. This kick-started a surge in orders and I knew it would be foolish to stop them. Even if I had no intention of going back, I decided to keep the clothing sales going. Hundreds of voices, out of the thousands I had connected with through social media, were very vocal in their belief that I should go back to the mountain in 2015. They made this abundantly clear at every opportunity.

I had already convinced myself that, if I were to return, I would try to do so immediately. I didn't want to wait a few years and try again. I wanted to keep the wheels of the wagon rolling. I told myself that this was a mere roadside stop to fix one of the wheels, but I knew that Tamara wouldn't buy that analogy, so I would need something stronger when the time came to announce my intention to return.

There was a more pressing reason to return in 2015. A rumour began circulating that the Ministry of Tourism in Nepal would honour the climbing permit for just one year. This meant that anyone, like me, who had an Everest climbing permit from Nepal in 2014 could return to the mountain the following year. Initially this offer was touted as being good for the next five years, which would have seen me through until 2019 if I wished to return. But the threat of this being downgraded to just one year was very real. In many ways it forced me (and no doubt countless other Everest 2014 climbers) to consider a swift return. The permit was worth $10,000 USD – or as recently announced $11,000 after the Ministry decided to do away with the higher individual permit cost of $25,000. In what was seen as a piece of propaganda by the Nepal government, an announcement went out in the world's press that climbing Everest was now $14,000 cheaper, as the individual permit fee had been slashed. The reality was that no one ever paid the $25,000 individual fee anyway, instead chipping in on a permit of seven or more climbers where the fee was just $10,000 per climber. So what was advertised as being a large drop in price to climb Everest was actually a $1,000 price rise, due to the fact that almost all Everest climbers paid just the $10,000 permit fee.

I was sitting on an $11,000 jump-start to return to Everest in 2015, and if the rumour was true, I didn't want to miss this opportunity. As well as winning over Tamara, I also needed to look into the finances involved to return. Even if the permit were in place, I still needed to find the money to cover my expenses on the mountain. This would cover the cost of everything from food, oxygen and Sherpa support through to Base Camp services, and everything required for passage up and down the mountain. I was pretty sure that, if I were going to go back, I would do so with Tim and Henry again – but this all came down to the cost.

Every penny of the expedition funds for 2014 was gone, and none of it was refundable. Had I signed on to do an eighteen-day trek around the Everest region with a reputable trekking company, spending a few days at Base Camp, I would have perhaps paid $3,000. Instead the same trip had cost me over $42,000, not including flights and equipment. One thing was for sure: I could not afford a similar amount again. As a returning client from the tragic 2014 aborted attempt, I knew this would give me special negotiating powers when it came to the cost. I also had something else to bring to the table, which I was confident would be a huge step in the right direction of driving down the cost to return.

Whilst at Base Camp a few days after the disaster in the Icefall, I went across to the neighbouring tents of Jagged Globe. One of their clients was a mutual friend of Michael Buttery, the climber from back home I had made friends with online. David Bradley, a 59-year-old finance director from Yorkshire, had reached the summit of Denali with Michael the previous year. I introduced myself and we had a brief chat about the situation as it was unfolding at the time. A few days later, David wandered across to our mess tent and I introduced him to Tim. I could tell from his line of questioning that he was curious as to just what we got for the money we paid across to Henry Todd and Himalayan Guides, compared to the fee he paid Jagged Globe. Having visited the Jagged Globe mess tent myself just a few days earlier, I had no obvious answer. When we were back home in the UK, I told David as much when he called me to enquire in more detail about being on Everest with Tim. I sang Tim's praises as a guide, and although our Base Camp services were basic, I reminded him that he still had to put one foot in front of the other and climb the mountain, whether he climbed with Jagged Globe or Tim Mosedale.

After out chat, David was keen to sign on for another attempt on Everest in 2015, with Tim as the guide. In doing so, he would be saving himself over $20,000. Not only that, our friend Michael was keen as well. With two potential clients to bring to the team, I was able to negotiate with Tim, who agreed a price for bringing two clients along. Tim also agreed to offer his guiding services for free if both David and Michael signed up. With the cost to return being a lot easier to swallow than the previous attempt, I set the wheels in motion for my plan to return. There was a major hurdle to overcome first, and that was Tamara's flat-out defiance against me going back.

One night on a warm evening in July, I invited Michael and his partner Joy round for dinner. Michael, who was Everest-bound the following year, was keen to chat with me about my experiences in Nepal during the ill-fated attempt a few months earlier. I was happy to oblige. I also hoped that the conversation would get round to the possibility of my return, which it duly did later in the evening.

As the wine flowed Michael certainly didn't mince his words:

"Tamara, why are you so hell-bent on him not going back? The lad deserves another chan—"

Tamara cut in before he could finish. "Because he had his chance and he could have died. He has two young daughters who rely on him. That is why!"

I sensed we were about to go over the same ground that had been well and truly discussed over the past few months.

"You won't win, Michael," I said across the table, to which Tamara gave me one of those stares that only a women can give. The type that lets you know you have crossed the line.

"It's not about winning or losing. It's about what is right for your family."

The situation was becoming quite fraught as Tamara stood up to go in the garden for some fresh air. "Ultimately I can't stop you from going back, Ellis," she said in parting. "But if you do, me and the girls won't be here when you come back."

Michael looked at me despondently, shaking his head. "You are fucked, mate."

As a husband and father, I understood her reasons for not wanting to see me return to Everest. In a nutshell, they came down to the possibility that I could die. Prior to 2014 and the tragic avalanche, climbers had died on Everest almost every year. Unfortunately, being there during the worst single loss of life in the mountain's history didn't do me any favours when it came to playing down death on the mountain.

It was hard to brush the year's disaster under the carpet as an unprecedented accident, the likes of which would probably not be seen again. Still, it didn't stop both Michael and me from trying.

"The probability of anything happening anywhere near the scale of this year again is the same as us winning the lottery. It won't happen," I said as Michael chipped in with how damned unlucky I had been.

As we discussed the thorny issue well past midnight, I noticed a slight change in Tamara's attitude. Had I finally been able to crack that tough exterior and break her stance? As we wished our guests a good night, and locked the front door, I knew I hadn't.

"That was an interesting evening, wasn't it?"

"It was," she said. "You are still not going back, though!"

A few nights later I spoke to my friend Mark Bradley. I needed someone to be unbiased one way or the other. Mark and his wife Jodi had been great confidantes to Tamara during my first attempt on the mountain. As a counselling Doctor of Psychology as well as a good lifelong friend, I knew he would have my best interests at heart. He listened intently to what I had to say before offering up his words of wisdom. On this occasion he realised the impossible position I was in.

"I completely get why you want to go back, and if I were in your shoes I would be feeling the same way," he said. "But, it could cost you your marriage, so ultimately it is your call. Is this worth more to you than your marriage?"

The words paralysed me. I didn't know how to respond. I wanted both. Why couldn't I go to Everest and keep my marriage intact?

"So this is lose, lose for me then. If I side with Tamara, I lose Everest, and if I choose Everest I lose my wife."

The mountain, and my unexplainable drive to climb it, was disrupting my life to a huge degree. If I wasn't careful I risked self-imploding, alienating everyone close to me in the process.

"I'll stand by you no matter what you decide to do, Ellis," was Mark's response. "You are my mate and I will support whatever decision you make – besides, I have a spare bedroom. You may need it."

I didn't want to force Tamara into giving me an ultimatum: *it's either the mountain or me, so choose.* But it was heading this way.

I guess I was hoping that in time Tamara would come round in her own way and give me her blessing for one last attempt. "2014 was supposed to be your one chance," she would say repeatedly to me during the summer. "This wasn't a two-year deal."

I would respond that I fully understood, but I felt that I didn't get my chance. After all, I hadn't even set foot on the mountain. That wasn't an attempt; it was stopped in its tracks before it had begun. This became my primary reason for needing to go back.

"And if you go back and reach Camp One, and then something else happens which stops you, will you want to go back again, Ellis?" she threw at me one night. "Where does this all stop?"

These prophetic words would later come back to haunt me, but at the time I assured her that if – and it was a big IF – that should happen, then of course that would be it.

A few weeks later I finally sensed that she was relenting when she questioned me on the finances and whether the climbing permit was definitely in place. Even though this looked to be in place, I still had to find the money, which I had agreed to pay directly to Henry.

As the summer months drew to a close, the clock began ticking down. I needed to lock in and commit. Once again I began Skype video-chatting with Ste Bock in Sydney. He shared his words of wisdom and scolded me if he saw any 'negative crap', as he would put it, from my Facebook updates. In mid-August I posted the following update to my page:

This is not looking good people. I need a lot of money, and even if I had that money I stand to lose a lot more than just cash if I do go back. Things are pretty bleak right now. I don't think I will be returning to the mountain.

An hour later Ste messaged me his thoughts:

I believe in you mate and will help. You just need to get rid of the bullshit distractions. Come up with a simple plan, use your strengths and deliver maximum intensity towards your plan. Remove any negativity from your life at the moment. I'm not seeing much positive stuff on FB and you need to be doing that daily – just go for it. Fight for your destiny, standing on your own feet… not crawling on your knees.

I admired and respected him greatly. After all, he was a man who had lived the same dream that I was pursuing. For Ste, the realisation of that dream came on the 23rd May 2010 at 8.30am. I was still holding out for that realisation, but speaking with Ste as often as I did was certainly helping me with a positive mindset. He would say to me: 'You have the heart of a champion', and 'You are an inspiration to so many people'. I took a lot of mental focus away from our video chats, and as my journey to Everest in 2015 truly started, he was right at the heart of my campaign, as an unseen driving force.

At the end of August, a miracle occurred which kick-started everything. I finally had the blessing and permission I had been seeking for the whole of the summer. Tamara told me that she wouldn't leave me if I went back after all, but that this was my very last chance.

"If you don't reach the summit this time, then you have to live with that," she added. "Can you live with that? Will me and the girls be enough for you?"

I assured her that they would be and that I loved them all in equal measure. I also promised that after 2015, Everest would be out of my system, one way or the other, summit or not.

On September 1st 2014 I posted an update to my Everest Dream Facebook page announcing my intention to return in 2015. However, I added that it wasn't a done deal and that I somehow needed to find a large amount of cash – either that or a pot of gold at the end of a rainbow. Either would do, I added.

I discovered a website for funding adventures called Trevolta. The website allowed you to set up a campaign where people could make donations towards a set goal. The maximum time you could run the campaign for was ninety days, so I had three months to raise as much money as I could. I figured it was worth a shot. This became the main project I ran with when I announced my intention to return.

With a highly active Facebook page, which was growing larger by the week, I was confident I could pitch my idea to the thousands of followers I had connected with. Throughout September I pushed and promoted the campaign as often as I felt comfortable doing so. Donations came through, but they weren't exactly flooding in.

I was offering T-shirts and hoodies in exchange for donations, but it wasn't working. Because I was essentially asking for money to cover my costs so I could go off climbing, I had a hard time with the ethics of it and I was reluctant to push it down people's throats. This ultimately was my undoing. I have always had a problem when it comes to asking for money, and as someone who needed to find a lot of money in a short space of time, this became a huge problem. I knew I needed to put my head on the chopping block and ask away, but I couldn't bring myself to do it. I didn't mind approaching large corporations and brands for sponsorship, but when it came to receiving donations from individuals it never sat easy.

An opportunity to earn my first significant amount towards the costs came about in the most unlikely of ways. A chap called Tony McMurray, who had been following my Everest journey through Facebook, offered me an interesting proposition. As the finance director for a large IT company based in Milton Keynes, he was sure he could swing it for me to be the inspirational after-dinner speaker at an inaugural IT conference in front of 200 IT executives. The talk was only two weeks away and they would cover all my expenses, including a hotel, and pay me a decent speaker's fee. Tony left it for me to sort out all the detail with the company's HR department. When the conversation switched to the fee, I asked for £20,000. Well, you have to try. When that was instantly dismissed, I came back with a more realistic expectation – £1,500. Without so much as a pause, the HR manager said, "Fine, no problem." The talk was on.

A few weeks later I gave a very nervy twenty-minute talk to a room full of IT professionals at Milton Keynes Stadium. I spoke about my whole dream to climb Everest and the events that had occurred earlier that year. I hadn't done many talks, compared to a professional after-dinner speaker, and I think it showed. I completely failed to seize the opportunity to sell myself. Executives from some of the UK's leading IT companies were in attendance, and I failed miserably to tell my story and make them feel compelled to help out. I cursed myself for messing up, even though I had just earned £1,500 for twenty minutes' work. It could have been so much more, but still it was a good start and I ultimately learned from the experience.

On stage in Milton Keynes

Feeling demoralised from my performance in Milton Keynes, I moped around for a week or so, allowing negative energy to fill my mind. I was on the brink of slipping into a depression when, one morning out of the blue, I received a message from an Everest climber by the name of Grant Rawlinson. I had got to know Grant a little over the past year or so, after he shared some advice with me on attracting sponsorship. Born in New Zealand, Grant had reached the summit of Everest by the North Ridge route in 2012. He covered his entire expedition costs through sponsorship, and he was happy to share some of the tactics that had worked for him. So far, though, nothing had worked for me. His message that morning got my attention straight away.

'Are you still looking for sponsorship? If so, I am going to send a company your way that is looking to sponsor an Everest climber.'

A Chinese tech firm had been in touch with Grant, saying that they wanted a climber on Everest to use their product and send back images of it in action. They were willing to cover the full expedition cost, plus any additional expenses. As I read further, I began to take it all with a pinch of salt. If it sounds too good to be true then it usually is, as the saying goes. Grant gave me the contact details for a lady from the company and told me I should contact her straight away.

Later that morning, I sent an email to the contact Grant had given me, making my introductions and informing them that I was hoping to return to climb the mountain in 2015. I added that I was looking for sponsorship, and if they were willing to provide it, I could offer them a lot in return. I played on the fact that I had almost 15,000 followers on Facebook to whom I could theoretically market their product – whatever it was. That same day a response came back, stating that they were deadly serious and that if Grant had endorsed me then that was good enough for them.

DU Apps Studio made apps for smartphones, specifically Samsung Android devices. One of their apps was a battery-saving app, which they guaranteed could increase battery power by up to 1000%. Their marketing claimed it to be the best battery-saving app in the world, and they wanted someone to use a Samsung phone on Everest, utilising this app, to show that it really was as good as it claimed. In return for testing the app and providing high-quality images for marketing purposes, they would pick up my entire cost. In an email exchange backwards and forwards for the next hour or so, I informed them that I didn't have a Samsung phone, and that I had damaged my digital SLR on my last trip to Everest. They responded adding that they would provide the phone, and I could shop around for a new camera and they would pick up the bill.

I was an amateur climber, who for twenty years had chased down a sponsorship deal to climb Everest with very limited success. I now had a company in China willing to cover my entire expedition cost, pay for my insurance and my flights and buy me a snazzy new camera, just so I could send back a few photos of me using a Samsung smartphone. It just didn't make sense. Why had they not approached someone from

China, or even a world-renowned climber who could pretty much guarantee a summit of the mountain, such as Kenton Cool? I could not believe the opportunity that had fallen my way. I asked for the company to lay out the offer in an email and I would come back to them. I was trying to play it cool, even though I knew that, if this was genuine, then they had me at 'Hello Ellis'.

I told Tamara that it looked like I was going back. I detected a bemused look. Like me, she also couldn't understand why a Chinese mobile app maker wanted to pay for me to climb Everest. But she was thrilled for me that they did.

I kept the news secret for a day or two, as I wanted to be pretty certain that this was going to happen. During this time, they asked all the right questions and I was confident I provided all the right answers. When I was sure that they were stepping in to be my principal sponsor for my attempt on Everest in 2015, I announced it on my Facebook page:

Since last week I have been in talks with an organisation who have agreed in principle to be my major sponsor for Everest 2015. I do not wish to say who this is just yet, just to be on the safe side. However, I will be shouting about it loud and clear once it's a done deal. They are an innovative company with amazing products and this opportunity is the chance of a lifetime. It has only taken me 15 years to find a sponsor like this. I don't want to say too much more in case I end up with egg on my face if this doesn't happen, but at the moment it is looking highly likely that I will be back on Everest next year. I will share more once I know more. It's almost game on time.

For the next week I bounced around as high as a kite. Further contact with the company only confirmed that this was going to happen.

Everything for once was going my way. I felt that finally this was my reward for sticking with this thing and never losing sight of my goal. Someone up there had at last taken notice, and declared in one divine thunderous voice, *'This guy deserves a break. Let's give him one.'*

But... remember this is me we are talking about, the guy who epitomises the saying, 'if it can go wrong, it will'. Two weeks later, it went wrong – very wrong.

The company in China went cold the minute the conversation switched to finances. I wanted to know how they proposed to pay me and when, as I had a timescale for transferring funds across to Nepal. For days I waited to hear back from them until finally, in one devastating email, they completely altered the conditions we had discussed. Instead, they proposed to pay me money only upon submission of photos, if they were deemed to be of good enough quality to satisfy their requirements. The higher and further into the climb I went, and the more value they felt they were receiving, then the more of the sponsorship money they would pay out. That wasn't sponsorship. It was a blatant attempt to be involved in an Everest attempt without having to fork out upfront for the privilege.

I felt crushed. For weeks now, I had allowed myself to bask in the feeling that I was once more Everest-bound. I had prayed that nothing would go wrong and derail the deal, but as I had never actually signed anything, I always knew it could come crashing down around me. I just didn't expect it to, especially not in the circumstances that it did. Of course, I couldn't agree to their terms. What they were proposing was preposterous and no climber in their right mind would have accepted those terms. I would have to pay for the climb myself, and then hope to claw back the money based on how well they thought I was promoting their company and product. They made it abundantly clear that they wanted a photo and video of their app in use on the summit of Everest. If this wasn't provided, they wouldn't pay out. I was crestfallen. Not for the first time in my life, I felt like the gullible idiot. I emailed back and told them I wasn't interested. I then openly shared my disappointment online and informed Tim. "You should never trust the Chinese," he said back to me.

At the beginning of November, I was back to square one. I needed to somehow pick myself up off the floor and go again. Just how I was going to do that I did not know. I was once again running out of time, and fast. In no mood to continue hunting for sponsorship, I buried myself in my training and consoled myself with the words spoken to me all those years ago on the end of that pier by the fisherman: "If this mountain of yours is meant for you, it will not pass you by."

I trained vigorously throughout the remainder of 2014, just as I had done in the final six months before leaving for the mountain the first time. I hammered the Stairmaster in the gym and did heavy pack work on the treadmill at maximum incline, carrying up to 25kg on my back and walking non-stop for two hours at a time.

At weekends I disappeared off to the moors of North Yorkshire, where I would go on long trail runs, usually incorporating several ascents of Roseberry Topping. This was tough on Tamara and the girls and it was one of the things about training for Everest that she found particularly hard – my being away from them at weekends, which should have been family time.

"It's just until after Everest is over," I would say.

"That's what you said last year," came back the sarcastic reply.

Ellis on Roseberry Topping

Still reeling from the disappointment of losing the Chinese sponsorship deal, things took a further turn for the worse when the Nepal government announced a new rule with the permit extension. The Ministry of Tourism said they would extend, by five years, group climbing permits that were issued to Everest expeditions during the last spring season. This meant that the same members of the expedition would have to scale Everest together within the next five years. If even one member of an expedition scaled the mountain, permits of the others would be cancelled. This was ludicrous.

As a few climbers from my 2014 permit were going back, this basically meant that unless I returned in 2015, my permit was gone. I would need to pay for a new permit for all subsequent years.

I started to become despondent once again. Maybe this dream wasn't meant to be for me after all.

I received a glimmer of hope a few days later when I received a $500 donation from an Australian writer by the name of Penner Choinski from the Gold Coast. The kindness of others never ceased to amaze me. Along with her donation, Penner sent me the following heartfelt message:

As a writer I must ignore unhelpful criticism and nay-sayers. Obstacles to success abound. Last year when things got painfully difficult for me, your efforts in the face of hard times gave me a model to follow. Here's to you! I really appreciate a person such as you and wish the world had more. Please take my contribution as a way to say Thank You. Ellis, I wish you the best of luck and success in 2015, and a safe return to home. Most of all I wish that your Everest Dream is fulfilled. Your persistence and determination is an inspiration.

Once more a complete stranger had brought me back from the precipice of failure. It made me more determined than ever to be back on the mountain in three months' time.

A week later and I was another £1,000 closer to my goal, thanks to a London taxi driver called Divyesh Ruparelia. As someone who was interested in the mountain, he had followed my journey and wanted to do his bit to help me return. These donations blew me away. Where I had failed miserably relating to organisations in the business world, I seemed to have far more success with the one group of people I was most shy about asking: the general public, or more specifically, my followers on social media.

On top of these donations, the Everest clothing range was selling through the roof. In December alone, I sold over 200 hoodies. All the money from clothing sales went directly into my Everest account, which was growing larger day by day.

Donations continued to come in through my campaign website, and in a 48-hour period alone, in mid-January, fifteen people donated over £500. I wasn't sure exactly why people felt compelled to help me, but I was speechless that they did.

By February, I still hadn't confirmed with Henry whether I would be going back to Everest or not. Although I would be climbing under the leadership of Tim, my deal to return was very much with Henry. As the permit was already taken care of, he was putting no pressure on me – I could travel to Kathmandu with the cash in my kit bag if necessary. This lack of a deadline was a welcome relief, and it allowed me to concentrate on bringing the money in, without any unnecessary distractions.

Getting Tamara on board had been a miracle in itself, and at one stage it looked highly unlikely. A few days into February, a second miracle involving Tamara occurred. I was happy enough that she was allowing me one more try, but she surprised me further when off her own back, she set up a separate fundraising campaign through GoFundMe, another crowdfunding platform. She wrote the following to further bolster her appeal:

Hi folks, for all those who said they would donate, even the smallest amount of money to see Ellis go back. Now is your chance! This is Tamara Stewart, Ellis's wife. As sponsorship is looking less likely in the 6 weeks left to raise the funds, I thought I would give this a go.

In the hope that Ellis achieves his dream, but also so his Mam and I (long suffering that we are) can stop hearing about it! Please DONATE if you can spare anything, in these hard financial times and share this for me and let's send him back to the mountain for one last try. Thanks, Tamara

I shared this on my Facebook page and it instantly reaped dividends. People began sharing the link for me, and the more shares I received, the more donations came in. By mid-February, with less than six weeks to go until departure, everyone was pulling out the stops. I had money coming in from the clothing sales, I had money coming in from people I didn't even know, and now through Tamara's fundraising page, donations began to come in from that. I was inching closer and closer to the target, yet I was still several thousand pounds short.

Before I left for Everest the previous year, I had applied for a marketing role with the outdoor clothing manufacturer Berghaus, based just twenty minutes from my front door. An interview invitation came through when I was actually on my way to Everest, so I couldn't make it. However, I got back in touch when I arrived home to see if they were still interested in seeing me, which they were. I spent an hour being interviewed by the company's global head of marketing, who was curious to find out why this wannabe Everest climber was keen to step back into a corporate career. At the time I didn't know I would be returning to the mountain, and went along in that frame of mind, ready for a new challenge, without Everest. I seemed to make an impression on the head of marketing and could tell she was wondering whether I would make a suitable marketing executive. She was impressed with my outdoor credentials and entrepreneurial spirit, but I think I was ultimately too much of a loose cannon to be considered a serious candidate. Although I didn't get the role, a year later I didn't let this stop me from approaching them to ask if they would supply me with clothing and equipment.

On all of my previous big climbing trips I wore anything and everything I could borrow, scrounge and buy from car boot sales. I didn't have a loyalty to any particular brand. Being cash poor meant I couldn't afford to be choosy. I adopted the saying 'whatever is going for free is fine by me'. This was my motto on all my expeditions. For Everest in 2015, I was finally hoping to buck that trend.

I initially asked Caroline, the head of marketing who had interviewed me over a year ago, if they could supply me with a few items to assist me with my return to the mountain. A day later she responded saying they would be happy to, and asked what I would need. I sent my list of requirements after browsing the extreme mountaineering category of the brand's website. I went for broke – what was the worst that could happen? They could only say no, or just send me one or two items on my list. A response came back a few hours later from the category-marketing manager saying he would see what he could do, but in principle it all looked OK.

A few days later, Berghaus agreed to supply me with all the clothing I needed for my attempt on Everest, including the high-altitude down suit, arguably the single most expensive piece of kit on a climber's list. I would be a walking billboard for the brand out in Nepal. It was highly fitting – all those years ago I had worked in the LD Mountain Centre in Newcastle, the birthplace of the iconic brand. I would hopefully now be off to climb the highest mountain in the world, a chap from the North-East, supported by an outdoor brand from the North-East. It was the perfect match, and I couldn't believe my luck.

Kit inspection before departure

By March, just three weeks until departure, everything was falling into place – everything apart from several thousand pounds. At the beginning of the month, I agreed to give a talk at a further-education college in my hometown for 16-18 year olds. I spoke that day as one of two guest speakers, and I was able to sit and watch the first speaker before I took to the stage.

The first speaker was a chap by the name of Chris Soley, the youthful-looking Managing Director of Cameron's, a large brewery in Hartlepool. He then sat through my talk, where I gave a rousing twenty-minute speech about having dreams and never giving up. I spoke briefly to Chris afterwards and he said how much he had enjoyed my talk, and that he thought it was fantastic that someone from the town was aiming to climb Everest. As I left the college, I thought to myself that it had to be worth a shot. The following day, I sent in my sponsorship proposal, marked for the Managing Director's attention. I then forgot all about it.

Tim called me later that day. He was becoming concerned that time was running out, and suggested I speak with Henry – who could pull the plug any time if he felt I wasn't going to be able to get the money together. I had put off speaking with Henry, but I knew I would have to eventually. I promised Tim I would speak with him later.

That evening I went to my local pub with Tamara. I needed some Dutch courage. As I sat with a drink in my hand, I began texting: *'Hi Henry, Ellis here. All is good. I have done extremely well with the fundraising so far and I am now only a few thousand pounds short of being able to pay you outright. I am confident I can get this money, but would there be a problem if I am not able to get it all before departure?'*

I signed off: *'I am happy to chat and discuss. Get in touch at your discretion, yours Ellis.'*

An hour later, after I had shared a bottle of wine with Tamara, Henry called back and left me a voicemail: "Ellis, I am coming to Hartlepool in a few days to see you, as I am currently in the country. We can discuss further, but if you can promise you will pay me, then I am happy to have you along. Keep up the training, see you soon."

Through my hazy, intoxicated mind, I listened to his message several times before the penny dropped. I gave the phone to Tamara, asking, "Does he say what I think he does?"

"He does," she replied. "You are going back to Everest."

With just three short weeks to go, I now knew categorically that I was returning to the mountain; a mountain that I had been forced to unceremoniously leave, without even stepping foot on, only twelve months previously. As tears of joy ran down my cheeks, Tamara gave me a hug and said how proud she was of me.

"You have made this happen. You deserve this," she said.

As I sipped my glass of claret, I slumped in my chair. Contentment breezed over me. This was abruptly shattered as I sat bolt upright.

"Holy shit. Henry Todd is coming to Hartlepool!"

Good news from Henry Todd

I arranged to meet Henry in a café down the road from my house. Having met Henry at Base Camp the previous year, I knew that he had a long and illustrious association with the mountain, and was as controversial as he was intimidating. My entire success on Everest hinged on this man, and it was important that I formed a good relationship with him. He arrived on time and we shared a coffee, discussing the logistics and plans for the upcoming Everest season. Henry informed me that a BBC journalist would be camping with us, but would predominantly be following a Gurkha expedition, aiming to put the first serving British Army Gurkha on the summit. Chatting with Henry that day was just what I needed and he welcomed me into his team with open arms. He informed me that he would do everything he could to help me reach the top.

"Providing you can keep bloody going, man," he said, "I will provide you with all the support in the world to make it happen."

As we parted, I went to the boot of my car and got out one of my Everest hoodies, which I gave to him.

"What's this?" he said.

I explained that it was one of the products from my range of Everest-inspired clothing, which had helped to fund my expedition costs. "Besides," I added, "We can't have you around camp wearing one of Russell Brice's HimEx hoodies when mine are so much better."

He laughed, and added: 'Well, it is my birthday. See you at Base Camp."

On 10th March I updated my Facebook page with the following:

Everything required for above Base Camp is now deposited with Tim, the expedition leader, and will be on its way to Kathmandu in a day or two. That's my down suit, big high-altitude boots and expedition sleeping bag to name but a few for high on the mountain.

I am currently searching for my return flights to Nepal, leaving on April 3rd and returning early June. This thing has now become very real.

I am really keen to get going but there is still a lot of preparation to do in the next three weeks before I depart. There are lots more hills to run, miles to bike and stairs to climb. I'll be writing blogs for Berghaus while out in Nepal, sending back updates as frequently as I am able to. It's almost time to get the show on the road for Everest Part 2. I'm praying and preparing for a much more satisfactory conclusion to my endeavours this time out. Stay tuned...

These frequent updates in the run up to the climb would illicit positive comments back.

A girl called Gill Nott added: '*We are behind you every step of the way and I think I speak for everyone when I say we are so proud of you for giving this your all. You deserve to stand on that summit more than anyone I know, all the very best.*'

I could write an entire book on all the comments I received from my followers in the run up to departure, and it was extremely motivating. I knew that, when I left for the mountain, far more people than just my family and friends wanted me to succeed this time round.

In the final week before departure, I tirelessly trained. Tamara's GoFundMe page brought in over £2,000, which was a huge bonus I never expected. My own fundraising had gone well too and I raised another £1,000 in the last month alone. With only days to go until my flight to Nepal, I was very close to being able to pay the balance for my trip. Further sales of Everest T-shirts inched me closer still.

When I received an email from Chris Soley, the brewery's managing director, I had almost forgotten that I had sent in my sponsorship proposal to the brewery a week or so earlier. He said that after seeing my talk and reading my proposal, Cameron's Brewery would be delighted to sponsor me. Chris went on to add that it was the brewery's 200th anniversary, and what better occasion to get behind a local guy's attempt to reach the top of the world.

A couple of days later I had a meeting with Chris and Yousef, Cameron's marketing manager, where we discussed what I could do for them through my attempt. In exchange for the publicity, the brewery offered me £2,000 towards the climb.

With just a few days to go before departure, I had finally managed something I had not been able to do in over fourteen years of trying, and that was to gain a significant sponsorship deal. It was all the more special that it came from a company in my hometown.

For Cameron's Brewery, I don't think it was about the exposure they would get from the deal. I think after hearing my talk that day, Chris just genuinely wanted to see me achieve my goal.

I had no family occasion to attend before departure this time. I had even managed to get my flights closer to home at Newcastle Airport. On the 2nd April 2015, I embraced Tamara, my girls and my mam at the airport and said I would see them all again really soon. This time I handled the emotion much better, as did Tamara, who kept it all together for the sake of the girls. I saw tears in Mam's eyes though.

I had two changes to make before I reached Kathmandu: Dubai, and Dhaka in Bangladesh. I had left it late to book my flights, so I had to take what I could get. Plus, it was a lot cheaper than flying direct. After updating my Facebook page to announce I was on my way, I boarded the plane for the first leg of the journey. I felt chilled and calm. Mentally and physically, I also felt stronger than the previous year. It was time to get the show on the road. This time, it was a show that I was sure was going all the way to the summit. I was finally in that zone, and I was ready.

Newcastle Departures Lounge in 2015

PART EIGHT: MOUNT EVEREST 2015

Winds in the East, there's a mist coming in, like something is brewing, about to begin – Bert

Arriving in Kathmandu had become as familiar to me as going away on holiday to my favourite destination. I arrived just after 2pm on 3rd April, having travelled for over twenty-four hours due to flight and transfer times. I was tired, but not unduly so. I was just thrilled and elated to be back so soon, ready to put behind me the disappointment of twelve months earlier.

My journey to the mountain this year would be different, as I would be trekking for the first ten days on my own. The plan was to meet up with Tim and the rest of this year's team at the Kongma La pass, where once again we would make an attempt on the trekking peak Pokalde, before crossing the pass back into the Khumbu Valley. This was more from financial necessity than anything else. I had worked out that it would be cheaper to do my own thing and meander my way up to Base Camp at my leisure. Tim was happy for me to do this as I had done the full eighteen-day trek previously, picking up all the little tips and tricks that four summits of the mountain had taught him.

As well as myself, Tim had another three clients on board, two of whom I knew. Young Alex Staniforth had made it back to the mountain for his second attempt back to back. There was never any doubt with Alex. When it came to sponsorship, he pretty much wrote the book on the subject. Where I had struggled in this area, Alex excelled. Here was a young guy who had overcome so much adversity in his short life already. Suffering from bad epilepsy as a child, along with a speech stammer, Alex learnt the hard way that kids can be cruel, and suffered bullying as a result. At nineteen years old, about to embark on his second attempt to climb Everest, he had shown a big middle finger to everyone who had ever put him down.

The second team member I knew was David Bradley, a Jagged Globe client last year, whom I had persuaded to return in 2015 with Tim. I was glad to see he had signed up.

Sadly, our friend Michael hadn't made it. He had every intention of being on the team, but the finances proved to be a bridge too far. A chap called Aeneaus Devenport was Tim's third client. I had never met him and Tim was keen for me to do so before arriving at Base Camp.

After I checked in to the Hotel Thamel, I unpacked all my kit and discovered that I had lost my iPhone. I must have left it on the plane. This was a blow, as it was my method of keeping in touch with back home and updating my social media. Without it, I was as good as off the grid for the next several weeks.

I had one full day to spend in Kathmandu before catching the flight to Lukla. I went to the Himalayan Guides offices, where I dropped off the money I owed to Henry and paid for my return Lukla flights.

Later that day, back in my hotel room, I packed and repacked my bag, and then repacked again. I came to an alarming consensus. My ultra-lightweight expedition backpack was far too heavy for me to carry. I would have struggled to carry it down the stairs of the hotel, let alone carry it all the way to Everest. I needed a porter.

I contacted the office again and asked if they could arrange for a porter once I arrived in Lukla. What was I thinking? A clear sign that I hadn't done my homework back in England. Just before I went to sleep, I accidentally nudged the bed across the slippery wooden floor, and the iPhone I assumed I had lost on the flight reappeared. I had been into a shop in Thamel earlier in the day to buy a replacement phone, which was now surplus to requirements. Sometimes I could be really careless.

The flight to Lukla went as planned the next day. Himalayan Guides were true to their word and managed to get me on the first flight leaving that day. By 7.30am I was sitting in the Paradise Lodge, eating toast and chatting with a group of Australian trekkers led by Jamling Tenzing Norgay, the son of Nepal's most famous Sherpa, Tenzing Norgay.

Rajan Rai had a cheery disposition and I could tell almost immediately that we would get on well together. He spoke very little English, but we communicated through the universal language of humour. From a small settlement called Chheskam in the Solukhumbu District, Rajan worked the main trail through to Everest Base Camp most of the year. For the next thirteen days Rajan and I would trek together towards the mountain. I agreed to pay Rajan 1,300 rupees a day to help me carry some of my kit, which wouldn't fit in my pack, all the way to Everest. He would also get a hot meal and bed for the evening at the teahouse where I stayed. It was nice to have some company on the trail, even if we couldn't string a conversation together.

"Rajan, tell me, have you climbed Everest?" I enquired. A blank look let me know he didn't understand. "You, climb, Everest," I said again, this time pausing after each word and using my fingers and hands to gesture climbing and Everest.

"Ah yes, lots," he said in broken English.

"Excellent," I added. "You can show me how then."

We both laughed. He didn't understand a word I had said.

Rajan Rai in Namche

For the second year in succession, I began the trek to Everest. I felt on top of the world as I left Lukla behind and headed to Monjo for my first night's stop. The sun shone for most of the four hours I was on the trail. I basked in the scenery all around me, deliriously lost in my thoughts. However, my good state of mind would not last.

During that first night at Monjo, whilst I lay in my room, the blackest of moods descended over me. I recognised instantly what is was, as I had experienced it the previous year, after the disaster in the Icefall. The debilitating sensation of homesickness had taken over once again. I told myself that this was ridiculous and I needed to snap out of it. It was only the first day on the trail for goodness' sake. How could I be homesick already? It was hard to describe the feeling. It was a paralysis that left me feeling totally alone and isolated from loved ones back home. Luckily, that night I had a signal on my mobile phone, so I was able to text home to Tamara for some reassuring words. I knew the feeling would pass, and I am glad it happened on the first night, because from then on in, if it were to occur again, I would be better prepared to deal with it.

My first glimpse of Everest this year presented itself through a clearing in the trees on the long steep path up to Namche. After a lunch stop in Namche, we quickly pushed on through to Kyanjuma, where I stayed for the next two nights. Tashi, the lodge owner, greeted me with an enthusiastic hug after recognising me from the previous year's trip. She went out of her way to make sure I was well looked after.

I stayed up late in the communal area of the lodge with a large group of trekkers, watching *Touching the Void*, the epic tale of mountaineering hardship. I also took advantage of a strong Wi-Fi signal to catch up with Tamara, Mam and Michael.

I updated my Facebook page with news of my progress so far, which prompted lots of comments.

'Every foot forward is a step to success. Slowly and surely your passion and desire for success will get you to the summit. Safe trekking all the way to the top.' – Simon Bennett (Facebook)

At Pangboche, I was privileged to have my own private blessing with the Lama Geshi, who was something of a legend to climbers on their way through to Everest and surrounding peaks. A large group had just left before I was invited to sit before him. It was an incredibly spiritual experience. With his blessing now secured, I didn't know if it would make any difference to my chances of success, but I did feel that regardless of the outcome, I would be safe. He placed a puja string around my neck and gave me a blessing card, which he asked me to take to the summit. I told him I would do my best.

Meeting Lama Geshi in Pangboche

In the lodge that evening I met up with Henry, and also Tom Martienssen, the BBC journalist who would be sharing Base Camp with us and reporting on the Gurkhas on the mountain and the Everest season in general.

During my second full day at Chukhung, I set out with Henry, Tom and Hans, a Singapore businessman who was a client of Henry's, to make the ascent of Chukhung Ri.

As we followed Henry most of the way up, the pace was very slow. Towards the top, I pushed on and felt in very good form. A short traverse to the right brought us to the highest point, at 5,400m, where we stayed for forty minutes or so soaking in the view. I spent a lot of the ascent chatting to Tom. At only twenty-four years old he had already lived an action-packed life. He was a well-spoken, likeable chap, with wispy blonde hair and an encyclopaedic knowledge of Middle Eastern affairs, which belied his young age.

As a former RAF infantry soldier, he had completed two tours of Afghanistan before coming to the attention of the BBC as a reporter. As a specialist in war-torn conflicts, I had no idea why he was on Everest – it didn't seem to fit his résumé. However, he took to the role with professionalism and was eager and enthusiastic.

Back down at the lodge later that day, Rob Casserley arrived, along with his wife MK and several clients. After suffering the disappointment of having to return home empty-handed the previous year, I was elated to see him back. Rob had been a great person to have around camp, especially after the stresses of the previous year's event. Also returning with Rob and MK was Daniel Wallace, a thirty-something Londoner, who was as driven to reach the top of Everest as I was. Other than MK, Dan was Rob's only true Everest client that year. The other clients with Rob were on permits to tackle Lobuche East and Island Peak.

As we sat around the lodge that evening, Rob presented me with an interesting proposition. One of his clients had decided to return home early, without making the ascent of Island Peak. This left one of the permits going free, which Rob asked if I would like to fill. Of course I jumped at the chance. The prospect of going over 6,000m before reaching Everest was a fantastic opportunity, and one that I eagerly grabbed with both hands.

Since arriving in Chukhung, I hadn't been able to speak with Tamara and the girls back home, or update my Facebook page. The Wi-Fi in the lodge wasn't working, which meant we all had to sit and chat with one another – a rarity in this technological era. I was missing my family, though, and not being able to speak with them was very frustrating.

That night I shared a room with Henry, as all the other rooms in the lodge were full. I was reading the Anatoli Boukreev account of the Everest '96 disaster, *The Climb,* when the very man soundly sleeping not more than three feet away was mentioned throughout the first chapter of the book. It was a surreal moment, only eclipsed by our coffee meeting back home in Hartlepool.

Throughout that night it snowed relentlessly. We woke to find four feet of fresh snow had settled outside. I had been due to meet up with Tim and the team the following day, to spend three nights in tents ascending Pokalde and crossing the Kongma La, but this was looking highly unlikely at midday as the snow continued to fall. I needed to get word to Tim, who was one village lower, that Rob had given me the chance to do

Island Peak. However, Tim sent one of his porters ahead with a note for me, which said that the snow had changed everything. We would no longer be crossing the pass, so Tim said that he would see me at Base Camp in five days' time. This was great news, as it meant I could join Rob and his team on Island Peak.

The next day the snow eased off, so Rob, Dan and an insanely fit American couple called Jennifer and John left the lodge to begin trekking to Island Peak Base Camp. I followed closely behind, conscious that I was an intruder in what would have become a close-knit group after recently ascending Lobuche East together. It became apparent how well acclimatised they were. They moved incredibly quickly – I struggled to keep up the pace. Rob and his clients had been on the trail for close to seventeen days, in contrast with my ten.

An average time to reach Island Peak Base Camp from Chukhung was around three and a half hours of steady trekking. We were sitting in the kitchen tent at IP Base Camp sipping hot tea just two hours after leaving Chukhung. I was totally exhausted as I stared into my mug, with alarm bells ringing loud and clear. The kitchen cooks brought us dal bhat, but I had completely lost my appetite and I struggled to force even a forkful into my mouth. After Rob did a quick kit check, we had the rest of the afternoon to relax and prepare for the ascent. We would be leaving at midnight that night.

I shared a tent for the rest of the day with Daniel Wallace, the Londoner who was also here to climb Everest. Dan was in a very closed-off mood as I tried to make conversation. I could see that he was upset. He got into his sleeping bag, zipped it up tight and turned his back on me.

At the time, I felt it was because he didn't particularly warm to my presence in his team. Dan was a direct paying client of Rob's and I wasn't. Technically, though, I wasn't a direct client of Tim's either, as I had negotiated my place on the mountain with Henry.

I still felt as though I wasn't welcome. It wasn't until Rob explained that two of the clients who had recently gone home early were Dan's brother and uncle. I suddenly understood why Dan was upset. It wasn't aimed at me as such, but it didn't help that I had taken his brother's permit. I would have felt the same.

After skipping dinner, as I couldn't face food, I tried my best to get some sleep, but no matter how much I tried I couldn't. My alarm went off at midnight; I was already wide awake. Again, I tried to force some food down, with a breakfast prepared by the cooks, but after a few mouthfuls I pushed my plate to one side. Rob noticed with a slightly concerned look.

As we left that night heading for the summit of Island Peak I didn't feel well at all, but I didn't let Rob know. I couldn't possibly fail on what was essentially a trekking peak. This would not do my Everest aspirations in a few weeks' time any good whatsoever.

I felt like I was overheating as the pace picked up to a similar speed to the previous day. I was tackling my biggest climb in fourteen years and things could not have started any worse. I was seriously depleted of energy, having not eaten anything for over twenty-four hours, and also borderline dehydrated, as I couldn't even hold water down. But my predicament wasn't the fault of Rob or his team. They were very well acclimatised and had prepared for this ascent. It was an opportunity that, in hindsight, I was foolish to have taken on so soon into my trekking and it was firmly biting me hard on the arse.

The next several hours will live long in my memory as my worst experience in the mountains to date. I struggled on to eventually reach a height of around 5,800m. How I managed to reach that high, I had no idea. I became a liability – not only to myself, but also to Rob and his team as I tripped and stumbled my way up Island Peak. I think had I not pulled the plug when I did, Rob would probably have done so anyway. Rob's concern at my welfare when we left was now compounded as a deeply worried look flashed across his face. I told him I was turning back, he knew it was the right call.

I wasn't his problem. I was someone else's client who had piggybacked onto one of his client's permits, although Rob would never have seen it that way. I didn't want my failure to reflect badly on him.

My performance annoyed me beyond belief as I made my way back down the mountain. Rob told one of his Sherpas to accompany me down to make sure I would be OK. As I turned my back on Island Peak and began the descent, I felt weak and disoriented. I vomited on several occasions and dropped my water bottle twice, which luckily the Sherpa with me was able to stop rolling away. I was in a really bad condition, and I hoped that by descending I would pull round.

As I collapsed back into my tent at first light, the damage was done. My confidence had taken a huge knock and I was seriously worried. As I lay there, I thought about quitting and going home. If this could happen at an altitude as low as Island Peak, then I would have zero chance of success on Everest. I had the towel of defeat ready to throw into the ring. I was as good as done.

I began to worry about what people back home would think. This could become very embarrassing for me. I was here to climb the highest mountain in the world, yet a trekking peak in Everest's shadow had humbled me and brought me to my knees. My aspirations completely unravelled around my feet. Did my ambition outweigh my ability? This question and more like it haunted my thoughts as I lay comatose in the tent, drifting in and out of sleep.

As long as I come out of this experience with at least one scrap of dignity intact, I will survive, I thought. I still had three full days before I had told Tim I would meet him and the rest of the team at Base Camp. I had time to recover from this, but it would take some serious soul searching to do so.

I left Island Peak Base Camp late afternoon, after I had managed to keep some food down. There was no sign of Rob and the others as I packed up and left, and I was sure Dan would appreciate a tent to himself coming down from the summit.

Feeling slightly better, I trekked back to Chukhung and checked back in to the lodge where we had been staying. MK was one of the first people to greet me; she had elected to rest instead of climbing Island Peak, on account of the fact that she had already done Lobuche East.

I told her what had happened to me, but she could sense I wasn't in the mood for conversation, so she quickly went back to her book.

Sat in the lodge feeling sorry for myself, I needed a pep talk, and I hadn't been able to contact anyone back home for almost six days now. Before I left for Nepal, I told Tamara that I would have ample opportunity to keep in touch, as I would be making use of the Wi-Fi in the teahouses and lodges. I told her not to panic if she hadn't heard from me for a few days, as I would no doubt soon be back online. However, this had been almost a week without word. I knew she and my mam would be panicking. I had to do something about it. I decided to check out of the lodge and descend back down to the village of Dingboche, where I could get a message home.

At the Mountain Paradise Lodge, I stumbled into the dining area, still feeling the effects of whatever it was that had struck me down on Island Peak. As I looked around for a seat, I heard a familiar voice:

"Now then trekker, how's it going?"

I spun round to see Tim. Alex looked ecstatic to see me and we gave each other a pat on the back. David Bradley stood up and shook my hand, but the third member of the team went for a more stand-off approach. I didn't know Aeneas at all and, as I hadn't trekked with the team, I hadn't had the opportunity to get to know him. I told Tim all about the drama on Island Peak, which I casually dismissed as nothing more than a short bout of sickness. I blamed my performance squarely on being ill, which Tim was happy to accept as the possible reason.

Tim informed me that Tamara had been in touch panicking about why my contact had stopped. She had even phoned the Himalayan Guides office in Kathmandu and spoken to Iswari, our expedition agent. I told Tim that it was my fault entirely, as I had told her there wouldn't be more than two to three days without contact.

"You need to contact her immediately and let her know you are fine," he added. "Tell her to remember the expedition's golden rule: no news is not bad news."

After a quick catch-up with Alex, I went to the bakery near to the lodge, where I could connect to Wi-Fi and get in touch with back home. I apologised to Tamara and explained that I had no signal in the previous lodge and then added a further delay due to my Island Peak debacle. She was mighty relieved to hear my voice and seeing and speaking with her and the girls improved my mood immediately. I told them that I loved them all and was thinking positive thoughts.

I updated my Facebook page, where I was honest about what had happened over the past week. As usual, comments flooded in and lifted my spirits. Chris Soley, the MD of Cameron's Brewery – the company that sponsored me at the eleventh hour – said he hoped I was back to full health soon and wished me the best of luck in getting to Base Camp. Kate Smith, my retired schoolteacher friend, replied with a longer response:

Thank goodness, my other boys will tell you I soon worry if I don't hear from them even though I know no news is good news. Sorry you have been a little unwell. Get it all over and done with as you go forward for bigger and better things. Our new puppy is keeping us busy and we had the whole family for a few days last week, which also kept us busy clearing up after them all. You were the No1 topic, but I was unable to tell them anything new. I am reading all things Everest and if you put all the items together I get a much better picture. Some of the photos appearing are great and show quite a thick depth of snow. Hope you are able to send us some musings now you have a couple of days before you start climbing for real. I would love to be there. Cheers Kate

I spent the rest of the day and night in Dingboche catching up with Tim and the team. It was good to see Alex, and we took ourselves off to the bakery at the bottom of the village for a catch-up over cake and coffee.

The following morning, after a breakfast that I struggled to eat in the lodge, Tim and the team packed up and set off for Lobuche. I told Tim I would soon follow, but needed some more time to sort stuff out and send a few emails.

In the Starbright Café, I spoke with my friend Michael back home via Skype, and gave him all the reasons why I felt I didn't reach the top of Island Peak.

I was just about to leave the bakery and head back to the lodge to pack my bag when Rob Casserley walked through the door. We hadn't seen one another since I turned back high on Island Peak, and he was clearly concerned for my welfare – so much so that, when he got back down to Chukhung from his successful climb of Island Peak and realised I wasn't there, he set off to look for me. Rob was keen to point out that I shouldn't read too much into what occurred.

"It happens. You got ill, you were unlucky."

He also added that he hoped I wouldn't be worried about it. But I was. How could I not be? I was taken aback that Rob had left the lodge in Chukhung, leaving his wife MK and clients to come and find me, a non-client, to make sure I was fine. This touched me greatly and it was a measure of his qualities as a guide.

For all he knew, I could have been on my way down, convinced my Everest dream was all over. Even though that thought had crossed my mind, I didn't share it with him. I needed to get myself back in the game mentally, and if I couldn't, then Everest was all over for me. I didn't have much time left.

That night, Rob planned a final dinner in a lodge at Pheriche for his two US Island Peak clients, Jennifer and John. Having successfully climbed both Lobuche East and Island Peak, it was the end of their adventure in Nepal. Rob, MK and

Dan would continue on up to Everest, as would I. Rob invited me to join them and said he wouldn't take no for an answer. This altered my final plans for reaching Everest. Tim and the rest of the team had already left Dingboche for Lobuche. I was still recovering from my illness and didn't fancy a long day's trekking, so I gladly accepted Rob's offer and emailed Tim to tell him I would see him at Base Camp the next day. I then made the short forty-five-minute trek over the ridge into Pheriche.

In the lodge I wrote in my journal, reflecting on events of the past few days. Tomorrow I would reach Base Camp, where the trip would change from a two-week trek into a mountaineering expedition with the aim of climbing the highest mountain in the world. It dawned on me that this would be the last lodge I would stay in until I came back down off the mountain.

Rajan and I tucked in to a great evening meal of fried chicken and chips, which Rob had paid to have brought up from lower down the valley. It was simply divine and I was happy that my appetite had returned with a vengeance.

Trekking in the Khumbu 2015

17th April 2015 – Day 13

So this was it: the day I would return to Everest after having to leave the mountain early due to a disaster in the Icefall almost one year ago. Before setting off on the long push up to Base Camp, I updated my Facebook page.

Day 13 – Today is the day I will arrive at Base Camp after 13 days of trekking. I have a long day ahead of me as I am currently in Pheriche, over 1,000 metres lower. It's normally recommended not to take a big jump in altitude like this, but I have been to over 5,000 metres three times already, so I am well acclimatised and ready to arrive. Next stop Everest, where hopefully this time it safely begins and concludes in around five weeks' time.

Again the usual messages of support followed my update:

'Enjoy every moment, but stay safe' – Sue Stamper

'Good luck mate. Been following your whole progress since day one' – Stephen Kitcher

'Fantastic, then the adventure really begins' – Steven McCarthy

'Enjoy fella. Hope the weather gods are smiling on you. Stay safe' – Paul Viney

'A journey begins with just a simple step' – John Davies

In total, the journey was around 14km – but with over 1,000m in height to gain, it would be a tough day. It started well enough as we strode through the beautiful wide-open valley heading up towards Lobuche, but I soon realised I hadn't recovered fully from whatever it was that had struck me down on Island Peak. Rob, MK and Dan powered on ahead, clearly feeling the benefit of their strong acclimatisation schedule and performance on Lobuche East and Island Peak. I, on the other hand, couldn't get any momentum going. My legs felt tired, and every step was painfully slow. What the bloody hell was going on? I didn't deserve this. Surely I was fitter and better than this? I struggled on to the village of Thukla at the relatively modest altitude of 4,600m, where we had a brief rest stop. I drank a hot lemon tea and ate a Kit Kat.

Rob enquired if I was OK, but when I couldn't even bring myself to finish the chocolate, I knew I wasn't.

"I'm fine," I said to Rob. "Just going at my own pace."

As we left Thukla the hill immediately beyond was a tough prospect. Rob and his team raced up with almost superhuman strength, but I didn't even try to keep up – it was futile. Rajan had to wait for me to catch up every 50m and he knew I was once more struggling.

"You OK, sir?" he would continually ask.

"Yes, and stop calling me sir," I would bark back.

At the top of the hill I rested amongst the many memorials: grim-reminders of how serious this expedition truly was. I located the memorial to Babu Chiri, the well-known Sherpa climber who had needlessly died on Everest in 2001. Babu had given me his cap and told me to never let go of my dream when I met him at Base Camp a year before his death.

As a tear filled my eye at the senselessness in all of this loss of life, I reached into my pack and placed that very cap on my head. Although I'm not really religious, I knelt down in front of his memorial and prayed. I read the words on his memorial: 'May his soul rest in peace and his dream be fulfilled'. I said a few words to the great man, hoping he would be able to hear me:

"Hi, you probably don't remember me but we met once at the bottom of the mountain. You gave me your cap and told me to dream big. Well, I did dream big, I never let go of that dream and now I am here to once more try to achieve it. But, I have got to level with you. I am really struggling here. Please help me out, and help me find the inspiration and the heart to keep going."

I didn't know if he would hear my words, but it made me feel better and it was a poignant moment on my way to the mountain.

Leaving the memorial cairns behind, Rob, MK and Dan were far out of sight, but the trail to Everest was packed. So I put my head down, stuck my headphones in and concentrated on putting one foot in front of the other. I spent the next hour through to Lobuche listening to the Irish band Kodaline, whom I had listened to incessantly since arriving in Nepal fifteen days earlier.

The trail into Lobuche was gentler, and I was able to pick up my pace as I made my way along the pleasant ablation valley where the village was set. It was in Lobuche the previous year that the terrible news of the avalanche reached us. I was hoping for no such news this time as I made my way to the lodge where I knew Rob and company would be.

I tried to stomach some food and ordered simple vegetable fried rice with a mug of hot lemon. I was able to drink, but solid food made me nauseous. Once again I pushed my plate away untouched. Weight had dropped off me at an alarming rate during the past week. My Berghaus trekking pants, which had fitted comfortably at the start of the trek, now refused to stay up, no matter how tight I pulled in the attached webbing belt.

Snow began to drift down as we left Lobuche together as a group. Before long, the views ahead up the Khumbu Glacier became obscured as a thick fog descended and covered up everything. The snow began to fall harder. The trek to Gorak Shep, the last stop before Base Camp, became unbearable. The extreme lethargy I'd suffered from on Island Peak returned with a vengeance, and I reached Gorak Shep completely crushed and soul-destroyed. I was convinced I was done. I could go no further with my journey to Everest. Whatever it was that was pinning me down had won. I had nothing left in the tank to battle it with. I collapsed into a seat next to Rob, opposite Dan and MK, and my emotions got the better of me. I wept uncontrollably.

This must have been awful for Rob. I apologised repeatedly, saying I would get my shit together and that it wasn't his problem. It wasn't! I wasn't Rob's client, yet our schedule to reach the mountain had thrown us together by chance. Rob tried his best to console me. It felt like my whole world was collapsing. Why was this happening to me? Everest had been my entire universe for over half of my life. I couldn't understand why now, at the hour of my calling, I felt so unbelievably out on a limb and exposed. I had done my time and put in the training, so I struggled to believe that it had anything to do with my fitness levels. If I was feeling like this down here at the foot of Everest, I had absolutely no chance on the mountain, and I knew it. I was praying for a miracle recovery.

Rob took me off to one side:

"Ellis, we all left Pheriche together this morning and we will all reach Base Camp together. I'll put you out at the front and we will walk behind you at your pace. No one will know anything about this," he added. "You are going to be fine. I have belief in you that you will pull through this."

I hoped so, but at that moment I didn't know where I was going to summon the inner resolve to continue. My self-implosion had rattled me to my very core. I thought I had always been a mentally strong person, but those past several days had been an incredibly testing period – not just of my trek to Everest but my entire life.

As we left Gorak Shep and headed out into the most ferocious snow storm I had seen in Nepal, I thought about the words Ste Bock had said to me in a message a few days earlier:

I wouldn't worry for a second if you become ill. Keep your focus and don't allow for any sense of doubt whatsoever (you know all this I'm sure). Remember, you need to remain inwardly focused (intensely so). You have fought hard to get here and deserve to be on her summit… you have proven that… so don't let anything get in your way. Strip back the layers and get into that mental zone brother…

I kept repeating the words '*strip back the layers and get into that mental zone*' as I trudged head first into a thick blanket of snow. As I did, I could feel myself growing stronger and I began to pick up my pace. Very little was said between any of us; we all kept our heads down, no doubt lost in our thoughts. Fifty minutes after leaving Gorak, the tents of Base Camp came into view as we followed the steep path that skirted the Khumbu Glacier that roared down the valley direct from the

Icefall. The snow hadn't relented all day and we finally stumbled into the Himalayan Guides' camp.

Two to three feet of snow covered Everest Base Camp. Loraine, a lady who had been trekking with Tim, was one of the first people to greet me. "Ellis, welcome. You have finally made it," she said as she threw her arms around me. This was the end of the road for Loraine, but as a reward for her efforts she got to spend two nights sleeping at Base Camp with the climbing team before trekking back out. Alex then came out of the mess tent to greet me, followed by David. Everybody who was on the permit for that year's attempt on Everest had now arrived at Base Camp. We had been the last few to arrive. With all the troops in place, the 2015 Himalayan Guides Everest Expedition could now begin.

Kumar, a cheerful-looking kitchen assistant, brought me a huge mug of milky tea and showed me to the mess tent. I was happy to follow. Rob patted me on the shoulder and whispered: "You'll be fine, Ellis, you big Northern Jessie," in his usual mocking Geordie accent. Normality had resumed. I was back, and this time I had no intention of leaving until I had at least tried to reach the top of the mountain.

Rajan and I said our goodbyes. I gave him a few thousand rupees for a tip, which put a huge smile on his face – a smile that broadened when I gave him the Samsung mobile phone I had bought in Kathmandu. He merrily skipped away in the snow, despite my pleas for him to stay and descend the following morning, when hopefully the snow would have passed.

I slept well that first night at Base Camp, and emerged from my tent the following morning a different person from the dejected and defeated one who had collapsed into it the night before.

The day would be an inauspicious one. Exactly a year earlier Everest had experienced its darkest day, when a large block of ice calved away from the western shoulder, killing sixteen Sherpas in its fall line. As a mark of respect, the mountain was peacefully quiet. With a full rest day to look forward to, it was an opportunity to spend time with the clients I would be sharing Base Camp with over the next several weeks.

Ingo, the Icelandic Bear Grylls, had returned for another attempt, bringing along his infectious personality. I was delighted to see him back. Ingo had a thirst for adventure unlike anyone I had seen. He was a real character and a breath of fresh air around camp – one of my favorite climbers from 2014 and I liked him immensely. On his website he describes himself as a climber and paragliding pilot who is driven by adventure. Coming from a small town called Akureyri in Northern Iceland, surrounded by snowy mountains, he was destined to one day attempt to climb Everest. He was back once more to try and cash in on our mutual dream.

I was pleased to see Henry around camp too and he was wearing the hoodie I had given him back in Hartlepool.

We shook hands as he said, "Welcome man, you feeling better?"

"Stacks, that mountain better look out!"

Henry smiled. "That's the spirit, cheers cheers man," he said as he strode off in the direction of the BBC communications tent.

Henry would always finish off any conversation with his double cheers. Tom, the BBC reporter who had shared my ascent of Chukhung Ri along with Henry, had been here a few days already and had settled well into Base Camp. He had already sent back a few video reports, which were run across the BBC world service. His communications tent was the envy of Base Camp. It consisted of a large dome tent housing the equipment, computers, batteries and satellite panels needed to edit, record and report back to the BBC in London. If anything should go wrong on the mountain that year, then the BBC would surely be the first to break the story worldwide.

As camps go on Everest, ours occupied a good spot directly beneath the Icefall, which roared up in all its ferocity directly in front. Unzipping my tent door, it was the first thing I saw, framing the entire view.

Positioned just in front of us were the tents of Adventure Consultants, the New Zealand guiding company caught up the disaster eighteen years earlier, and with whom I had climbed Aconcagua in 2001. To the left of us the British Army G200 Gurkha team became our immediate neighbours along with

Jagged Globe, the UK guiding company. To our immediate right was the camp of Madison Mountaineering, who had a large number of clients on both Everest and Lhotse, including the US climber Alan Arnette who was hoping to climb the latter.

We were right at the heart of action in Base Camp, with all the leading players in the Everest climbing business located tightly together. IMG and HimEx, the other two big commercial outfits, tended to keep themselves more isolated at the other end of camp: this would prove to be a piece of luck one week later.

I spent much of the day relaxing in my tent. The following day Tim planned for us to do some ladder and ropework practice on the glacier beneath the Icefall, so I was happy to use the day to generally laze around and become accustomed to my new surroundings. I took the short, but breathless, walk to the Wi-Fi tent at the entrance to Base Camp.

An industrious communications company called Everest Link was selling Wi-Fi access on scratch cards. I purchased a 5GB card, thinking this would be plenty for me to keep in touch with loved ones and friends back home and update my social media channels. I wasn't planning on writing essay-length blog posts, just short and frequent updates to keep people up to speed with the expedition as it evolved.

I took a few photos of the view from the front of my tent and shared an update:

Day 14 – Relaxing day at Base Camp. It was a tough walk in yesterday. The last two hours into camp were in a complete whiteout with driving snow. In fact, Base Camp is covered in the stuff. Today is the 1st anniversary to the 16 Sherpa souls who lost their lives up in the Icefall last year. Out of respect no one is moving anywhere today. So it's kick back time; sort out your living space in your tent so it's as comfortable as can be for the next five days and sort out kit so it's ready to go. This thing now feels very real.

For the first time people responded with a few questions, now I had arrived on the mountain. A chap called Mark Johnson asked me if there was a new longer but safer route up the Icefall. Alistair Musgrave wanted to know if there was an increased risk of things going wrong with so much fresh snowfall. It was amazing that perfect strangers back home were following along with all my updates and, once again, there were plenty of words of encouragement:

'All at Cameron's behind you. No need to look around.' – David Soley

'Keep going. Safe journey. Follow your dream.' – Maria O Sullivan

'The BBC had the anniversary yesterday. Very sombre. Good luck.' – Carl Bevan

Over the next few days, I completely threw myself into life as an Everest climber. The ladder and abseiling practice went well and I even got to jumar up and down a fixed line. It wasn't difficult to grasp 'down' at the modest altitude of Base

Camp, but high on Everest, when your brain is in a hypoxic state, it could be fatal to make a mistake. It was therefore paramount that jumar-climbing became second nature now, before the stakes were raised.

On the 20th April, my third full day at Base Camp, Tim and the rest of our team trekked up to Pumori ABC, which gave a spectacular view back across to Everest. Perched at a high point of 5,750m, similar to the altitude I reached on Island Peak, I felt fantastic, with no symptoms at all of the type that took me down over a week earlier. I found the trek up a breeze and I was one of the first from our group to reach Pumori ABC.

There were plenty of climbers already there, soaking in the view and resting. I noticed one I hadn't seen for fourteen years, and I was keen to say hello.

"Guy Cotter, how's it going?" I said as I reached out my hand.

There was a pause of two to three seconds. "Ellis, wow. I am great. How are you?" he said back, as he suddenly realised that we had climbed together on Aconcagua.

We spent a few minutes chatting. He said that it was great to finally see me on Everest, to which he added, "You deserve it." Before he stood up to descend back to Base Camp with the rest of his Adventure Consultants team, he told me to take it easy as he disappeared off down the steep slope. "If there is anything you need, you know where I am," he shouted back up.

The trek that day did wonders to restore my confidence and it answered one glaring question for me. I now knew I was fit enough, and that what happened to me on Island Peak – and possibly on the final day into Base Camp – had been altitude-induced sickness. I now knew the warning signs to look out for and I was determined not to get ill again, although this was largely outside of my control.

Back in the mess tent later, Tim laid out the plans for the coming days. The following day would see our puja ceremony. This is an auspicious event for Everest climbers and one which the Sherpas thoroughly delight in. We weren't allowed anywhere near the mountain until we had attended the ceremony.

The day after, Tim added, would be our first introduction to the Icefall. A shudder went through the team. We all knew it was coming. We would have to tame this beast several times in the coming days and weeks. I was anxious to get going anyway and a nervous excitement filled my mind. After our first push up into the ice, we would then have two days downtime where further practice would take place lower down on the glacier, making sure we were prepared and ready before moving up to Camp One on the 25th.

Everything was now in place; we knew when we would venture into the lion's den, providing things went smoothly. I was confident that this year would be a good one. It had to be. I wasn't coming back for a third attempt.

I had experienced a puja on Everest in 2014 and it was a day of great celebration amongst the Sherpas. As I sat and watched this year's ceremony unfolding, I became fixated on the Icefall. There was a lot of activity and I could see climbers strung out throughout the route. They must have been descending climbers and Sherpas, as it was far too late in the day to be heading up. The entire journey down to Base Camp, for a fit acclimatised climber, takes around ninety minutes. Going up to Camp One takes a minimum of three and a half hours, and that was motoring. I used the zoom lens on my camera to study the route I would be treading the very next day. No matter how much I stared at the frozen labyrinth, it still intimidated me. It looked every bit as committing as it absolutely was. For most climbers scaling Everest from Nepal, it was the part of the mountain that filled them with the most dread. The fear levels had risen a few notches higher after the ice avalanche twelve months earlier. This type of thinking did nothing to calm my fears, so I stopped looking and became immersed in the puja.

Ellis being blessed during the puja

Our entire Nepali expedition team was introduced to us, one by one, from the kitchen assistants and cooks through to the climbing Sherpas who would be accompanying us on the mountain. I recalled a few of them from the previous year. Pasang Temba, who was much older than some of the younger members of the team, was our Camp Two cook, and had done this job for many years. Rumour had it that 2015 was to be his last on the mountain. He was partially deaf and communicated in nods and gestures. He was a cheerful addition to the team, and I had nothing but the utmost respect for the man – anyone who had climbed up and down through the Icefall as many times as he had deserved a knighthood, in my opinion.

Once the climbing equipment had been blessed, puja strings were placed around the neck of each climber and a local lama gave us all a blessing. The mountain was as good as open for business. To conclude the ceremony, someone organised a team photo. Henry had wandered off so Rob took the picture; I think they both saw this as a bad sign. The last time a team photo had been taken in a similar manner, a team member perished on the mountain.

22nd April 2015

I woke at 4.00am, knowing that a few hours later I would be breaking new ground in my attempt to reach the roof of the world. Kumar brought out milky tea and toast and I forced it down, even though my appetite was virtually non-existent at such an ungodly hour. Rob and his team were also leaving for a move into the Icefall. The mess tent was a hive of activity, but the only sound was the clink and clank of metal on metal as climbers got into their harnesses. Everyone was silently contemplating the climb ahead. This was why we were here. Years of dreaming and training were about to be put to the ultimate test.

Himalayan Guides Everest Team 2015

I was keen to get going, but we didn't leave the mess tent until gone 5.30am. It took forty minutes to hit the bottom of the ice from our camp. All you could hear was the sound of fresh snow being crushed beneath our feet as we wove our way in and out of other camps. We passed the tents of the Icefall Doctors, which were eerily silent; the occupants either fast asleep, or up on the mountain already. At crampon point we rested to fit our crampons onto our boots. At 6.15am I began climbing through the clear blue ice that guarded passage into the jaws of the route. With Tim out front, the four of us followed along like ducklings. For the most part, lower down in the Icefall I didn't need to attach a jumar – the mechanical ascending device – to the rope. I just clipped a karabiner on and slid my hand along until the next anchor point. This allowed me to move very quickly, and it was only when the route steepened, or we came across a ladder, that I needed to be more secure by attaching my jumar.

For years I had read about this section on Everest. I had seen photos and films of climbers balanced precariously, inching slowly across the ladders, but when I was climbing through this section it was like nothing I had ever imagined. It was hard to deny the sheer staggering beauty of the scenery all around. Yet as I moved slowly higher, I didn't allow my mind to wander too far from the thought that this part of the mountain could wipe me out in a second. My mind stayed razor sharp as I repeatedly told myself *strip back the layers and get in the mental zone,* over and over. I had no idea what it meant, but I said it again and again anyway.

The sun's heat began to make its presence known a few hours in, and the temperature within the Icefall soared. As I crossed several ladders, my confidence soared with it. David, or Alex, pulled the rope taut at either side of the ladder and I then gingerly stepped onto the first rung, carefully placing each foot until I stood back on solid snow on the other side. I then returned the favour by holding the rope so they could cross. I paid no attention to the gaping chasm of the crevasse beneath my feet; I was too focused on my step placement to notice.

Ellis: first rotation in the Icefall

By mid-morning we reached a wide, flat part of the Icefall. My watch showed that we had reached 5,850m: the highest point so far on that year's expedition. After declaring a job well done, Tim indicated that we had gone far enough and we would now head back down. His words prompted a pang of disappointment. I was enjoying myself too much and wanted to push on. I felt very strong and confident; my first foray into the Icefall could not have gone better.

It was far easier to descend through the ice than it was to ascend, and in no time I was back in my tent, knocking the snow and ice from my crampons. In total, we must have crossed half a dozen ladders that morning. It felt good to have finally stepped onto the mountain after the huge disappointment of the previous year. As I stared up at the mountain, trying to pinpoint exactly where we had just been, I offered a quick thanks to the mountain gods for being kind that morning. For the rest of the day, I felt truly alive. The crushing sensation of defeat on Island Peak was now a distant memory, defeated by climbing into the Icefall. As psychological boosts go, this could not have been any better. I now had forty-eight hours' rest to look forward to, and I planned to make the most of it.

Every morning without fail, since arriving at Base Camp, I woke at first light. This was usually at 5.30am. I would lie awake, refusing to get out of my warm sleeping bag, until the sun hit my tent, which was around 7.30am. Occasionally, an early-morning avalanche saw me rush for the zipper and fling open the tent door, where a plume of powder rising up from the valley floor would get my full attention. This was normally at the bottom of the Lho La, a 6,000m pass between Nepal and Tibet, although you would have to be mad to attempt to cross into Tibet this way.

Avalanches regularly crashed down all around Base Camp, at all times of the day. The longer you stayed at Base Camp, the more you got used to it. The wall of Pumori and Lingtren, which linked the two peaks towering over Base

Camp, was fairly active, with at least one avalanche a day thundering down to the valley floor. The distance from these peaks protected Base Camp from this threat, and I felt happy enough to just watch in awe.

After breakfast the next morning, Rob Casserley commented on how well I had moved in the ice the previous day, which further added to my renewed confidence. As I relaxed in the mess tent for the rest of the morning, I was sure that the worst days of the trip were behind me. Since the trek up to Pumori ABC, I felt a whole lot better about things, and I was now in a much stronger place mentally.

Tim set up a rope on a nearby ice pinnacle after lunch, and we spent a few hours climbing up and abseiling down in our crampons, brushing up on the basics before we ascended higher onto the mountain. It was tiring work under the relentless heat of the mid-afternoon sun, which reflected off the glacier ice. This only made the situation worse by adding to the oven-like temperatures. Once the sun had set, the temperature on Everest could drop in minutes, but in the full mid-day glare, it was unbearable. I hadn't come to Everest to be baked alive! If I had wanted heat, I would have gone to the Middle East.

The next day dawned with the clearest blue skies. Looking up into the Icefall, I found myself wishing I were one of the climbers nearing the top. Teams had been moving up and down the mountain for a number of days now, as most of the main teams had all concluded their puja ceremonies.

Everest 2015 was now in full swing and the mood throughout Base Camp was one of optimism. The Icefall was in great condition and the route had been moved across to the right to avoid some of the danger areas, which lurked on, or near, its western side. There was no reason to think that it would be anything other than a normal season on the mountain – which implied a few hundred westerners reaching the summit, with a few inevitable deaths, which always accompanied the summits. There was no getting away from the fact that this mountain killed people. That had been Tamara's main concern before I went back out there. She had witnessed it to an appalling degree twelve months earlier, and I couldn't believe I had actually persuaded her to change her mind about my return trip. *As long as I don't die, everything will be OK, I* reasoned, *or Tamara will kill me herself.*

On my last full day at Base Camp, before moving up to Camp One, I wandered down to visit a neighbouring camp. Tony McMurray, the finance director who had arranged for me to speak at his company's IT event in Milton Keynes, was in Nepal trekking with a large group. I knew there was a chance that our paths might cross and I had kept in touch with him in case the opportunity arose. I found him attending a puja ceremony with a team of Indian climbers. Tony and his group of trekkers were allowed to stay at Base Camp for a few days, undoubtedly the highlight of their trip. When I was introduced to the rest of his group, I felt like royalty; as I was there to climb the mountain, they looked at me with admiration. But I wasn't any different to a single one of them. We all had dreams of being there and seeing Everest. My dream just took me a bit further up the mountain, I hoped.

I spent a great morning with Tony and his team, which was made more special by attending another puja ceremony and being blessed again.

Ellis with Tony McMurray at Base Camp

Back in the mess tent that afternoon, we sorted out the food we needed for the next three days and nights on the mountain. The following day, we would push up through the Icefall to Camp One, where we would stay the night before moving further up the mountain to spend two nights at Camp Two. These rotations were all part of the grand plan of acclimatisation to the ever-increasing altitude. Spending a night at Camp One, at just a smidgen under 6,000m, would allow me to adapt to sleeping 600m higher than Base Camp. The tents of Camp One are generally regarded as a staging post for pushing further up the mountain. Camp One's location at the top of the Icefall means it is penned in by the west shoulder of Everest on its left and Nuptse on its right, both of which have regular avalanches. It is not a camp that you want to spend much time at. As climbers become more acclimatised the further into the season they go, Camp One is bypassed altogether, with most climbers moving up to Camp Two from Base Camp in one push. I was not at that stage yet, and needed to spend at least one night at Camp One. As I retired to my tent for the rest of the afternoon after sorting my kit, the nervous anticipation at what lay ahead was palpable.

The Wi-Fi signal at Base Camp had been hit and miss all week but, before I tried to get some sleep, I was able to get a quick message out to Tamara and my girls and update my Everest page:

All is well. I am looking forward to the next few days on the mountain, away from Base Camp as I continue with my goal to climb this mountain. Wish me luck, onwards and upwards. Ellis

I set my alarm for 4.00am and made sure I knew where all my kit was. Before sleep consumed me, I read some of the responses to my earlier update. Climbing on this mountain the following day meant everything to me. But I also knew it meant a lot to the followers back home who had so far been extremely supportive of my endeavours:

'All our thoughts, best wishes and prayers go out to you. Remember the mountain will always be there, just make sure you come back safe' – Jonathan Atterbury

'WOW, so jealous right now. Good luck and stay safe Ellis. On top of the world.' – Paul Viney

'Finally!!! So happy for you, reach for the stars and stay safe. xx' – Jan Baron

'Living the dream, best of luck! See you on the flip side.' – Colin Murphy

25th April 2015

I didn't sleep much through the night, and lay awake tossing and turning. The sound of a few distant avalanches kept my mind far too active. When the time came to get ready and start sorting my pack, I was fully in the mental zone ready for the mountain. The few hiccups I had endured on the way to Everest had played heavy on my mind, but now was not the time to let the demons descend. *I can do this. I wouldn't be here if I couldn't,* I silently told myself. I headed for the mess tent as focused and determined as I had ever been about anything in my life. I knew that, if I didn't perform today and reach Camp One, then my Everest dream would be over.

Every climber under the umbrella of Himalayan Guides left that morning, heading into the ice. Rolf Oostra and his client Jo Bradshaw were the first to leave an hour earlier. Next to leave was my team, with Tim leading the way through the maze of tents to reach the bottom of the Icefall. Rob Casserley, MK and Dan, along with their climbing sirdar, Thundu, were the last to leave the mess tent. Rob also had Ingo and Tom, the BBC Journalist, in tow. Tom was only allowed to go through the Icefall to Camp Two. He wasn't on a full climbing permit, and was therefore not allowed to go any higher. But by going through the Icefall, he put himself at the heart of the Everest universe for that year's attempts. This morning that universe was about to explode spectacularly.

I started moving through the relatively easy terrain at the bottom of the route, feeling very good. There were no indications that I would struggle. For the first forty minutes or so, I kept tight to the heels of David Bradley, who was directly in front of me. One thing I picked up on straight away was how quiet the Icefall was. Not many teams had decided to head up that day, most electing for a rest day at Base Camp. The teams located around our camp had already moved up to the higher camps the day earlier. This consisted of most of the Madison Mountaineering contingency, Adventure Consultants and the large G200 Gurkha team. Our central area of Base Camp had been serenely peaceful as we wove our way through it an hour earlier.

By early morning a thick, low mist began to fill the Icefall, creating an eerie atmosphere. Three days earlier, the ice had looked spectacular against the clearest blue high-altitude sky. Today it looked menacing and forbidding. Every step up took a monumental effort, and my lungs screamed. Just walking around Base Camp was tough, but up here it was another level completely. Every ounce of effort hurt. As the group began to naturally spread out, Alex and I remained at the back of the line. Alex was also feeling the full effects of the altitude; we had both performed much better a few days ago, but today for some reason we were struggling.

I inched slowly up the mountain, my pace sluggish. My mind wandered to the Al Pacino movie *Any Given Sunday,* about an American Football team. There is a scene in which Al Pacino's character is giving his team a half-time berating. He gives the players a speech about life being a game of inches. I knew most of it by heart so began reciting it to myself as I painfully plodded on.

We are in hell right now, gentlemen, believe me, and we can stay here and get the shit kicked out of us or we can climb out of hell, one inch at a time. On this team, we fight for that inch. On this team, we tear ourselves and everyone around us to pieces for that inch. We claw with our finger nails for that inch. Cause we know when we add up all those inches, that's going to make the fucking difference between winning and losing, between living and dying…

It gave me a boost as I moved up the rope. The ladders to cross lower down in the Icefall had been fairly straightforward, most about five or so rungs in length. I never found the exposure beneath my feet unduly scary, as I was so wrapped up in concentration – carefully placing my feet on each rung in my heavy boots and crampons. I rounded one large serac that leaned menacingly, appearing as though it would topple at any moment, obliterating any unfortunate climber in its path. I hurried around it as best I could, as I had done a few days earlier. I heard it creak and groan as I quickly got out of its way. This extra effort meant I had to take a moment to rest, in an area I hoped would be safe.

By now the rest of my team were out of sight. Rob Casserley and his team caught up and went past Alex and me. Rob enquired how we were both doing. Rob, MK and Dan had been very strong so far – as I had found out first hand – and even here in the Icefall they went past without so much as a break of stride. Even Tom, the BBC reporter, appeared to be very strong.

With his group moving away into the mist, Rob suddenly climbed back down to our position to make absolutely sure we were OK.

"I'm fine," I shot back. "Just having a bad day in the office, but I'll be fine."

Alex responded with something similar. Rob then practically ran back up on the front points of his crampons to join his team. *Unbelievable,* I remember thinking, envious of how natural Rob was at altitude. You don't reach the summit of Everest eight times without being supremely fit and built for the mountains. Rob certainly was that.

We reached the point where we had turned back days earlier and I welcomed the break as I removed my pack and slumped into the snow. Tim crackled into life on the VHF radio I was carrying.

"Good, good," he replied to our altitude check. "Just keep coming, you're almost there."

Resting in the snow allowed my mind to wander and I immediately thought back to 2014. The Sherpas who were killed in the Icefall had also been sat resting, with packs off. A shudder ran down my spine. I rose to my feet and began moving again, worried about the possibility of something toppling down on us. For most of the morning visibility had been virtually zero. Even if something did start to topple, we would be able to hear it – but we certainly wouldn't see it, until it was too late. '*Life is a game of inches*' became my mantra, and I recalled the entire scene over and over as I moved further up the route.

I was extremely tired by the time we hit a bottleneck at a ladder. A blind Korean climber and his team understandably took a long time to make the simple crossing. Alex and I had to patiently wait our turn before being allowed to cross. We quickly moved past them, clipping back in to the safety of the fixed rope. Due to my tiredness, and the fact that everything was cloaked in a thick fog, I had taken very few photos. I only had my iPhone and had taken one shot early in the morning just as I began climbing, but that was it. Alex had moved ahead at one point, and I was waiting for two descending climbers to come down a short vertical ladder, so I could cross a narrow snow bridge and make my way up the ladder in turn. I took my phone out and snapped a shot of one of the climbers coming down.

A short while later I caught back up to Alex, who had waited for me to reappear at the top of the ladder.

"Man this is so tough," I said between gasping breaths.

"Yeah, a lot tougher than I expected it be."

"Not far to go now." But I was trying to convince myself more than him.

At another ladder crossing – they increased in frequency towards the top of the route – Tim called on the radio again, asking where we were. With no obvious visual reference to call on, all I could do was give the altitude that was showing on my watch.

The Icefall – 25th April 2015, 11.15am

I knew that we couldn't be far from reaching the safety of Camp One, but at each corner we turned and serac we moved past, another ladder would come into view – each far steeper than any we had encountered earlier. We found Tim at the top of one of these ladders. He had held back from the rest of the team and was waiting for Alex and me.

"How you doing, guys?"

"Could be better," I grumbled back, totally shattered and longing for the respite that Camp One would bring.

"Look, we haven't got far to go now."

He told Alex to go ahead as I took my pack off, so I could get to my water bottle. I took several huge gulps and applied some lip balm. Even through a thick layer of cloud I could feel the skin on my lips burning.

As we moved off together, we said very little. I plodded on slowly as I had done all morning. "Take your time, there is no rush," I heard from behind. I didn't know whether he was being sarcastic or serious.

We approached the first of the two steepest ladders on the entire route up to Camp One. Lashed end to end up a steep ice cliff, three ladders barred entry to the last but one ice shelf before the Icefall gave way to the gentler sloping start of the Western Cwm. I had dreamed about this moment for years, imagining what it would be like to take those final steps to the top of the Icefall. I had imagined emerging into a valley that had bewitched climbers for years with its beauty. As I forced myself forward towards that moment, all I could feel were my tired legs refusing to move, and my head full of the fear of failure. This was not what I had in mind.

We reached the bottom of the final ladder, and I summoned all my energy to scale it. Towards the top, the grip in my hands went slack and I struggled to hold onto the last few ice-slick rungs.

I made it to the top, just. Alex was no longer visible, having moved off into the distance some 30m ahead. Everywhere I looked was a sea of white and grey. Nothing was discernible. The impressive West Ridge of Everest, which was directly in front, was completely obscured from view. I waited for Tim to clamber up the ladder so we could continue the final leg of the journey into camp. I had started out that morning at 5.30am and it was now almost midday. It had taken me over six hours to climb through the Icefall – not terrible for my first time, but below average at best. Rob Casserley had mentioned that he could go from Base Camp to Camp Two in just under four hours. I was well off that mark, and knew it.

Tim and I both clipped back in to the safety rope after moving away from the cliff edge, and slowly began the final push to Camp One on less steep terrain. I am not sure which of us felt it first, but we both simultaneously halted in our tracks.

"Stop," Tim uttered.

We both stood motionless. This wasn't good, standing as we were on a large flat shelf, surrounded by crevasses. My first thought was that the whole area was about to collapse from under our feet. I could hear cracks all around, booming from every direction. Then I felt the ground moving beneath my boots. I knew this was serious, but in my tired state I didn't fully grasp our predicament.

Tim jolted me back to reality. "We need to move or we are screwed." I could hear the worry in his shout.

"Move – where to? I am exhausted."

Looking around, there was nothing we could do. We were at the full mercy of whatever the mountain was about to throw at us. My mind became a blur of emotions as it dawned on me that I could be about to die. Not many climbers have survived collapses in the Icefall. Just when I had almost given in to my fate, the ground stopped moving as suddenly as it had begun.

I really believed that we had just experienced an isolated incident confined to our part of the glacier. Thinking I had just had a lucky escape, I was about to say to Tim that we should get the hell out of there when I began to hear a sound I had heard a hundred times before in the Himalayan mountains. There was no doubt in my mind what I was listening to. It was the unmistakable sound of an avalanche hurtling down the mountain.

Once again we stood rooted to the spot. With the visibility as bad as it was, neither Tim nor I had any idea where it was coming from. The sound was all around, and increased in loudness until it was almost on top of us. For the second time in a matter of minutes, I once again became convinced I was about to die. I also knew that whatever was happening on the mountain was far bigger than just a serac collapse.

And then it hit. The powerful air blast, which seemed to last for several seconds, knocked me off my feet and down onto all fours. Convinced I was about to be buried by a powerful avalanche, I began to think of everyone back home, in particular Tamara, the girls, Aaron, and my mam. Intense guilt swept over me. I had convinced Tamara that this wasn't going to happen. I told her that what had happened on Everest in 2014, sad as it was, was an unprecedented incident and unlikely to occur again. As I crouched on all fours, peering down into a crevasse, all I could think was what an idiot I had been. How could I do this to my family? I was about to leave Tamara a widow, plus the girls and Aaron fatherless, and all because of my insatiable appetite to stand on a tiny piece of our planet 8,850m high. In what I thought was the moment of my death, it no longer made any sense.

Powder snow began to rain down on us both, pinning us to the ice. I began to cough and splutter and hyperventilate – possibly the body's natural defence mechanism when thinking that it is about to shut down. I faced away from the torrent of snow. At first I thought this was the front end of a much larger avalanche about to crash down on us, but when the snow began to dissipate after thirty seconds or so, I began once more to think of survival.

Once it had stopped, the reverberations of the avalanche gently drifted out. I stood up and began to brush myself down. Every bit of me was covered in a crust of snow. I looked at Tim as he slowly rose to his feet and did the same. We had both been extremely lucky. Either the avalanche had stopped short, or it had shot straight overhead. Either way, I didn't care. All that mattered was that I was still alive and I was still breathing.

"I am done with the mountain," I muttered to Tim, shocked and disoriented in the aftermath.

"Give it a few days before making any rash decisions," was Tim's response.

After composing ourselves we continued on our way upward. It seemed like the only thing to do. Unsure whether Alex and the rest of our team had survived, my mind became numb with fear that they hadn't. The mountain guide in Tim kicked into full gear as he moved out in front of me, treading carefully, checking that the ground we were stepping on was solid. With a new layer of snow covering everything, crevasses were hidden and it would have been easy to step into one, thinking it was solid ground. We continued in this manner for fifteen minutes or so before Tim's radio burst into life. Aeneas, who had been with David Bradley at the time the avalanche hit, asked if we were OK. Tim replied that we were fine and would be at camp soon. I trudged on in a complete state of shock until a few figures emerged in the distance. It was David and Aeneas, who looked as shell-shocked as I felt.

Reeling from all we had just experienced, we gave each other a tap on the back, glad that we were all still here. Alex was OK too, Aeneas informed us. A few minutes later Rob and Rolfe arrived. They had selflessly left Camp One to look for those of us who still hadn't reached the tents, and much to their relief they found us all together.

"My God, guys," Rob said, "I thought you were all gone."

The emotions got the better of one or two of us, and tears filled my eyes as Rob put his arm around my shoulder.

"Did you feel the ground moving?" Rolfe asked.

"Yeah, what the hell was that?" I said.

"Earthquake," Rob said. "A big one at that."

I couldn't believe what I was hearing. Of all the reasons why I might not be able to climb this mountain, an earthquake didn't even cross my mind. We stood chatting for a few seconds before Tim motioned that we should get to the tents of Camp One, where we could regroup and hopefully get further news from Base Camp. Upon reaching our tents, there was more rejoicing with the rest of Rob's team, who had already reached Camp One when the earthquake struck. Everybody looked stunned. Adventure Consultants and the Gurkha team had already been at Camp One for a night, so there were a lot of climbers up there when we all emerged through the thick mist.

Aftershocks would surely follow the main earthquake. The thin nylon wall of a tent would offer no protection should any of these aftershocks trigger further avalanches. Tim showed David and me to a tent, where he told us to get in and start melting snow for a drink. As I did, I heard Rob directly outside my tent speaking on the radio, trying to get hold of Henry down at Base Camp.

"Henry, come in over, this is Rob at Camp One. Are you OK? Over." He repeated it one more time before Henry responded.

I struggled to pick up on all the words Henry said, but I heard the ones that counted: "Total destruction, Base Camp completely destroyed and multiple fatalities."

If I didn't already realise just how grim the situation truly was, I did now. Knowing that people had just died beneath my very feet down at Base Camp was as serious as this thing could get. I felt sick to my stomach. As I struggled to light the gas stove to melt snow, the situation we were now all a part of slowly sank in. Thousands of miles away back home, Tamara would be waking up to the news that there had been an earthquake in Nepal, with loss of life on Everest. She would undoubtedly panic, as would all my loved ones and friends. Stuck as I was at Camp One on the side of Everest, there was nothing I could do to quell that panic. Tamara was just receiving the news in the worst way imaginable.

It was the night before; little did I know the events that would come to pass. I was attending a ball at a local school. My aunt was babysitting and staying the night. "Go out," she said. "Enjoy yourself," she said. "Let your hair down," she said. I had been feeling pretty tense and anxious, so 'Why not?' I thought.

A couple of cocktails later and I ended up in a little bit of a heated debate with one of Ellis's friends. After the tragic events that took place during the 2014 season, I told Ellis that I didn't want him to go back. How could he risk his life when he had young children? They needed their father and I was adamant he should not go again. I think I even said at one point: "If you go, I will divorce you!" Ellis's friend wanted to discuss this and why I had let him go. Let him go! As if it was ever in my control.

This then led to a few more drinks; needless to say I was feeling rather tipsy.

The following morning – the morning of the 25th April – I was in a delicate state. My aunt laughed, adding that it was self inflicted, when I received a phone call from Alex's mum Debbie. 'Strange for her to be phoning so early,' I thought. The time was a little after 7.00am.

She had been a fabulous confidant so far; we were helping each other, discussing our hopes for Ellis and Alex, but also our fears. Debbie was in contact with Alex via a satphone. Ellis and I did not have this luxury. Each time she heard from Alex, she asked about Ellis and then contacted me.

With a cold flannel across my forehead, I laid on the couch to answer the call. At first I was confused. Debbie was talking about not worrying, and they were OK at Camp One. I had not seen the news and had no knowledge of the horrific events that were unfolding in Nepal. I sat up, giving my full attention to what Debbie was saying. She explained about the earthquake and the little information she knew at that point. I called Ellis's mum and told her what I had learned. I told her what we always said to each other: "No news is good news," and to go about her day as normal. I was here if she wanted to come over.

I turned on the TV and was confronted with awful images coming out of Nepal, with the death toll increasing by the minute. I felt sick – such devastation and those poor people. My thoughts then turned back to Ellis. There was no mention of Everest. What had happened there? What was going on? Was he safe? I had so many questions.

As the afternoon wore on, more information reached us up at Camp One. The earthquake had not only destroyed our tents down at Base Camp, but had also destroyed large parts of Kathmandu, where the death toll ran into thousands. Over our radios, Henry told us that three of our own support team had been killed: Pasang Temba, the Camp Two cook; Kumar, the jovial kitchen hand who always brought our meals to the table with a smile; and Tenzing, one of our climbing Sherpas. I simply couldn't comprehend what I was hearing.

I logged on to Twitter, trying to see if there was anything trending specifically about Everest. People were indeed tweeting about Everest. 'Deaths at Base Camp' and 'aftershocks'. What turned me cold was a tweet that stated Camp One had been wiped out by aftershocks. Camp One was gone. I kept saying to myself: "Debbie has spoken to them, they are OK," but I also knew they were at Camp One and, according to Twitter, Camp One was gone

For most of that first day up on the mountain, I remained inside my tent with David. Outside was a hive of activity, with climbers frantically trying to find out more about the situation as it unfolded. It was clear that this was a huge incident with global implications.

The tents at Camp One were lined up next to one another in a row. The tent I occupied with David was at one end, and the closest to the huge ice wall of Nuptse. If an avalanche was going to hit Camp One, chances were that it would come from the West Shoulder of Everest, at the opposite side to the glacier. This did nothing to make me feel any more reassured. As recently at 2012, Camp One had taken a direct hit from an avalanche, which originated from Nuptse. It destroyed many of the tents. One Sherpa was swept into a crevasse but fortunately was rescued, suffering no more than a few broken ribs. Luckily, most of the climbers were further up the mountain and not in the tents when the avalanche hit.

Knowing that an avalanche could hit this camp was a sombre thought. Even without the threat of aftershocks, Camp One wasn't a good place to be stranded. With the ever-present threat of a shock hitting, it was almost suicidal being here. We all sensed it, which added to the stress and anxiety.

Talk outside the tent switched to the possibility of being able to climb back down the Icefall the following morning. I remember thinking: *The following morning, for God's sake! Does that mean we have to stay up here tonight?* My optimism plummeted even further at that moment in time. We all hunkered down in our tents, unsure just what was going to happen. Rumours began to circulate that helicopters would be needed to evacuate us all off the mountain. Through that long, dark night, the helicopters did not come. Inside our tent, nerves were frayed to the wire. Every distant roar would have me and David sitting bolt upright, fearing the worst. Was this the one that was finally going to wipe us out?

In the next tent to ours, Rob Casserley spoke gently to his wife MK: "I think we are done with Everest, my love." Like me, Rob and MK had both been there twelve months earlier, and were once more caught up in disaster on the slopes of the mountain. In 2014 they became involved in the rescue effort in the Icefall after the deadly avalanche. In an ironic twist of fate, they were themselves now waiting to be rescued at the top of the Icefall.

I didn't get a wink of sleep that first night at Camp One. Too many thoughts running through my mind prevented my brain from shutting down. Had the avalanche that brushed past us been the one that had destroyed Base Camp? What would we find if we made it back down there? What would the rest of the valley be like? These questions, and more like them, raced through my confused mind.

The following hours were a bit of a blur. The phone kept ringing with both family and friends asking if Ellis was OK and news reporters wanting a comment. I kept saying, "Phone my mobile so the landline is free," or "No comment, I want to keep the line free." The Sun newspaper even came to the house; I answered the door with girls in tow, as they thought it was their friend calling to play. The reporter was asking how we were and how the children were taking the news. I repeated no comment and said the children were not aware of the situation. This of course led to lots of questions from the girls, I explained what had happened in Nepal, but said it was not near Everest and Daddy was fine.

The sun nudged out from above Lhotse early the next morning, but it brought no relief. Although grateful to still be alive, until I was down off the mountain, I couldn't allow myself to relax. For the first time since arriving at the tents the previous day, the view ahead up the Western Cwm showed itself in all its glory. The picture postcard view I had seen so many times on a computer screen, or in the glossy pages of a book, looked so enticing. Rob commented on how much snow was on the Lhotse face this year – more than he could recall seeing in a long time. It didn't matter any more. It was a Lhotse face we wouldn't get to tread on. The expedition was over. How could any team continue in these conditions?

The view up the Western Cwm – April 26th

Helicopters began to arrive, ferrying climbers down the mountain. The sound of the Fishtail high-altitude helicopter became a constant roar in the morning sky. Since we arrived, the expedition leaders from each team had met every few hours to discuss the situation. Climbing back through the Icefall was the number-one topic, but as yet no decision had been made. Damian Benagas, one half of Benegas Brothers Expeditions, had been behind me with a team of clients in the

Icefall the day we had climbed up. A very strong and accomplished climber and guide, he volunteered to go back into the Icefall to assess its condition. We would sit and wait. As climbers began to leave two at a time in the back of the stripped-out helicopter, my mood went from doom and gloom to excitement at the prospect that we may get out of this.

A decision was made to evacuate my tent companion, David Bradley, on one of the first choppers to leave that morning with members of Adventure Consultants. Before returning to Everest that year, David had an operation to have a coronary stent fitted. As a result, he needed to take Clopidogrel medication daily to prevent the blood from clotting. However, his medication was down at Base Camp. Not wanting to take any chances with his health, he was flown down at the first opportunity.

This dampened my recently renewed good mood, as I now had no tent companion. As far as I knew, we could be stuck up there for days, and with no one to converse with through the long nights, the prospect filled me with dread. I didn't want to die alone, should an avalanche hit.

Family came to the house so we were all together and not alone. The hardest part was trying not to convey my fear to Lara and Isla. I did not want them to be frightened and think their dad was in harm's way or even dead. Outwardly smiling and playing games, inwardly crying and feeling sick.

Later that day the weather clagged in again, and the snow began to fall once more. The conditions became eerily similar to the day we had climbed up through the Icefall. Lying in my tent, I stared at my feet in my high-altitude boots poking out in the vestibule area. I took a photo with my phone. The tedium of the moment is plainly evident when I look back at the image.

Waiting to be rescued at Camp One

The helicopter continued with its heroic mission of picking up two climbers at a time. I envied those rescued.

Just as I relaxed my mind and shut my eyes, I once more felt an uneasy sensation beneath my body. I looked at the tent zipper, which began to flap violently. "Everybody in!" I heard being shouted outside. The whole mountain started to shake. Staying in my tent with the zip shut was the last thing I wanted to do. I sprang from the tent fearing that this may be it. Thick cloud completely obscured the wall of Nuptse, but there was no mistaking the roar of an inevitable avalanche. I didn't know where to go. I just knew I didn't want to be on my own.

I dived towards the entrance of Rob and MK's tent, next to mine, and just crouched down next to it. If I was going to die, at least I would almost be with others. I heard Tim shout out from his tent: "One above, one below," a clear reference to the avalanches that were thundering down all around. I shut my eyes tight and prayed. I took the puja string from around my neck and placed it to my lips. "Please, not now," I quietly said. I wasn't the most religious of people, but right at that moment I prayed hard to my god to hear my prayer – a god I hoped would take pity on us all, trapped on Mount Everest. I gripped tightly to the outside of the tent. Seconds later there was quiet once more. The avalanches released by the largest aftershock so far had thankfully missed us, causing no more damage than a light dusting of snow to each tent. However, I could take no more. I was a nervous wreck. I didn't want to be in my tent on my own for one second longer. I went across to Ingo and Dan's tent and asked if they would mind if I joined them, telling Ingo I couldn't bear being inside my tent on my own with this going on. He warmly welcomed me in, as I knew he would.

I spent the rest of the afternoon sharing the cramped tent space with Ingo and Dan. Neither protested, understanding the emotions we were all experiencing. The last time I shared a tent with Dan had been at Island Peak Base Camp, now a distant memory. This occasion was very different. We both spoke about how our families must be feeling back home. Like me, Dan had young children, and like Tamara, Dan's wife would have been equally as worried. Alex was the only member of our team who had a satphone, and upon arriving at Camp One, he allowed us all to make a brief call home to tell our families that we were OK. I got through to Tamara, but I don't think she heard me. I could hear her repeatedly say: 'Ellis, is that you? Hello, hello!" before the line disconnected.

That Sunday afternoon in the tent with Ingo and Dan, I got another chance to try again. Alex once more let us all make a short call home, but with a dwindling battery, we promised we would be quick. Dan spoke to his wife first. The relief and elation at being able to speak with her was evident in his voice, which began to break with the raw emotion of it all. I then got my turn.

What seemed like days later, an important call arrived. As soon as I heard Ellis's voice I started to cry. I now know how I react to pure relief – I cry. Ellis kept saying "I'm OK, don't cry," but I just couldn't help myself. He only spoke briefly to say he had been hit by an avalanche but was OK and had made it to Camp One. They were waiting to be evacuated out as there was no longer a safe route down.

I hoped my conversation with Tamara had reassured her that I was OK. I wasn't aware how much she knew, but the wider story must have been world news. The earthquake in Nepal dominated the headlines. Just a few rich climbers on Everest, satisfying over-inflated egos, – that's how I fully expected the media to report on us. In the pecking order of those most in need, I anticipated us to be at the bottom of the list. We had got ourselves into this mess by climbing Everest, therefore we could jolly well get ourselves out of it. I wouldn't know the full story until a few days later.

In the immediate aftermath of the aftershock, my thoughts shifted to Damian Benegas, who was down in the Icefall when the mountain moved again. Luckily, he had survived once more and made it back to Camp One. "One thing is for sure," he said in a meeting of the leaders, "we won't be climbing back down the Icefall." Most of the route had been destroyed in the initial earthquake and resulting avalanches. What was left intact had now been taken out by the secondary quake.

Our only way out of this would be in the back of that Fishtail helicopter. This brought some comfort and relief, as I didn't want to go anywhere near the Icefall after my experience the last time I was in it.

That afternoon Rob tried tirelessly on the radio to get hold of Bhola, our representative from Himalayan Guides, who was down at Base Camp dealing with a million issues. They had not only sorted out our expedition logistics, but also those of Adventure Consultants and Madison Mountaineering. It must have been a stressful time for all concerned, especially having to contend with the deaths of three staff members from our own team, as well as a fatality within the Madison team. Eventually, Rob managed to get through, and gave us the news we had been praying for: the helicopter would pick us all up and take us down to Base Camp. I became ecstatic at the news.

"The only thing is," Rob added, "it won't be until tomorrow morning now."

I instantly became deflated. The afternoon cloud had moved up the Icefall to our position, which meant it was now too dangerous for the pilot to continue flying. It was great news that we were getting out of there, but I would have to endure one more night before our rescue. The thought of it filled me with fear.

Damian Benegas wandered across to our large group, stood outside chatting and enquired if we could spare a gas canister. Without thinking, I offered him mine. I had planned to share an evening dinner with Ingo and Dan and therefore wouldn't need my full canister. It was the least I could do after the guy had been down into the jaws of the Icefall. But Tim scolded me.

"We are going down tomorrow," I said. "I won't need it."

"Yes, but you don't know that. Do not take anything for granted up here." He was right, of course. I hoped it wouldn't come back to bite me.

With supplies diminishing, we only had enough food to last one more night. We spoke about moving further up the mountain to Camp Two, where we would have fresh food and supplies, but no one was particularly keen on that idea. The helicopter the next morning would be our salvation. I just needed to get through the longest night of my life first.

Camp One before the longest night

I stayed with Ingo and Dan as long as I could. When I knew I was beginning to outstay my welcome, I went back to the loneliness of my own tent. As the temperature plummeted, I pulled my sleeping bag tight around my neck. *Just one more night and you are out of here,* I began to tell myself. My senses sharpened to every noise outside the tent. I became convinced I could feel the ground beneath me start to move on several occasions, but luckily this didn't come to pass. As the night wore on, my restlessness increased. I kept looking at the time on my watch, praying for the morning to put me out of this misery. To calm myself down, I began to think about being back at home. I longed to hold my two girls again, and I focused on that as I imagined their smiles. I then imagined Tamara saying: "I bloody well told you so." This made me chuckle for the first time in days.

As the night's doom and darkness gave way to the morning light, I must have finally drifted off to sleep. The next thing I remember was the unmistakable swoosh of a helicopter blade slicing through the thin air. "Shit!" I said, as I scrambled out of my sleeping bag and began to squash everything into my pack. I checked the time: it was only 8.40am. *Phew! What a relief,* I thought. The day before, Rob had informed me that Alex and I would be on the third flight down that morning, so to be at the makeshift landing pad at the top of the Icefall for 9.30am. I calmed slightly, until Rob poked his head in the door of my tent.

"Ellis," he shouted, "get up to the pad immediately, you are out of here."

Oh shit, here we go again.

I got dressed as quickly as I could and threw my pack on. I didn't even have time to speak to anyone. As I left, Tim gave me a two-man tent to take down with me. As we didn't know what to expect at Base Camp, we all had to carry a tent down, in case we needed one. None of us knew what we were flying down to. We knew it was a scene of complete destruction, as Henry had told us so over the radio. I was about to discover just what that meant.

Getting to where the helicopter would pick us up was tiring work. I had watched for the last two days as climbers had left in their droves, wondering when it would be my turn. I had to keep stopping every few metres to catch my breath. I was frantic to get there, believing I might miss my spot. When Alex and I finally made it, we joined the back of a line of several climbers, all waiting for their short flight down. A few minutes later, the helicopter landed and Rob ushered us forward. He physically hurled us both inside, his instructions drowned out by the rush and noise of the blades sweeping a few feet overhead. After our packs and the tents were thrown in, we were up and off down. The pain of the climb up a few days earlier vanished beneath us in minutes. I looked at Alex and shook my head in disbelief. I then patted him on the shoulder.

"We couldn't have done any more," I said. "It's just not meant to be."

A few minutes later, the helicopter touched down at the far side of Base Camp, the point farthest away from our tents. We quickly exited the helicopter and the pilot pulled back on the stick and was away once more, heading back up the mountain. Then, what should have been relief at being rescued instantly turned to horror as the full scale of the destruction became evident.

Everywhere I looked I could see devastation on an unimaginable scale. What the hell had hit this place? It looked like one of those towns that had been flattened by a tornado, except this was no twister. The avalanche had torn through camp with a force so powerful that nothing in its path would have stood a chance.

One of the first people I saw was Tom, the BBC reporter, who was busy with his camera snapping pictures of all the carnage. All we could do was look at one another in horror. I slowly moved through the camp, which a few days earlier had been alive with the buzz and hope of a few hundred climbers. Now it was like moving through a derelict ghost town, most of its occupants long gone. A couple of grosbeaks, a bird native to that part of Nepal, sat perched on a rock eyeing me with curiosity as I shuffled past, barely able to lift my feet. My scant reserves of energy had been knocked out of me with the dash up to the landing pad, and now with the trudge back to the site of our tents. The weight in my pack pulled me back, which I counterbalanced with the tent I carried out front in my arms. As I reached the point where I thought our tents should have been, I heard a voice shouting out.

"Are you OK? Stay there."

I looked up to see one of the Nepali officers from the Gurkha team coming to my aid. He took the tent and pack from me, gave me a hot drink and told me to follow him. Five minutes later I slumped to the ground at the site of the G200 Gurkha Base Camp. They had managed to partially assemble their mess tent, where they had a small working kitchen distributing noodles and tea. I was given a hot bowl of noodles as soon as I collapsed onto the glacier.

I sat and tried to shovel a spoonful of noodles into my mouth, but my appetite once again let me down. A few Gurkhas, who had witnessed and survived the avalanche, explained the full horror of what had occurred to me.

All the death and damage wasn't caused by an avalanche that came down from Everest, but by an avalanche released from the main ridge connecting Pumori and Lingtren, the two peaks directly opposite Everest and the Icefall. When the ground began to move, most people at Base Camp instinctively looked towards Everest, where the Icefall funnelled avalanches from above. Fearing the worst for those of us on our way through the Icefall, it was almost too late to react when a thousand tons of snow and rock smashed through camp from the opposite side to where they were looking. People had no time to react. The full staggering horror of it all shook me to my core.

Although I had just lived through the two darkest days of my life to date, it was nothing compared to what those at Base Camp had endured. It was a complete role reversal of the previous year. In 2014, climbers and support staff reacted in horror to the huge loss of life up in the Icefall. This year, those of us who had been in the Icefall were now reacting with that same horror to the devastating loss of life down at Base Camp.

Henry, and the rest of our team who survived, had been incredibly lucky. Henry nursed a broken hand, a paper cut compared to some of the horrific injuries suffered by others. As I would later learn, at least twenty-two people lost their lives on this day, the darkest and deadliest day in the mountain's history. Ten of them were Nepali, further adding to the suffering caused in 2014, when sixteen had been killed.

When I arrived at what had been our own camp, I was moved to the point of tears. I didn't want to know the specifics of how they died, but Pasang Temba Sherpa, Kumar Rai and Tenzing Tengien Bhote had all been tragically killed. Henry,

Kame (our expedition sirdar) and the rest of our team had to deal with the immediate aftermath. This must have been extremely harrowing. I didn't push Henry on the specifics. The man was clearly traumatised.

I spoke with David Bradley, who had spent the night there after getting the helicopter down the previous morning. He looked unnerved and edgy as he described how every sound outside had the whole camp on tenterhooks. I could tell by his voice that he didn't want to stay there any longer than necessary.

As more of the team began to emerge from Camp One, hardly anyone spoke; all were lost in their own worlds. Although all of our tents were smashed to a pulp, most of our kit was recoverable. I had placed most of my belongings in a duffel bag, which I had left in the vestibule area of my tent. I found my duffel intact by the side of a small glacial pond. The contents were barely touched. Others did not fare so well. The BBC communications tent was obliterated and with it thousands of pounds' worth of BBC technology. Tom looked incredulous as he sifted through the wreckage of what only days earlier had been his connection hub to the outside world, where he had been able to send back video reports on the Gurkha team and Base Camp. It was the last footage taken of our camp intact.

With nothing to do other than try to retrieve our belongings – what was left of them – we spent a few hours frantically digging and chipping away at the ice which now concealed our tents. I found my small action camera encased in a block of ice. Convinced it wouldn't work, I chipped off the ice and flung it into my pack. Tim had lost a large amount of cash from one of his barrels and he was desperate to try to find it.

Had Rob and MK been in their tent, they would have been crushed to death by the large boulder now wedged firmly in the middle of it – or what was left of it. Flaps of yellow nylon fluttered away from underneath. The whole scene was totally catastrophic. It felt like a morgue and I was keen to leave at the first opportunity. I gave my ice axe to Jo Bradshaw so she could set to work on trying to recover her belongings.

Dan was also keen to leave Base Camp. Along with David, the three of us looked into the possibility of chartering a helicopter back to Lukla. I couldn't face the trek out and wanted to return to my family as soon as I could. I was done with Everest.

A mountain that had been a driving force for most of my adult life, and a scene of joy and elation after reaching Base Camp for the first time fifteen years earlier, had for the past two years become a place of heartache and tragedy. I wanted to turn my back on Everest and walk away for good. I felt nothing but contempt staring up at the Icefall. I was grateful I had survived when so many hadn't, but felt bitter at the shattered conclusion to my dream. Lukla and the flight to Kathmandu couldn't come soon enough.

Dan and I trudged wearily to the helipad at the far side of Base Camp. This part of Base Camp had been spared the full ferocity of the avalanche and was largely intact. We found Bhola, who was no doubt busy dealing with several other issues. As we enquired into the possibility of getting a helicopter down to Lukla, I noticed a body on the ground wrapped in a blue tarpaulin. Not knowing who the poor individual was, and the sheer terror they must have felt when a wall of snow came towards them, I offered up a silent prayer. That could so easily have been any one of us.

Bhola told us to gather our belongings and be at the landing site at the other end of Base Camp in one hour. I rushed back as fast I could and told David he needed to be ready to go soon.

As well as my backpack, I had two large duffel bags, which I struggled to carry to the crest of the hill where the helicopter would land. Ingo saw me struggling and came straight over. He lifted both my duffel bags onto his shoulder and, without saying a word, carried them straight to the top of the hill for me. He didn't need to do that, but that's the type of person he is: always the first to offer help when needed.

The helicopter was due to land, but we were still waiting twenty minutes later. Another twenty minutes and there was still no sign of the helicopter. Bhola radioed ahead to find out where it was. He reported to us that the pilot may have grounded for the night due to the clouds rolling in. We could wait and see, or come back at first light and be one of the first out. Dan gave up and begrudgingly made his way back towards our makeshift camp for the night. David and I decided to leave and trek down to Gorak Shep, where Bhola said the pilot could collect us in the morning. I wanted to feel safe within the four walls of the lodge at Gorak Shep, should another quake or large aftershock hit. It was preferential to being inside a tent.

As we left, I looked back across at the Icefall. I took one last photo, cursing that for the second year in succession the mountain would remain unclimbed. Further down the glacier the summit of Everest appeared, its entire southern face illuminated by a brilliant setting sun. It looked stunning. As I turned my back on the mountain one last time, I wondered if I would ever return. This time, I very much doubted it.

Further down the path towards Gorak Shep, we approached a climber who was also heading down, but appeared to be in no rush. As we got nearer he looked familiar to me. I realised it was Alan Arnette, the climber from Colorado in the US who, when not climbing mountains, reported on other people climbing mountains. Thinking back to when he had interviewed me in 2014, I said a quick hello. He didn't seem to be in any kind of mood to communicate – understandable given the circumstances. Alan had been part of the Madison Mountaineering team, whose team doctor was killed when the avalanche swept through Base Camp. At just twenty-eight years old, Eve Girawong had her whole life to live, yet she was killed – ironically by living her life to the full on an Everest expedition. I hadn't met her, yet she was in my thoughts as I left Base Camp far behind.

It felt good to be back on the terra firma of a solid lodge floor, and the lodge was surprisingly busy in light of what had happened just days earlier. I expected everyone to be at Lukla, in a mad scramble to escape the hills. Yet tourists sat around idly chatting and laughing as if nothing had happened. The Madison team had also made it down to the lodge, with some hoping to be picked up and flown out the following morning. As well as Alan Arnette, I recognised another two climbers in the team. Randall and Hayley Ercanbrack were a US father and daughter who had hopes of summiting together. Randall was struck down with pulmonary edema up at Camp Two and was evacuated down to Base Camp after the earthquake hit. They were reunited down in Base Camp after Hayley and the rest of the Madison team walked down from Camp Two to Camp One to board the rescue helicopters.

I slept reasonably well that first night back in the lodge. Every unfamiliar sound outside still had me alert and jumpy though. (This would continue for the first few weeks back home.) The next morning, we all congregated in the lodge dining area, hopeful that we would soon be sat in the back of a helicopter on its way down to Lukla. The Madison group were a friendly enough bunch, but they could be loud. So for the rest of that morning David and I spent time outside the lodge, where it was quieter. We were both still in a state of shock. Just three days ago I had been on my way to achieving the dream of a lifetime. Now I was sitting outside of the Himalayan Lodge in Gorak Shep, waiting for a helicopter to whisk me away from

Everest. The speed and finality with which my twenty-year dream had collapsed was staggering.

That day we waited and waited and it looked as though, once again, no helicopter would be coming for us. Finally, the *whoosh whoosh* sound of our ride out got nearer and nearer from up the valley. At last, we were on our way. Or so we thought! The pilot told us he would drop us at Pheriche and come back for us, as he had to go back up to Base Camp to pick up another couple of passengers. Hayley and her father Randall also shared the short ride down to Pheriche.

We disembarked and found the nearest lodge. Thirty minutes later the helicopter was back. I was pretty sure one of those two passengers would be Dan. What I wasn't expecting, was another Dan to be on board.

Daniel Fredinburg was a thirty-three-year-old Google executive from the US who had also been on Everest the previous year. As well as working for Google, Daniel was a keen climate activist, and on the 24th April 2015 he had unfurled a flag on the summit of Kala Patthar for a charity he had co-founded, Save the Ice. The following day he suffered a fatal head wound, killing him instantly when the avalanche from Pumori smashed into Base Camp. He didn't even have time to leave his tent and make a run for it, although that would probably have been futile anyway. As Dan Wallace got out of the helicopter, he motioned to us to give him a hand. We went across and helped carry Dan Fredinburg's body out of the helicopter, and laid him on the ground. Seconds later, the helicopter was off again, perhaps continuing on its grim task of bringing more dead bodies down from the mountain.

Dan Fredinburg was respectfully wrapped in a blue tarpaulin and, as he lay on the ground of the valley floor in Pheriche, all I could think to say was: "Rest in peace, buddy." He didn't deserve this. He was there like we all were; to live life to the full. He had paid the ultimate price for the pursuit of that fullness. It could have been any one of us lying there that day on the valley floor. On Everest in 2015, only luck decided who lived and who died. Dan had been unlucky. Had he not been in his tent when the earthquake struck, he might have survived.

As we waited in one of the village lodges for our onward helicopter, I reunited with my Irish friend Paul Devaney. The last time we had seen one another, I was in a bad state after my Island Peak attempt. I was mighty relieved that he had survived. I knew at least nineteen people had been killed at Base Camp. There was a good chance Paul could have been on that list. Paul knew we had been up on the mountain, but his information on survivors was sketchy. For the second year running, like me, Paul's dream of climbing Everest had been dramatically halted.

"What more can we do to climb this mountain?" he said to me as we embraced.

"Maybe it's telling us something," I replied.

Paul and I only had a few fleeting moments together before Dan rushed into the lodge looking for David and me. "Come on, we need to go now!"

Twenty minutes after boarding the helicopter, we touched down on the landing pad next to the main runway at Lukla. As we clambered out, with the world's press staring through the perimeter fencing, we placed Dan Fredinburg's body on the ground. Within seconds a dozen Nepali policemen swarmed around the body and us. They wanted to know who he was and what had happened to him. Dan Wallace said very little, reiterating over and over that he was an American citizen who had been part of a different team to us. As our agent from Himalayan Guides found us and took us away from the melee, I noticed that a few of the policemen had opened up the tarpaulin that covered Dan Fredinburg. After they had checked for ID, he was quickly covered back up and carried away from the prying eyes of any press who may have been watching.

Lukla was, as I had expected, extremely busy. I had never seen the place so teeming with life. When the earthquake hit most tourists and trekkers aborted their trips and returned to Lukla, hoping to fly out as soon as possible. As I trudged wearily up the steps to the Paradise Lodge, I didn't know when I would be getting out of there. I figured it would be a long wait, judging by the number of people swarming all around the airport.

I couldn't face dealing with anyone. I wanted to forget about everything that had happened over the past seventy-two hours. I was able to get a message home to Tamara that I had made it to Lukla and was now waiting to get back to Kathmandu, but I did not know when that would be.

Later that day Henry arrived in the lodge with his arm in a sling. He had been incredibly lucky to emerge with just a broken hand. The shock of everything that had happened to this beautiful country was just too much to bear. Lukla had suffered minimal damage, but as I found out over the coming days, other parts of rural Nepal had been decimated, with serious loss of life.

On the 29th April 2015, the fourth day since the earthquake, I wandered around the streets and sidewalks of Lukla, trying my best to keep myself from thinking about the terrible events I had been caught up in. I went into the Starbucks coffee shop and bought a Wi-Fi card. I figured it was time to update my Facebook page. The second I connected, messages began to stream in from all around the world, with most people expressing concern for my welfare. I typed away and added the following:

This is Ellis. Thank you for all your messages of concern. I am currently in Lukla, awaiting a flight out to Kathmandu. It's been a horrendous few days since the earthquake hit. I was near the top of the Icefall when it hit, but was able to recover and continue on to Camp One, where we waited for two days before being flown off the mountain. Final pictures of the trip included. Thanks everyone for your support.

I added two pictures: one I took at Camp One, of my feet poking out of the tent just minutes before the large aftershock hit; and the second of the climber coming down a ladder in the Icefall, before the main earthquake struck. They seemed fitting.

Ellis, Brian is more than pleased to hear you are safe and sound. Brian was very worried about the Icefall and you being lifted out by helicopter, so great to hear that you are safe and heading home to your family and friends soon. Stay safe. We will catch up again on your return.
– Stephen Gittins (Brian Blessed's manager)

Glad to hear you are OK. My year 5 class has been following you for a couple of weeks as we are learning about explorers! We are in the North-East too! They were so worried about you and were so relieved you are safe :) Tomorrow they are holding a cake sale to raise funds for the relief. They are amazing children :) Thank you for helping to inspire little minds to never give up on their dreams!
– Carolyn Thompson

Namaste, condolences but at least you are alive! You will have a far bigger story to tell having experienced the last few days, but I can feel your disappointment for the outcome of not standing on the summit. I guess it's more about the journey than the destination. Keep safe.
– Jeremy Hepworth

I received hundreds of comments, all in a similar vein. It touched me greatly that all these people had been supporting me, and that they took their time to respond to my updates.

On my last full day in Lukla, I met up with Tony McMurray and his group. They were overjoyed to see me and welcomed me into their lodge with open arms. I shared a beer with Tony and we had our photo taken together. He added it to Facebook with the caption *'Great sharing a beer with a great friend and mountain hero of mine. Could have been so much different.'*

I had never been called a hero before, and despite many comments suggesting it, I was no hero. I was just a normal chap who tried to climb a mountain, but had been unlucky twice. Or lucky, depending on how you see things.

That last night in Lukla I shared a meal with Henry and Tom. David, Dan and I had been told to be ready the following morning for the flight back to Kathmandu. In a fitting end to my time in the mountains, Peter Hillary – the son of the legendary New Zealand Everest climber Sir Edmund Hillary – sat at the table next to ours. The last time I had been at this lodge, on my way to the mountain, I said hello to Jamling, the son of Tenzing Norgay. Now I was speaking with the son of the other groundbreaking pioneer who first climbed the mountain in 1953. It was a surreal but satisfying moment.

Indian Air Force at Lukla

The following day, after waiting several hours at the airport building and adjacent coffee shop, we were finally summoned down onto the runway. Along with several members of the Madison team, Himalayan Guides had chartered a plane to take us out of Lukla. They had been unable to get us out to Kathmandu due to the sheer volume of travellers waiting to leave. Instead, we took the short flight to Biratnagar, the second largest city in Nepal, on the Indian border. We looked completely misplaced as we walked across the runway to the airport building. The heat and humidity were oppressive. I glanced down at Dan's feet – he was still wearing his high-altitude climbing boots.

"I don't think you are going to need them any more," I joked.

He sniggered. "Yeah, you're probably right."

The tension of the past few days eased slightly as we sat in the airport building chatting with Hayley and her father Randall, waiting for our onward flight to Kathmandu. A few hours later, after another short flight, we touched down in a city I had grown to love. This time I didn't know what to expect. How much of Kathmandu was left standing? I wasn't meant to be back here for at least another month, yet once again fate had intervened. And this time Mother Nature herself had played a very cruel hand.

Iswari, our agent, picked us up from Tribhuvan, the international airport, and drove us back to Thamel in the heart of the tourist district. The drive was heartbreaking. Large areas of the city had been completely reduced to rubble. Open areas had been transformed into tented communities, with people sheltering under tarpaulins, too afraid to return indoors. Since the main earthquake almost a week earlier, there had been hundreds of small aftershocks, which kept the city's population on a knife-edge. Iswari informed us that he had been sleeping with his entire family in a tent in his back yard. I felt physically sick seeing all the destruction to the city. Thousands of people had just been going about their daily business when disaster struck. Why could life be so cruel? For most of the residents of Nepal's most populous city, the nightmare had only just begun. The monsoon rains were due to come, only adding to the problems. I wanted to do something to help, but knew I could do this better at home, once I had taken stock of all that had happened during my time in Nepal.

After collecting our personal belongings from the Manaslu Hotel, which was left largely untouched by the earthquake, we were immediately driven back to the airport.

Dan had been on the phone to his brother in London trying to get us on the next flight out to the UK that night. International flights were landing and departing from Kathmandu so we didn't see any reason why we couldn't leave. The city had been brought to its knees, and neither Dan, David nor I was keen to stay. Tom had also caught the flight back to Kathmandu and the BBC were keen to get their man back to London as soon as they could.

In the departures terminal, the four of us were able to buy scats for a flight to London Heathrow leaving that night. The extra cost to fly back in business class was minimal, so we all upgraded. Staring at the exquisite food menu, whilst sat in the comfortable seat of the plane, felt so wrong. I wasn't meant to be there. I should have been up on the mountain, melting snow and eating boil-in-the-bag meals, preparing my body to go higher in my goal to achieve a lifetime's quest. However, I knew that I was extremely lucky to be alive.

As nice as the flight home was, I wished the circumstances could have been so different. Through the pages of the English newspapers, I discovered more about the full terror that Nepal had endured. The village of Langtang, – which I hadn't visited personally, but which was extremely popular with trekkers – had been wiped off the map. Just one building was left standing. Hundreds of people had lost their lives there alone.

As the plane cruised at 38,000ft towards the UK, home could not come soon enough. I longed to pick up my two girls and hug them tight. As that thought filled my mind, I drifted off to sleep trying to blot out the painful memories of a dream shattered in the cruellest of ways.

Perhaps I should have paid more attention to the rest of the words from the Mary Poppins song that I had used for my campaign to return to the mountain:

Winds in the East, there's a mist coming in, like something is brewing, about to begin, Can't put my finger on what lies in store, but I feel what's to happen, all happened before.

PART NINE: THE END OF THE ROAD

New beginnings are often disguised as painful endings – Lao Tzu

O n the 25th April 2015, at approximately 11.56am Nepal Standard Time, a killer earthquake with a magnitude of 7.8 struck Nepal. The ground shook violently for 50 seconds.

Once it subsided, large areas of the country were decimated. The earthquake caused untold damage and destruction on an unimaginable scale. Its epicentre was 49 miles north-west of Kathmandu. Over 9,000 people were killed, with a further 21,000 injured.

By being where I was that day in the Icefall at the exact moment the earthquake occurred, I could not – under usual circumstances – have been on a worse section of Mount Everest. I was nearing the top of the ice after a torturous climb up from Base Camp. The Icefall had been the scene of indescribable tragedy only the year before, when I was three hours away from the mountain on my first attempt.

It had an appalling record over the years for extinguishing human life. This vertical 2,000ft labyrinth of moving ice guarded passage to the upper slopes of the mountain. Everyone hopeful of climbing Everest from Nepal by the South Col route has no choice but to ascend the Icefall a number of times during the duration of an expedition.

The Icefall on a good day was not a great place to be. On a bad day, it was an unbelievably bad and positively stupid place to be. The 25th April 2015 was to become one such day. But it wasn't the worst place to be that day.

A few thousand feet beneath my feet at Base Camp, a place I had left earlier that morning, a catastrophic avalanche of a scale never before seen on Everest caused widespread destruction.

Once the snow and rock from the avalanche had settled, twenty-two people would not be going home. Although I did not realise it at the time, I had just become part of the deadliest season in the mountain's history for the second year running, with the death toll about to outstrip the previous year.

As part of a group of climbers who became stranded on the mountain, cut off from safety by the earthquake, our only way down was by helicopter. We simply didn't know how long we would be stranded – at the time we weren't sure that rescue would come at all.

They say that lightning doesn't strike twice. In 2014 and 2015, on the world's highest mountain, that rulebook was torn to shreds and thrown out.

I returned home an empty and soul-crushed version of the person who left a month earlier on the trip of a lifetime.

From Heathrow, David and I caught the express train to Paddington, and from there a short taxi journey took us to King's Cross. As we dragged our heavy expedition bags across the floor of the train station, we must have looked like weary troops returning from battle. With just half an hour to wait for our next train, my friend Ste McCarthy travelled halfway across London on his lunch break to buy us both a coffee. He looked shocked at our appearance. I hadn't studied myself in a mirror for weeks. I would save that horror for home.

The long train journey home took us to Thirsk in North Yorkshire, where David's wife Helen met him.

"Daddy, Daddy!" I heard as I stepped down from the train onto the platform. I looked up to see the sweetest sight in weeks. A sight at one stage I thought I would never see again. As I swept my two daughters up into my arms, tears began to roll down my cheeks.

"Why you crying, Daddy?" enquired Isla, my youngest.

"Because I am so happy to see you."

As I held them both tight it was hard to believe that, just six days earlier, I had been up at Camp One on the world's highest mountain.

Michael, the mutual friend of David and me, drove the girls, Tamara and my mam the short journey from our home in Hartlepool.

I embraced my mam, and then Tamara.

Tamara looked me in the eye, took a deep breath, and said simply: "That is it, no more."

It was hard to disagree. "Are you sure? I might reach Camp Two next time."

I smiled. Tamara didn't.

It was as emotional a reunion as I thought it would be. We went back to David's, who lived not far from the train station. Over coffee, David and I tried our best to answer all the questions that came our way.

Homecoming: Ellis with Lara and Isla

Later that afternoon, I placed my bags down in the hallway of my home in Hartlepool. The house phone rang incessantly with family and friends keen to know I was back home. Tamara fended all the calls, recognising I wasn't in the mood to chat. Before I took myself off to bed, Tamara took a photo of me, sat in the living room, holding the girls. I added it to my Facebook page with the following short caption: '*Home, nothing more to say right now. Sleep calls.*'

'You may not have reached the summit but you never gave up. You can't beat Mother Nature. Enjoy being home with your girls. Maybe take up golf now!' – Craig Gill

'Welcome home Ellis. God loves a trier and you have definitely tried. Enjoy time with your girls and keep smiling. You should be proud for what you have accomplished. I know I am proud for you.' – Jane Dickinson

'To a hero's welcome I can imagine. You're an absolute inspiration buddy. Glad you're home safe.' – Craig Simpson

'Standing on the summit of Everest, or snuggled up on the settee with your two beautiful children – no contest.' – Jonathan Atterbury

After the best night's sleep in weeks, I woke early the next day suffering the effects of travelling. Having lost all sense of time, Tamara informed me that it was a Saturday. I took the girls shopping to a nearby Toys R Us and bought them each a talking dolphin, after which we went to TGI Fridays restaurant, where I ate my body weight in chicken and sweet potato fries.

On Sunday a friend organised a welcome-home party in our local family pub. In a cornered-off section, everyone who meant something to me came to welcome me home: another gesture that deeply touched me. There was a notable absentee, Tamara's Aunty Anne.

The following week, as I settled back into my home life, everyone wanted to know my version of events. The local newspaper ran a front-page article with the headline: *'Avalanche survivor back home safely'*. Media teams from Look North and Tyne Tees News – the two local TV news programmes – came to the house to interview me. I wanted to temporarily blank out the outside world, but I knew that events in Nepal had been global news. I was still being swept along on a tide of grief, raw emotion and the memory of those few days on Everest. The experiences I went through hadn't fully sunk in yet. It would be weeks before they finally did.

One day I was alone at home when Tamara's Aunty Anne walked through the door. I hadn't seen her since I had been home, as she didn't come to my welcome-home party. I assumed that she had popped in to visit Tamara and the girls, her great nieces. I told her the girls weren't in.

Not one to mince her words, she said: "It's actually you I want to see." She apologised for not attending the pub to welcome me home the other week, "But," she went on to add, "I was fucking angry with you, and didn't want to see you!"

Well that's a nice welcome home if ever I heard one.

She went on to say how she had been with Tamara on the day of the earthquake, and had then spent two days watching my wife in a state of mental exhaustion and near collapse. She added that, although she could appreciate I went through my own hell up on the mountain, I had no idea just what I had put Tamara and the girls through. I could see her point and she was only saying what others close to us probably wanted to say themselves – the only difference being that Aunty Anne had the balls to say it. I took the scolding in the well-intentioned way it was meant to be received. She finished by saying: "If you ever go back, I will break your fucking legs so you can't walk again!" Later that same day, Tamara's father told me the same thing, albeit in a less violent way.

Since I had been home, I hadn't said much online about all that had happened. I was receiving messages on a daily basis from well-wishers; all keen to know that I was OK. So, I figured that it was time to update my blog and Everest Dream Facebook page, which I did on May 5th with the following:

I have had four full days at home since returning from Everest and Nepal and in this time I have been able to reflect on the disaster that occurred whilst attempting to climb the mountain. I do not wish to dwell on my own experiences in the Icefall on that fateful Saturday; suffice to say that it was the worst two to three minutes of my life to date. However, this was nothing compared to what those at Base Camp had to endure.

Over the past few years I have tried to convey the steps needed, and emotions experienced, in attempting to climb the highest mountain in the world. But not only that, I hope I was also able to share with you the preparation for such a task. Through my two attempts, I hope I did a pretty good job of sharing all of this with you. The outpouring of support and goodwill directed towards me this past week or so, and indeed after 2014, lets me know that I achieved my aims and then some. I didn't need to step foot onto the summit to achieve my dream. Maybe it's not about the summit after all.

Being able to share this incredible journey with you all, twice, through the wonderful nation of Nepal, and receiving all your kind comments and feedback was extremely gratifying. I am so glad I was able to share all of this with so many wonderful likeminded individuals.

When I returned home from last year's tragic climb I took a few months to decide on whether to return to Everest or not. This year I need no such time. I can hand on heart say that I will not be returning for a third attempt. I have reached the end of my journey in regards to attempting to climb the mountain; yet in a way I feel I have lived through and achieved far more than I ever set out to all those years ago.

My personal experiences in Nepal these past two years will stay with me for the rest of my days. I take into my heart all those whom I met who moved me and added some magic spark to my endeavours including plenty of you.

A lot of you gave so generously in allowing me to have these shots at achieving this dream, so it is now my turn to try and give something back. With almost 15,000 subscribers to this page I want to try to do some good from this. So it is my intention to send some money back into Nepal for the families of the three staff that we so tragically lost at Base Camp: Pasang Temba, Tenzing and Kumar.

Two days later, I added one final product to the Everest Dream clothing range. Working with a friend of mine, Mike, who ran a screen-printing business in Cheshire, we turned a photo of the Nepali staff from my expedition, including the three who perished, into a T-shirt design. I incorporated the words: '*Only In The Darkness, Can You See The Stars*', along with '*Nepal 25-04-15*'. Mike donated 150 T-shirts and printed each one for free. I then began to promote and market them through the power of social media. Sales instantly began to flood in. Within a week I had sold eighty of them to people all around the world. Donating all proceeds through the Juniper Fund – the US-based charity that climbers Dave Morton and Melissa Arnott co-founded – meant that nearly all of the money raised could be distributed to the three families of the staff members we lost on Everest. The Juniper Fund works exclusively for the benefit of Nepali workers tragically killed in the mountains of Nepal. It was the perfect charity with which to align my efforts.

Over the next month I sold all 150 T-shirts that Mike had initially donated. So successful was the campaign that Mike had to print an additional fifty, which we sold throughout July. In total the *Only in the Darkness* T-shirt raised over $3,500 for the Juniper Fund. It wasn't a staggering amount of money but in Nepal that money could go a long way. Throughout the rest of the summer, people who had bought one of the T-shirts sent me photos of themselves wearing it. It was a nice end to the campaign and I added them all to my Facebook page. It showed a great solidarity for the people of Nepal.

My page, which I expected to fizzle out once the charity T-shirt campaign had run its course, showed no signs of slowing down and was still growing. I was gaining new likes week-to-week. In the time I had been home, I gained another 2,000 followers. Did they know something I didn't? Maybe I could keep this community of Everest-lovers going after all. People had bought into not only my dream to climb Everest, but me as a person.

I had always considered writing a book at the conclusion to my Everest adventure, but as things ended dramatically on both occasions, I shelved the idea. After all, who wants to read about Everest when someone doesn't reach the summit? It was only after repeatedly being asked when the book was out that I started to give the possibility some serious consideration.

In mid-June, six weeks after returning home I made my decision known:

I have decided to pen a book titled The Everest Dream – *two years of heartache and tragedy on the world's highest mountain. This will be about the past 15 years of my life and the build up to the last two years of Everest attempts. It will be all about the steps I took to get the $70,000 together to have two attempts back-to-back on the mountain, as well as what played out during the actual attempts. I will speak from the heart about all the trials and tribulations I went through, and the strain of being caught up in two years of disaster and the effect it had on my family.*

A day later the responses blew me away. I received a staggering number of comments to the news, every single one of them positive. I even received offers of help with finding a publisher.

Of the many comments I received back, one in particular stood out. It was from a chap by the name of Kevin Marchant, who said the following:

Would make a good read. Some of the most popular British stories are about failure: Shackleton, Scott, Titanic, Light Brigade etc. There are too many to name, but you get the idea. I think as a nation we celebrate the person who tries and fails, rather than the person who succeeds. Twice you have tried and both times failed, not by your own lack of ability but by events out of any human's control. You have done yourself proud.

Throughout the start of summer, as I began writing the book, I also immersed myself in spending time with my family. I refused any offer of doing a public talk. I didn't feel ready to stand up and speak to a room full of strangers about my experiences on Everest. In time I would, but June was too soon for me to even think about it.

On July 15th 2015, I gave my first talk since returning home from the mountain. It was to the local Rotary Club, but I was still nervous. I hadn't done any public speaking since March, when I spoke to the group of college students. That was the talk that secured my sponsorship with the brewery.

There were just twenty or so members of the Rotary Club in attendance, but I spoke as candidly as I could about my experience. It dawned on me that I was now talking about Everest in the past tense. It was no longer an event on the horizon, as it had been for the past several years. I was now on the other side of that dream and it saddened me to think about a life without the mountain. By the end of the month I had also finished the introduction to the book.

In August, I began running again. Freed from the constraints of training to climb the world's highest mountain, I simply enjoyed plodding along the sea front. Everywhere I went, people who knew me began asking if I would go back for a third attempt. I was pretty confident, this time, that no would mean no. I had been lucky twice, although I didn't feel lucky; I didn't want to chance that luck a third time. Besides, even if I didn't have a wife, two young girls and a son to consider, the fundraising had been such an exhausting and demoralising experience. I doubted very much that I would have the energy, or the inclination, to pull together the funds for one more try.

Everest, the big Hollywood production based on the events of 1996, was released at the cinema in the autumn. I took Tamara to see it. As we sat and watched the scenes involving Beck Weathers, I saw similarities to my own story. Beck was a pathologist from Texas, who ended up being left high on the mountain, as everyone who came across him assumed he was dead. A client of Adventure Consultants that fateful year, he had an insatiable drive to climb the mountain, and it became the centre of his universe, much to the dismay of his long-suffering wife and children.

I looked across at Tamara with my mouth full of popcorn; she stared at me and gave me *that* look that only wives can give.

"That could have been you," she said, as she dropped my hand and folded her arms.

In late September, I was invited to give my Everest talk at an outdoor festival called the Alpkit Big Shakeout in

Derbyshire. I had never heard of it before, but it looked like a fun opportunity to have a few nights away and speak to some enthusiastic outdoor lovers. I was due to give my talk at 7.30pm, which also coincided with an England v Wales rugby international match.

The Alpkit speaking slots were kicked off by Andy Kirkpatrick, the British mountaineer and big-wall climber, who gave a talk in the main area of the festival. If I were to give a direct comparison with Glastonbury, the famous British music festival, Kirkpatrick was on the Pyramid stage and I was on the smallest stage possible. Only around fifteen people sat and listened to my story. I was floored and dejected. I vowed that I would never speak at an outdoor event again.

In the late autumn of 2015, I attended the book launch of Brian Blessed's autobiography in North Yorkshire. His book, *Absolute Pandemonium,* summed him up perfectly. After everything he had done for me, I wanted to show my appreciation by attending his talk. Plus, it was about time I met him face-to-face to thank him for everything he had done. I took my mam with me for the evening, as I knew she would also like to meet him. After Brian's talk, in which he waxed lyrical about his entire life to date, I was going to buy a copy of his book and get it signed by him. However, the queue was out of the door and winding its way down Ilkley High Street. I told Mam that we should go, as it would be ages before we could speak with him; plus, we had a fairly long drive to get back home. I was almost out of the door, when his publicist asked me to come back and wait, as Brian would be delighted to see me. I decided to wait. And I am glad I did. When we finally spoke, he informed me that he had mentioned me in his book. In the postscript, he spoke about the events on Everest six months earlier, clearly mentioning my name and his support of my attempt. I said I was honoured and humbled. I was, deeply.

Meeting Brian Blessed

My expeditions to Everest – the mountain of dreams as I affectionately called the mountain – became journeys to a mountain of nightmares. But in the process they became voyages of discovery.

On both expeditions I experienced what it was like to be caught up in a major global news story, being swept along on a tide of grief and emotion – deep emotion at what occurred on the mountain I had grown to love, and sorrow at losing people in our teams.

Despite the sad conclusions, these were life-affirming events, through the good times and the overwhelmingly bad times.

It has taken me the best part of four major mountaineering expeditions – twice to Everest herself and a lifetime of dreaming – to finally realise· that reaching the summit of any mountain is a distant second to the overall experience of the journey.

Although the end goal of every mountaineering trip is to reach the top of the mountain, this is only a small part of the adventure. My dream to climb Everest ended up being so much more than the pursuit of reaching a tiny piece of snow and rock the size of a billiard table.

What I take away from these experiences is what I have learned about life – my life in particular, the person I was and the person I have become. I learned these valuable lessons the hard way, ultimately learning that life is not always about the achievement of dreams and aspirations. It is more often than not about the entire process and the steps we take to achieve the goal, regardless of whether it is achieved or not. It is about the places we visit, the people we meet and the cultures and values we experience along the way. That is the true essence of any dream we set out to achieve.

The experiences I lived through, on my two expeditions to Everest, have defined me in ways I couldn't possibly have imagined when I set out to achieve my dream over twenty years ago.

A wise man once said that *'it is better to live one day as a tiger, than a thousand as a sheep'*. I have very few regrets about going to Everest. My only regret is choosing to go during the two most disastrous seasons in the mountain's history. With no crystal ball to consult, there was sadly not much I could have done about that.

I am living proof that if you want something strongly enough, it will happen. It may not be today, it may not be tomorrow, but *if you want the rainbow, you must be prepared to put up with the rain.* In a way, I guess I achieved all I set out to and then some, and I didn't need to step onto a mountain summit to do so. If you followed along with my attempts on the mountain, you know that I was not a 'professional mountaineer'. I would not even have referred to myself as a mountaineer by the true definition of the word.

However, through the steps I took and the life path I put myself on, I was able to travel to Nepal and attempt to climb the world's highest mountain – not once, but twice in consecutive years. For that I will always be incredibly proud.

I hope that you are able to take some inspiration from this, and maybe set forth on your own Everest adventure, whatever that may be. If I was able to get myself into a position to live out my dream, then why can't you? Climbing Everest, or trying to achieve some other equally monumental goal, is certainly achievable if you put your mind to it. You just need to commit the time and energy required and block out the background noise.

I hope that you will have gleaned from these pages that being tenacious and stubborn does pay off in the end. And I guess that is a life lesson we can apply to a lot of scenarios and goals.

On both occasions I left for Nepal, I was financially stretched. I was seriously overdrawn in both my business and personal bank accounts. I also left for Everest with my family deeply anxious and worried about what they viewed as a selfish and dangerous venture. Accusations by others such as 'being self-centred' and 'not being a responsible parent' rang loud in my ears.

There were a hundred reasons not to go, and only one reason *to* go. That one reason overpowered all others by a country mile. I wanted to climb Everest for me. It was the challenge I had personally set myself, and only I could achieve it. Nothing was going to distract me from the thing I had painstakingly prepared for, and dreamed about, for almost my entire life.

For now, I have reached the end of my journey and my dream to stand on top of the world. Is this mountain out of my system? No. Will it ever be out of my system? Probably not. You do not live through all that I have without it permanently leaving its mark. Will I ever go back and attempt to climb the mountain again? I do not know! At this exact moment in time, I have to say no, but who knows what the tide may bring again one day? One thing I have learned in this life is that anything can happen. Everest will always be there, enticing future generations to its steep icy ramparts. Where there is a challenge, people will always go. The highest mountain in the world will always have a pull factor for generations to come. I didn't reach the summit, and although it took me a while to get over the disappointment of that, in time I have found it easier to accept.

After all, when it comes to Everest, it's not about the summit. It's taking the journey in the first place; that is the *real* achievement of the dream. In my eyes anyway.

EPILOGUE

In the spring of 2016, climbers returned to Nepal in the hope of climbing Everest, ending a two-year drought.

With everything in place, the climbing got underway. The threat of a third disaster must have weighed heavy on climbers' minds. The season settled in and, by mid-April, climbers entered the Icefall. As the month drew to a close, there had been no major incidents on the mountain – not of the kind that would draw world attention. As this normal season progressed, it looked highly likely that the first summits of the season wouldn't be too far away. The rope-fixing Sherpas pushed the route beyond the South Col and up the final summit ridge as May rolled around. On May 11th, a team of nine Sherpas reached the summit, the first from Nepal in three years of trying. Kenton Cool followed this a day later – successfully guiding a client to the top – and in doing so, reaching the summit for the twelfth time. Several minutes later, a Mexican climber and his Sherpa joined them. After two years of disaster and large loss of life, Everest was finally playing ball.

Over the next two weeks, hundreds of western climbers reached the summit, most for the first time, achieving life dreams in the process. On May 19th, Tim Mosedale made his fifth summit, along with a single client.

Shortly afterwards, my friend Michael messaged me: "I know you will be hurting right now. I'm sorry mate. Sometimes this life sucks."

In July 2016, I closed the final chapter to my Everest dream when I attended Holyrood Palace in Edinburgh to present Duke of Edinburgh Gold Awards to a group of young achievers. It was a huge honour to be asked and I was thrilled to have the opportunity to meet HRH himself, Prince Phillip, Duke of Edinburgh. Tamara and my mam attended with me, and I could see how proud they were as I stood on the lawn of the palace and gave an inspirational speech to thirty young people and their families. I was then presented to HRH, whom I spoke to for a minute or so. He asked me if I had reached the summit. I told him that sadly I hadn't, due to avalanches and earthquakes. "Well at least you survived to tell the tale, far better story anyway," he said as he scuttled off.

Ellis meeting HRH the Duke of Edinburgh

July 30th 2016

As I sat at my computer typing away, the sun streaming in through the open windows of my study, I nervously typed the final few words into an email I was poised to send:

Tim, is the permit still good for 2017? I am thinking about giving this mountain one last try.'

Before I could send it, my daughter Lara ran into the room and threw her arms tight around me. "I love you so much, Daddy."

I pressed delete and switched off the computer. My real Everest was here at home, where it had been all this time.

ACKNOWLEDGEMENTS

Witing this book has been a painstaking love affair over a fifteen-month period of my life – fifteen long, hard months slaving away at the keyboard night after night. I will never get this time back, so I want to say a huge thank you for making it worth my while by buying this book and reading the whole thing. Unless you have just skipped straight to the back of the book, that is. In which case go back to the front, put the kettle on, put your feet up and read a few chapters. You will hopefully like what you read. I have bared my soul, warts and all, and tried to take you the reader on the emotional journey of my two attempts to climb an obscenely large and downright dangerous lump of rock and ice, thousands of miles away from my family and home comforts. The dangerous element played its part oh so well, don't you think?

These expeditions happened thanks to a cast of many players. I simply could not have undertaken such a project – twice – without all the support I received. There are far too many of you to mention in the few pages confined to the end my story, so I won't even attempt to. But please know that I am extremely grateful.

I would like to mention the key players that helped – not only to enable the realisation of my dream to step foot on the mountain, but who also gave their time and expertise in the production of the book. I love you all dearly.

Firstly to my long-suffering soulmate, my beautiful Tamara, I am sorry I have put you through fifteen years of pain, suffering and worry. One day I will make this up to you. I am sorry about everything that happened on Everest too. I would not have been able to attempt to climb this mountain without your unwavering love and support. You shielded our daughters from all the angst that you went through and I want you to know I am grateful you did this.

To my mam, Ann, I hope through my exploits I made you proud – despite the worry, the sleepless nights and the constant times you had to listen to me talk about the mountain. I would not have been on Everest without your unbiased and unconditional love, that only a mother and son share. Thank you Mam.

To the Everest climbers whom I looked to for inspiration during my campaigns, you made the impossible possible for me, and helped me to believe. Ste Bock in Sydney, you are a legend. Thanks for the many video chats at some ungodly hour from your office in Sydney. Your motivating words kept me firmly on track when it appeared as though I was about to stumble.

To David Tait, thanks for the training schedule, which helped me to prepare for the mountain. I would not have been able to kick the arse out of the Stairmaster without being inspired by your exploits.

Bonita Norris and Sam Lipscombe for taking time out from your schedules to offer your help and guidance with the fundraising. I am indebted to you both.

To my official patron Brian Blessed it was an honour to be mentioned in your autobiography. The exposure that you were able to give my campaign to reach the mountain twice was massively appreciated. You took my Everest Dream and placed it in front of thousands of people that I simply would not have been able to.

To Chris Soley, and everyone at Cameron's Brewery, thank you for the financial support towards Everest 2015. I was honoured to represent an organisation from my hometown, and I have no doubt I would have been the first person to open a bottle of Strongarm Ale on the summit of the world.

The outdoor gear manufacturer Berghaus made sure I left for Everest in 2015 with some of the most sophisticated and technical clothing and equipment available anywhere. Maybe one day, this kit will see action again.

Thanks to everyone on my Everest Dream Facebook page who followed along with the whole crazy journey. In particular to those who went above and beyond by providing emotional and financial support, especially Mick Buttery, Divyesh Ruparelia, Kate Smith, Gary Bourne, Penner Choinski, Tony McMurray and Ingram Micro, Simon Lewis, Colin Wallace, Paul Arnold, Anne Ganley and Ben Mitchell.

Paul Huckleberry Everitt, thanks for the crazy month that was the Nurofen voting competition. You kept it interesting to the very end, and I wish there could have been two winners.

For the nights sat in the Tall Ships listening to me go on and on about this bloody mountain I give special thanks to my patient good friend Mark Bradley. I am sure there must have been times when you felt like telling me to shut up. But you never did, the sign of a true friend.

I must also give a mention to Andrew Drummond and Sharon Pinchen for writing and performing a beautiful song about my Everest Dream. I was very touched by the song and I will listen to it forever more.

I give thanks to Henry Todd, for allowing me the opportunity to return to Everest at the first time of asking, and for travelling to meet me in Hartlepool that day. That must have been quite the bizarre experience.

To Tim Mosedale, thanks for believing that I had the ability to climb the mountain and for steering a steady ship through choppy seas in both years. To Himalayan Guides for overseeing the logistics of both Everest climbs and for enabling a way out of the country after the earthquake, I am deeply indebted.

Emma Finn, you are an absolute star. For reading each page of this book and correcting all the many schoolboy errors I made I can never repay you. Bill must be happy he now has wife back.

To Alex Roddie, the book's editor, for your invaluable critique of that first draft and for your skill in helping to make the writing shine I offer sincere thanks and much appreciation.

Thanks also to Everest climber and author Mark Horrell for your advice on the very early chapters, and for pointing me in a more professional direction.

To Mike Donovan for your help in bringing to life my vision for a T-shirt to commemorate those we lost that day on the mountain I give special thanks.

Tom McGuire did a sterling job bringing his photography skills to the table and took some great PR shots before I left for both expeditions. In fact one of those shots is on page three of this book.

I give a huge thanks to every one of you who followed me on Facebook, Twitter and my blog. If you donated to my cause, and purchased one of my T-shirts, hoodies, beer mats, framed pictures or anything else I was able to sell you to keep the fires of my dream burning, I am grateful. You helped to make Everest Dream one of the most popular and followed of all Mount Everest social media campaigns. Through the highs and lows of the double disaster your comments made me feel highly appreciated and loved, and I will never forget the compassion that was shown to me when things went wrong.

In late September 2016 I launched a pre-sale campaign for this book. The following individuals all generously donated the maximum amount to receive a copy, which also helped towards the book's editing costs. I am forever grateful.

Lynne and Maas Shaheen, Eden & Milo Shaheen, Mark Bradley, Steven McCarthy, Tony & Deb Stewart, Chris Soley, David Soley, Ed Simpson, Linda Crennan, Dan Reynolds, Gary Ferguson, Hazel Grace, Simon Lewis, Ben Palmer, Gary Ringrose, Paul Singer, Gareth Lowe, Colm Simpson, Nigel Summersby, Pinna & Chris Napoli, James Allen, Jeffers Ford, Tony McMurray, Kate Smith, Simon Ablard, Mike Brennan, Martin & Louise Dyson, Neale Johnson, Paul Thomas, Penner Choinski, Carl Wilcock, Mike Bamber, Graeme Forth, Kevin Molloy, Drum.

INDEX

M

N

Printed in Great Britain
by Amazon